JOAN BAKEWELL
NICHOLAS GARNHAM

# The New Priesthood

## BRITISH TELEVISION TODAY

ALLEN LANE THE PENGUIN PRESS

First published in 1970

Allen Lane The Penguin Press
Vigo Street, London W1

ISBN 0 7139 0047 4

Printed by Latimer Trend & Co. Ltd Plymouth

Set in Monotype Times New Roman

# CONTENTS

# PREFACE

We did the interviews for this book between October 1969 and April 1970. Particular programme and policy issues will therefore refer to that period of time. However, apart from such specifics, we do not feel that the style and content of British television will have changed fundamentally by the time this book is published.

We have shared the interviews throughout the book: we do not always share the same point of view. Hence the comments at the opening of each chapter are individually credited. The interviews within each chapter are the work of us both.

J. B./N. G.

# Introduction

The members were to be distributed throughout the country, so as not to leave even the smallest integral part or division without a resident guide, guardian and instructor: the objects and final intention of the whole order being these – to preserve the stores and to guard the treasures of past civilization, and thus to bind the present with the past; to perfect and add to the same and thus to connect the present with the future; but especially to diffuse through the whole community and to every native entitled to its laws and rights, that quantity and quality of knowledge which was indispensable, both for the understanding of these rights and for the performance of the duties correspondent.

Thus Coleridge described the function of the Clerisy, the members of his National Church. It is this noble concept that stands like a shadow behind the idea of public service broadcasting in Britain and still influences the debate about the proper function of television. Lord Reith was able to mould the BBC in the way he did and British broadcasting took on its own individual moral tone, because it responded to a deep current in the intellectual life of this country. The BBC was created as the embodiment of a long-standing cultural tradition that stemmed from the reaction of Burke, Cobbett and Coleridge to the industrialization of Britain. Raymond Williams, who delineated this tradition in *Culture and Society*, described it as:

the emergence of culture as an abstraction and an absolute: an emergence which, in a very complex way, merges two general responses – first, the recognition of the practical separation of certain moral and intellectual activities from the driven impetus of a new kind of society; second, the emphasis of these activities, as a court of human appeal, to be set over the processes of practical social judgement and yet to offer itself as a mitigating and rallying alternative.

1

These are noble ideals, but they depend for their fulfilment upon accepting, if only temporarily, an intellectual and artistic *élite*, a nobility of culture rather than of birth. This our society is no longer prepared to do, which accounts in part for the period of stress through which the idea of public service broadcasting is passing. The tradition that underlay the original Reithian concept has died and a new society is in the process of giving birth to a new and more egalitarian tradition, a new definition of the role of cultural priesthood.

But the growth of this new tradition is hampered by a fashionable helplessness. One of the most significant characteristics of modern thought has been the rejection of the romantic notion of individuality and the steady devaluation of the concept of individual will and individual responsibilities. An increasing stress has been laid upon the conditioning structures within which individuals operate; for Marx the structure was economic, for Darwin biological, for Freud psychological. These are all, in their different ways, valuable methods for assessing our experiences, but they have themselves become conditioning factors, reintroducing a debilitating feeling of helplessness before a predetermined fate. The old gods have risen again. Our unhappiness is now caused, not by an angry Jove or a spiteful Apollo, but by market forces or an unhappy childhood.

It is this conditioning that accounts for Marshall McLuhan's widespread influence. He appeals in the field of communications to just that fashionable helplessness. His most celebrated epigram, 'the medium is the message', is very close in tone to the gnomic utterances of Old Testament prophets. It is an invitation, not to thought or argument, but to worship: 'In the beginning was the word', 'I am the Alpha and the Omega'. Now television is erected as a new golden calf to be worshipped or reviled to taste. But neither the worshipping nor the reviling will discriminate. Television is television is television. It is hardly surprising that Madison Avenue should have clasped McLuhan to its lush bosom, for it is in their best interest that a critical examination of media content should be avoided.

We would not wish to deny the importance of much of McLuhan's work. No one can now write about television uninfluenced by what he has written. Of course it is true and important that the forms we use to communicate condition what is communicated. But to say that 'the medium is the message' is like saying 'you should not drink and drive' without specifying what it is you should not drink. To regard all television as of equal value is like failing to discriminate between milk, sulphuric acid or alcohol. And yet even those who have never heard of McLuhan talk in his terms. Television, they say, trivializes or (alternatively) television has been a great educator; television reinforces social attitudes, television has encouraged permissiveness, television should be less violent, television should be impartial, television should be this or that. Such statements are neither right nor wrong. They are not even self-contradictory. They are simply meaningless, for television is not a single entity, but a multiplicity of programmes, each with a different function. Television is, at one time or another, newspaper, magazine, cinema, theatre, music-hall, cabaret, sports arena, concert hall and even lecture room.

It is often forgotten that this multiplicity of programmes is produced not by some mysterious body known as the BBC or Granada or Thames, but by individual writers, producers and directors. This book looks at British television from the point of view of those people who make it what it is: the programme-makers themselves, and also the engineers, the administrators and financiers whose decisions shape the context in which the programmes are created. It is based upon the proposition of personal responsibility and activism, that is to say, as television is created by individual human beings, they can change it if they so desire.

There is no doubt that the Annan Inquiry – regrettably now cancelled – was set up in response to a growing weight of opinion that all is not well in broadcasting and that we need to think very seriously about what functions we want television to fulfil and how best it can fulfil them. Before we decide on any change of direction let us try to find out how and why television has developed in the way it has, from those in the best position to know, those who are responsible for the way it is. In previous inquiries the opinion of those, who, day after day, actually make television programmes was the last to be sought. This mistake must not be repeated, nor that of assuming that the ideas of the official representatives of the present system coincide with the ideas of those they employ.

The range of opinion in this book is neither exhaustive nor is it

3

a perfect cross-section, but it is, we think, representative. There are important areas that we haven't dealt with at all, such as educational and children's television. This is not because we are not aware of their importance, but because, for reasons of space, we had to keep to what we saw as the mainstream. The aim of the book, as a contribution to the debate on the future of British television, could not be better expressed than in this extract from an interview with Tony Smith, the Editor of *24 Hours*.

There is quite properly and fascinatingly this huge discussion going on at the moment about the ethics of television – about its role in society and about how it should be organized in the future. In this discussion there are two voices to be heard, that of government and that of the broadcasting authorities. The practitioners do not have a voice and are not allowed to have a voice. The Board of Governors of the BBC and the senior members of the BBC accept on our behalf all the moral, spiritual and intellectual responsibilities for the craft which we perform. It's like no other profession that I can think of. Now what I happen to feel quite strongly is that the broadcasters have an enormous contribution to make to this discussion in the light of their professional experience. It's most important that the point of view of the broadcaster is expressed, because it is so different from what it is imagined to be, even by people occupying positions of authority within the world of television who themselves used to be producers.

Once you move into being an administrator over an institution your interests (in both senses of the word) alter, and so do your attitudes on the whole range of questions that are currently under discussion. Everyone should take part in this discussion. The last thing I'm trying to do is put forward an élitist argument, but I am saying that the one group that isn't being allowed to participate is the very group of people who fill the screen with the very thing that's being discussed.

# 1 · BBC Television Begins

In 1936, when rumours were current that Sir John Reith was contemplating leaving his position as Director-General of the BBC, he received a letter from Sir Ernest Benn: 'You hold the biggest job ever since the days of the creation, and in my humble view it is your duty to continue to hold it. If you relinquish control then the BBC will become a full-blown government department.' Such exaggeration and pessimism were unjustified. Sir John Reith did resign from the BBC which did not subsequently go under to government control. Nevertheless the apprehension was perhaps called for. Sir John Reith spent the late 1920s and much of the 1930s defending the independence of the BBC.

It was often under attack from politicians of both right and left. Chamberlain complained to Reith that the BBC gave undue prominence to political attacks on him. Attlee complained in the Ullswater Report of 1936 that in the economic crisis of 1931 the BBC allowed a series of talks all in support of the then government. In 1937 Tory MPs were up in arms complaining that, in the news bulletins about the Spanish Civil War, the BBC was biased in favour of the Republican cause. Nothing, it seems is new – but the emphasis has shifted. Throughout his autobiography, in which he records in detail his successful struggle to keep the BBC free of government influence, Lord Reith makes almost no reference to a new development which was taking place at that very time. Throughout the late 1920s and the early 1930s television was gathering strength. Today it bears the brunt of that same public criticism and political attack.

For many years the development of television was confused by the emergence of two systems of transmitting pictures. The first, invented by John Logie Baird, was successfully demonstrated to

5

the Royal Institution in January 1926. Post Office engineers, when they saw similar demonstrations in 1928, were impressed enough to ask the BBC to allow one of its stations to be used for further experiments. The BBC engineers, not impressed by the standards of Baird's pictures, dragged their feet, but under mounting criticism in the press finally made 2LO available for some transmissions in 1929.

The second system, EMI, was demonstrated to the BBC in 1933 and proved far more satisfactory. None the less, the Selsdon Committee, reporting in 1935 on the future organization of a television service, recommended that the BBC should develop the two systems in parallel. The BBC was made exclusively responsible for the development of television and settled on Alexandra Palace as its television station. From there, the first regular BBC television service – the first in the world – began in November 1936. For three months the Baird and EMI–Marconi systems were used during alternate weeks, but at the end of that time the Baird system was discarded.

Today Lord Reith, Director-General from 1922 to 1938, looks back on the development of television as partly the reason for his leaving the BBC when he did. He hated it then, regarding it as inconsequent and trivial: and today he knows his worst fears were justified. Perhaps, he thinks, some good might have come of it if it had not been allowed to run away with itself. For today the BBC is not running television, television is running the BBC. And, more and more, television will be running the country. The sheer abundance of it appalls him: had he his way it would be greatly restricted in hours so that excellence of quality could be sustained through the competition for the privilege of a few hours. As it is, he feels television must carry a large part of the blame for what he calls the decline in our intellectual and ethical standards, which he regards as absolute tragedy.

None the less, in the 1930s Lord Reith was determined that the BBC should pioneer television development, if for no other reason than to keep ahead of America. He was proud to found the first service in the world, while the Americans held back and waited to learn from the BBC's mistakes. Despite his loathing of the amount and content of television programmes today, Lord Reith's allegiance to the BBC structure is still great. Standards declined, he believed, a year before ITV began, when the BBC was hoping to defend its monopoly by establishing an undeniable popularity. There was absolutely no call at all for the BBC monopoly to be broken – apart from the insistent lobbying of a group of Tory back-benchers, including a number connected with advertising agencies. He feels that had the BBC mounted a public relations operation on the same scale as the commercials the monopoly would have been preserved and the subsequent decline in standards avoided. Lord Woolton, who was responsible for introducing the ITV Act and commercial broadcasting, he considers as doing more ethical and intellectual harm than any other man of his day. He speaks of standards, taste and value to society – the rigorous principles on which he based broadcasting and which are still very meaningful within the BBC hierarchy. As to the size of the BBC, he says that managing 10,000 is no different in principle from managing 1,000; and he thinks its powers are not excessive. He dismissed the suggestion of an independent public watchdog as nonsense. He is still today the dogmatic, highly principled and great man who founded the world's first and largest broadcasting organization. But he cannot stand 80 or 85 per cent of present-day television.

Lord Reith's appointee as the first BBC Director of Television was Gerald Cock – who appointed Cecil Madden to be his programme organizer. Cecil Madden remembers the very beginning of television.

# Cecil Madden

Assistant to three Controllers of Television, from 1937 onwards.

In August 1936 Gerald Cock sent for all the people who had been engaged to be the first staff of television. We came from all sorts of worlds – the theatre, radio, films, current affairs. There was a bit of everything. But I was really a senior man. Now Cock brought us all into the Council Chamber in Broadcasting House and he said to each one, 'This is your title, this is what I expect you to be.' In my case I was Programme Organizer and Senior Producer. He said, 'You will not have to do any programmes until about November. What I advise you to do is to get into cars, go out to Alexandra Palace [which is about half an hour away from Broadcasting House] and see your offices and just look round.' So we all did just that. We piled into cars and we all rushed round there in a state of high enthusiasm. My office was a substantial room, and next to his on the third floor. I walked in. There was absolutely no furniture in it and the phone was ringing. I went over to it lifted it up and there was Gerald Cock again. He said, 'Cecil, I've got something very important to say. The Radio Show at Olympia is going to be a dead failure. They can't sell the stands. They have appealed to the BBC to have television there and I have agreed that we will do television for the Radio Show at Radio Olympia, which opens in ten days' time.' So I rang up a fellow called Ronnie Hill who was writing songs a lot at that time and I said I wanted an absolutely brand new song to open television with. What could he do? He said, 'I'll ring you back,' and a few minutes later he hummed a song to me over the phone. He said, 'I've thought of a title for it. I'm going to call it "Here's Looking at You",' and I said, 'What a marvellous title!' So we called the first show *Here's Looking at You.*

We had to give twenty performances of it, twice a day from Alexandra Palace to the Radio Show, but we had to do it on alternate days in the two studios with different systems. So with differently placed Control Rooms I had to do it one day in one direction and the next day quite differently. So a lot of people saw television very quickly. Tremendous numbers went to the Radio Show and saw it in rooms with sets everywhere. Of course, the actual viewers who had bought television sets, about 300 stalwarts, naturally had great crowds in every night drinking them out of house and home. And that was really how it opened. The official ceremonies came in November.

I only had £1,000 to make all the programmes for the entire week, so that I could only put, say, £100 into a top programme and roughly allocate about £100 a day. Money went a lot further in those days than it does now, and we somehow managed. Now the next thing we did was we said that we must be allowed to experiment. I wanted this topical magazine *Picture Page*, and we did it twice a week for seven years. So it had a pretty good success.

*Did anyone conceive at that time that television would take over from radio?*

Well, I certainly did. But, of course, the difficulty was that Broadcasting House was not absolutely friendly and they resented having to pay out money for it. They looked on us as the mad lot out there getting all the publicity, getting in all the newspapers, getting all the interest.

There were two schools of thought about programmes in those days. There was the school of thought that said start small and get big, and there was the other school of thought to which I certainly belonged which was that although there weren't very many viewers there was the press. We had the enthusiasm, therefore let us spend all the money that we had and do things in as big a way as we can, fast, so as to make an impact. The very first week I was able to put on the first studio ballet, the first studio play and the first studio opera, together with all the magazines and all the bits and pieces, so that we really had a stunning opening week by any standards and people were clawing the ceilings to watch programmes everywhere.

*What was your view of the role of television or what the balance of programmes should be in those days?*

That it should be based on the writer. I created the slogan 'a play a day', and it was a very good one. Some plays were short, some plays were very long, but the drama was there right the way through. I felt that the writer would never let you down, and it was entirely up to you whether you let him down. So television in these early days was very firmly based on what we might call show-biz. In those days we were a small staff and had not enough money, so it was absolutely impossible to organize it any other way. But we did make an arrangement with the film companies – Paramount, Gaumont-British, Movietone – and we did have the current cinema newsreels.

After the war television resumed, in June 1946, with the Victory Parade. Then there was the royal wedding, Prince Philip and Princess Elizabeth. The next thing was that television up to that point had all been in London. So we had to go out into the provinces. The Midlands came in 1949. In 1950 we were able to do a programme from Calais, which was quite a big technical achievement then. In 1950 we started Children's Television on a daily basis. In 1951 we had Manchester, 1952 we had Scotland, then came Wales and the West Country, and in 1953 television was given an enormous boost by the Coronation. In 1954 another great high spot was Eurovision, which gave us eight countries. Of course, it is more now but it was important then. In 1955 we were doing colour tests.

We had not, until 1938, brought Sundays in. We had that one day off. Then came the great battle with Broadcasting House: what would the programmes be on Sundays? Broadcasting House was quite adamant that it should be what they did on Sundays, which was a bit of Palm Court, a bit of religion, and I take credit for having fought a very hard fight to say that it should be drama. For years this was established and it was known as the Sunday Night Play and the Sunday Night Play has not really been licked today. It is still what you need and in those days we repeated it on Thursday.

*What do you think of the standard of television now?*

I think it is extremely good. I do not think it is light weight. I think that when anything really important comes up, such as the death of a President or the astronauts, all hands go to the helm in all countries and the artistic standards are really very good.

*What did people in the BBC feel when ITV was founded?*

They did not like it. They could see that a lot of their staff was going to go. Those of us who had, shall we say, good reputations had splendid offers made to us. Some went, and I think the exodus was a very good thing: it enabled the BBC to take on new people, and it gave the trained people a chance. The competition was certainly extremely good for the BBC and I personally decided to stay with the BBC because it was the kind of organization I liked. It suited me very well. But I think that it was a tremendously good thing all round, and anybody who said that it would dilute talent is talking absolute nonsense.

# 2 · Engineering

It should never be forgotten that television is, before anything else, a technology. The medium may not be the message, but it certainly precedes it. The institution of television rests upon a technological base. The BBC Charter and the Television Act are the means by which governments share out scarce frequencies. Their very scarcity forces government to intervene in broadcasting more directly than in any other communication medium. Only technical advances, in such fields as satellite transmission, cable systems and video-cassettes, can free it from that servitude.

When BBC television started the world's first regular television service in 1936, a monopoly was inevitable; the 405-line transmission filled the whole band-width then available to the engineers. As the engineers have pushed further into the VHF and UHF ranges, thus opening up more usable space, so new television services such as ITV and BBC 2 have become possible.

In setting up the late lamented inquiry into broadcasting, the then Minister of Posts and Telecommunications above all stressed the need to investigate thoroughly the new and exciting technical options facing the television industry. After previous inquiries it was the evidence and reports on programme standards and philosophy which received publicity. This is, of course, only proper, since the justification of any television system, however technically sophisticated, is, in the end, the programmes it transmits.

However, it is the technical decisions taken by these successive inquiries which are crucial and determine the future shape of broadcasting. Programme-makers tend to fall into two groups in their response to the technological future. One greets the future, like a junkie his fix, and talks as if an all-electronic McLuhanite dream-world of 100-channel TV and computer-controlled tape-

11

libraries will be with us, if not tomorrow, at least the day after tomorrow, and ignores the way in which technology advances within a much more slowly moving framework of general social and economic change. As engineers never hesitate to point out, the viewer is not seeing a substantially different picture to that seen in 1936. The history of colour shows that because something is technically possible it does not mean that it either will or should happen.

The other group is short-sighted rather than far-sighted. It either plays down the possibility of change because it doesn't really like change of any sort; it wishes to continue making the same programmes in the same way. Or it feels that such matters can safely be left to the engineers. But such decisions can radically affect programme policy. For instance, once an organization like the BBC has invested heavily in electronic studios, it is committed to keeping those studios fully occupied even if a majority of producers should want to make their programmes on location with film cameras. The shape of BBC and ITV regions is dictated not by philosophy but by transmitter-range. In the wider economic context the way in which wire services and video-cassette production are financed and marketed can radically determine the sort of work that programme-makers will be free to do, cf. the development of the Grade–ATV–EMI complex. Programme policy and artistic decisions can be rapidly changed but, owing to the large sums of capital investment involved, major technical decisions are in the main irreversible. So although television engineers do their work unsung in the background, their achievements taken for granted by the millions who watch the programmes, the developments they pioneer have shaped and will continue to shape the course of British television.

Study of the development of British television highlights the fact that producing a picture is one thing, actually distributing that picture to an audience is quite another. In the period up to 1939 the main problems of live television production were solved, but when the station went off the air at the outbreak of war the range of transmission was still restricted to the thirty miles around the Alexandra Palace mast.

So after the war the first priority was to start building a real national network. In this field another useful lesson was learnt, that technology crucial for television is often the by-product of work in other fields. The necessary development of micro-waves was a by-product of war-time work on radar, and their development was financed by the growing demand for long-distance telephone circuits. In the same way, satellite transmissions are a spin-off from Cold War rocketry, and the future development of cable systems will probably receive its impetus not from the demands of television but from the commercial needs of the Post Office to move into the rapidly growing data-processing and information storage markets.

The build-up of the BBC's national network was held up by government restriction on investment. Replacing bombed houses was more important than building transmitters, but between 1949 and 1952 the basic national network was completed. Here technical history has a direct bearing upon the arguments as to what effect the foundation of ITV had on the BBC. It is often claimed that ITV, by making popular programmes, speeded the spread of television, a medium which the BBC, still in the thrall of radio, had never taken seriously. But the spread of television depended on the construction of transmitters. Once national coverage had been achieved in 1952 the annual percentage growth in set-owners remained constant throughout the 1950s at about 9 per cent. This growth would have had an inevitable effect on programmes whether ITV was there or not. Until television achieved national coverage, the BBC was right to regard radio as the principal news and entertainment medium. Increased current affairs coverage on television during the 1950s was based upon a growing audience and therefore on an assumption of increased power and influence. ITV's rapid growth was based upon the solid foundation laid by the BBC engineers.

The history of television transmission has been one of ever-increasing range. Now that we have seen live transmission from the moon, the technical imagination, investment and energy which went into that rapid development will, one hopes, be concentrated on increasing the diversity of transmissions.

On the programme-making side the most important technical development was recording. Until the introduction of Ampex magnetic recording in 1959–60, British television was still largely a live medium. Recording was originally developed in the United

States as a means of solving the problem of time differences across the continent; in order to network shows across the country some method of recording had to be found. The impetus was economic not artistic. Film recording was first used in Britain for the Coronation in 1953, but it was seen purely as a tool for the purpose of repeats and sales. It did not seriously challenge the belief that television was essentially a live medium. Indeed, a whole theology was erected to justify television's existence as an autonomous art in terms of its liveness. But, increasingly, programme-makers began to exploit the editing possibilities that recording offered, and television aesthetics, especially in drama, drew closer to those of the cinema. However, while recording offered the artist greater freedom it also encouraged the economic development of the programme factory. Recording was exploited because it offered management the maximum use of scarce resources. On the other hand, recording also offers the possibility of much wider diversification of production facilities. Large centralized complexes such as BBC Television Centre are products of the era of live television. Once you can deliver a programme in a can or on a tape, all a television network requires are some video-machines and telecines, and a presentation gallery.

The new technical possibilities facing television in the transmission field – satellites, cable system and cassettes – may well have as profound an influence on the future of communications in the next thirty-five years as EMI's original development has had on the last thirty-five years. But just because something is technically possible let us not imagine that it will happen. As the history of the change-over to 625 lines and colour shows, technical progress in television is evolutionary rather than revolutionary. By examining the evolution of the past perhaps we can plan for the future we want.

# Howard Bridgewater

1946, Engineer in Charge, TV Outside Broadcasts; 1952, Superintendent Engineer, TV Regions and Outside Broadcasts; 1962–8, Chief Engineer, BBC TV.

I worked with Baird for four years until 1932 and for the last two to three years of that period we had started some experimental broadcasts from a little studio. Just head-and-shoulder views of people each day, very simple things, but fascinating for the experimenters who in those days even made their own sets, adapted from radio sets. And they were thrilled just to see anything at all coming through in a flickering kind of way. After these experiments, a certain amount of pressure was put on the BBC by the Baird people, who said that the BBC should do more to encourage television. At that time all it was doing was to provide the use of the Brooklands Park medium-wave transmitters after broadcasting hours. So with some prompts from the Postmaster General, and rather against their will for reasons one can understand because of the doubts about the long-term usefulness of this mechanical system, the BBC did take over the responsibility for the programmes, and they built or rather adapted one of their own studios for the purpose. And we then started two or three years of the same kind of experimental transmissions. We had a very bright and imaginative producer called Eustace Robb. He really got the last ounce out of the system, far more than we ever dreamed was possible – crude still, but at least he made the programmes interesting. He got important people along, Russian ballet and all sorts of things, you never dreamed you could make anything of. But with great care in the scenery and the make-up and so on he overcame the limitations.

*How many cameras did you have then?*

Oh, only one.

*How many people were actually watching at that time?*

We never really knew. A thousand sets had been sold by the Baird company, and there were kits that you could buy to make up, so probably there were three or four thousand viewers.

*Did you, and other people working on, it foresee at that time it was going to be a great national medium?*

No, I don't think I did. Baird always used to say it was going to be, but I think he was a man of vision in that respect. I think we all thought that it's got to come sooner or later and improvements

*Engineering*

must come, but I don't think we could have predicted they would come as soon as they did or be as important and as widespread.

*History shows that although Baird was first in the field his mechanical system wasn't the right answer. When did you first become aware of the rival electronic system?*

I think we really became aware of the electronic possibilities seriously in 1934 when EMI were able to demonstrate the progress they had made on improving the iconoscope camera. Although it was based on an American invention I think what they had produced by 1934 and 1935 was more complete than was then available in America itself. It was really ready to be considered seriously for the establishment of a broadcasting system: electronic cameras, where you could have as many as you liked in the studio and mix them, electronic cathode ray tube viewing, everything – and the transmitter, they even designed that, too, in conjunction with Marconi. . . . So they could offer a complete package.

The Selsdon Committee then recommended that the BBC should set itself up with a television service on short wave, and also recommended that they should try two systems alternately: the EMI, of course, the one that really gave rise to the whole study, but they also recommended that Baird's should be tried alongside. Well, by this time Baird, seeing the way the wind was blowing, knew they had to try and keep in competition and they had extended their mechanical system to 240 lines, repeating twenty-five times per second, which wasn't bad for definition, but was still flickery. The EMI system was 405 lines repeating fifty times per second. The effect of fifty repetitions was to take them outside the flicker area. You can't really see flicker at fifty, unless the picture is very, very bright. So you couldn't say Baird was strongly in competition, but at that time one can well understand how a committee would be reluctant to sweep aside Baird, who had been leading the field doing everything pioneering, and so on, exclusively in favour of EMI who looked foreign.

*How sophisticated had television become by the time you went off the air in 1939?*

By the time we went off the air we were operating only the EMI system, because the Baird tests lasted about two or three months,

16

and were stopped. So we were operating two electronic studios at Alexandra Palace, and by then we also had two outside broadcast units. The first OB was of the Coronation in 1937 and since then we'd gone everywhere possible within the range of the one transmitter that you could use. The short-wave transmitter was trundled around with the OB unit and fired the signal back to a receiver on top of the mast at the Alexandra Palace. Well, it had to be more or less in optical range, and I believe the longest distance we ever achieved was about twenty-nine miles. But we had done Epsom Races and all the Wimbledon tennis and many events in London like the Cenotaph ceremonies and shows in theatres. Incidentally, it wasn't only the radio link that was used, cable technique had also come along. Underground cables went through London and around the West End. One could hook on to a special cable that had been laid for this purpose by the Post Office. And that was very useful indeed. It went through Whitehall, Victoria Station, the Albert Hall, Hyde Park Corner and places like that where you were likely to want an OB, and then the BBC itself devised a means of spurring from this sort of ring main up to another mile or two using ordinary telephone lines.

So by 1939 we really were doing quite an enterprising service, both from the studios with plays which were quite advanced, Shakespeare and ballets, things of that sort, and OBs doing many kinds of sport, pageantry, Lord Mayor's Shows, anything which was available. The only limitation being the distance.

*Did you still feel television was rather eccentric?*

By that time I think we were certainly beginning to feel that television was coming on fast and was going to be more and more accepted by the public. I don't expect we could see the development was going to be so fast, and of course the war made some difference. Radar had become so prominent and developed so far, we didn't realize how much effect that would have on post-war television.

*How did it have such an effect?*

Because radar was using pulse techniques and in fact a number of us that worked in television both in the BBC and in industry, EMI and so on, went into the RAF and the Army and other

17

services and government research places, to work on radar, because we could adapt ourselves so easily to it, and I think this helped radar get off the ground quickly in this country and establish a lead over the Germans. But then radar became such an industry and so much knowledge of electronics came as a result of the pressures of war, that by the end of the war there was a very large force of advanced technical manpower waiting to do something else.

*When the war ended what were the chief technical problems facing television?*

I think it would be true to say that the main problem was extending television throughout the country. We were still confined to the London area. It was important to cover the country, and this was one of the big plans that were made early on, first Sutton Coldfield and then other stations throughout the country. That all had to be planned, some years in advance. The Post Office had to lay cables for the purpose and design the equipment.

At that time I was working on the outside broadcast side, and our problem was getting better equipment. We wanted vans laid out more like control rooms where you'd sit at desks, and have proper facilities. It was all more like a mobile laboratory, rows of racks with equipment on them, people standing about and walking up and down. There was no kind of production control facility except in a very crude way. But also we wanted more sensitive cameras. Although the electronic camera we had before the war was wonderful compared with anything we had ever known, they had very serious limitations. The original iconoscope was not sensitive enough for outside broadcast purposes, we wanted something working in much lower light conditions. It was also very tricky to operate particularly outside – in the studio you could tame it but it needed very great skills to work it properly. You could manage if the lighting was under control and it was very even, but if you got sudden changes in light and the sun going in and out and cameras panning in on different subjects as you have on outside broadcasts, you got very strange effects that we called 'tilt and bend'. That probably doesn't convey anything, but great shadows came across the screen, purely due to difficulties in design of the electronic pick-up tubes. So one of the priorities was to get better cameras. We did, thanks again to some work done in America by the same RCA laboratories who produced the camera called the image-orthicon.

*The other problem I imagine with* OBs *was the question of range?*

The first approach to the problem was to get micro-wave links. These were fairly easy to set up over optical paths from one hilltop to another, or from tops of buildings. You could operate them back to back and stretch them out across the country. These links were again a by-product of the war, of radar, and the first one we had came from America. I think the first extensive use we made of micro-wave links was the OB from Calais which was in the summer of 1950 – the first time in fact it had come across the water. It was also the first example of the use of several micro-wave links in tandem. Thereafter it was really only a question of acquiring more equipment and learning the know-how of operating it easily.

*In later years what were the most exciting developments on the engineering side of television?*

Sending pictures over long distances. This has always seemed to me to be the real stuff of television, seeing something happening at a remote point. That is why outside broadcasts always have a great fascination. I played quite a large part in working with the European broadcasting organizations, planning and getting Eurovision going, and it was extremely exciting to see pictures direct from Rome – not recorded you see, you were really seeing things happening. Then the next thing was the satellite which enabled you to see live pictures from America and soon after that from Japan and then Australia and so on. And finally the moon.

# Dr R. D. A. Maurice

Head of Research Department, BBC.

# G. G. Goriot

Chief Engineer, Research and Development, BBC.

*The most revolutionary technical development in television production was recording, first on film and then on tape. It changed the whole nature of the medium.*

MAURICE: In the early 1950s it wasn't possible to record video signals on to magnetic tape. There was, moreover, a race to produce a good system of recording, for the Coronation, because it was realized that this would have a good archival and export value. We devised 'suppressed field' recording just in time but, of course, this consisted of images recorded on photographic film.

*But how long did that form of recording last before it was superseded by tape?*

GORIOT: RCA were the first to demonstrate recording on magnetic tape. It was a longitudinal recording, in which the tape raced through it at a high enough speed to allow you to do a single track longitudinal recording. We developed a longitudinal recording system called VERA. But the timing of it was such that we'd scarcely demonstrated the thing before Ampex came out with what undoubtedly has been the solution to the problem. They used the rotating heads to make an adequately high head-to-tape velocity and thus to enable the speed of the tape itself to be reduced back to the standard sound-recording figure of fifteen inches a second.

*You just hadn't thought of that particular solution?*

GORIOT: No, never occurred to us.

# Howard Bridgewater

The first recording was done on film. It started as a means of recording a complete production which was still made live. It wasn't originally used at all for storing and then putting out the programmes when it suited you. It was simply used as a means of providing repeats.

Well, then obviously people's imaginations got to work, they began to see that there was great value in repeating, but also there was value in not putting programmes out live at all. Instead, you could record at a time of day when it suited you, and so that led to the need for a good recording system. Stimulated, I think, by the excellence of tape, and the convenience and ease of using tape of course – stopping and starting, cutting – then people got the idea in a big way of stop/start recording, which is, I suppose, universal now. Very rare now to go through a studio production from beginning to end without stopping.

\*

*The prime advantage of recording is not so much artistic as economic, as Neville Watson explains.*

# Neville Watson

Chief Engineer, BBC TV.

What has been adapted is the method of operating the studio. They have got to a system whereby the rehearsal takes place on one day for a thirty-minute output and then on the next day final rehearsals and recording. This is the pattern, and by doing this they have enabled the output of the studios to be very greatly increased. We reckon to do thirty minutes in a day. Just one day in the studio and all the scenery is whipped out overnight, all the lights are re-set overnight and the next day a whole new production goes into the studio. Now for live broadcasting that would be quite impossible. This is where the economy is – not in the use of the apparatus, not in the number of technical staff that you use, but in the amount of production that you get out of a given set of

*Engineering*

facilities. This is really by far the most productive centre of television presumably in the world.

*One always has it drummed into one that the organization of broadcasting is conditioned by the scarcity of available channels. How many channels are in fact available?*

The distribution of television on 625 lines is crammed in this country in groups of four channels in any one area. In London, for example, there are channels 23, 26, 29 and 33 and you could have four programmes on 625 lines – four separate ones on those channels. This was a government decision. Three of those channels are now allocated, two to the BBC for 1 and 2 and the third one to ITA. The fourth one is idle and this applies over the whole country. This thing is very complicated and very carefully planned to allow four channels to be provided over the whole country to a degree.

*You say it was a government decision. What other decisions could they have made?*

Well, they could, as they have in most countries on the continent, have allocated them in groups of three. You could have made provision for only three programmes on the 625 line. In this country, you see, we have the tremendous embarrassment of having a 405-line service as well. And this is using up what is called band 1 which is where BBC 1 is on 405 lines and then there's a band 3 which is largely used by Independent Television. Now those cannot be used for 625-line transmission until we've got a duplicated service on 625 lines which gives virtually the same coverage as the 405-line service at the present time. The government in due course can take a decision to close down the 405-line service.

*When the government decide to close down 405 transmission, will that free two more networks?*

No. A 625-line transmission requires a wider channel than a 405-line. So that if one could replan the existing bands 1 and 3 which are at present carrying 405, one would get less channels. There are also other reasons why perhaps we would get less still than the straight arithmetic swap. Some of the channels in band 1 are rather seriously interfered with by distant transmitters at certain times of the year due to the condition of the reflecting layers. My guess is that we could use bands 1 and 3 for one more programme being made in the distant future on 625 lines.

*One way of getting round the scarcity of frequencies is the use of a wire system, I imagine. Do you think transmitted television as we now know it will be superseded by universal wire television?*

No, I don't. Certainly not within the next ten or twenty years. The capital investment in providing a single coaxial cable into everybody's home is enormous. I always think when people make optimistic forecasts about a development of that kind that, to date, we've only succeeded in getting telephones into about one third of the homes in this country and that's a much cheaper business than putting in a coaxial cable. Even if you cover a populous area such as London, what are you going to do about the vast underpopulated rural areas of this country? In particular, Wales and Scotland, where the costs of putting in an underground cable network would be enormous. I think we will be stuck with the broadcasting system as it is for a long time to come.

After all, things do persist – things don't change as much in my view as people think they do. The great majority of viewers in this country are still looking at a 405-line picture which first appeared on the air no less than thirty-four years ago – it's a very persistent thing, isn't it? Using the same broadcasting channels as were used then when we started at Alexandra Palace – the channel was identical with the one we're using in the London area now. So things do persist and the reason why they persist, of course, is pretty simple. It is that people have an enormous capital investment and it is very difficult to replace a capital investment at all quickly. Even the most wealthy organization has to do it relatively slowly. And we must never forget that the big investment in television broadcasting is in the viewer's homes – not in the capital equipment that the broadcasters use, although that's substantial. When you are talking of, say, twenty million homes, each investing something of the order of, in black and white, say, £70 you're talking about a large sum of money which makes anything that we do look comparatively small.

*Then do you think satellites will come before coaxial cables?*

I think they will. It's a huge capital investment if it has to be a competing system with an existing land-based network. If one didn't have an existing network and were able to assess the situation from scratch I think that, at this very point in time, it might be cheaper to use a satellite than to set up a land-based network. So we are already at that stage. But, of course, it has to compete with its extra capital investment. Incidentally, the investment by the viewers will again be considerable because a rather special receiver would be needed. The satellite cannot send out its signals on the same channels that are being used on land-based networks. So there are real problems. Undoubtedly this may well come, but it ought to be done as a co-ordinated inter-government system. I mean, absolute chaos could result if individual governments just stuck up big broadcasting satellites, because they can't be made to cover just one country. They spill over like our transmitters do, and while they don't give a first-class service outside the area for which they're designed, they nevertheless would put up a very strong interfering signal over a very much wider area than that. Also, there's a limited number of satellites that can be put up there – space is already beginning to get used quite a lot and there is a limited space for these satellites, because they all have to be in the same orbit.

# Maurice and Goriot

*How do you see the video-cassette field developing?*

GORIOT: There are two aspects of this: one is the domestic market, the consumer market for people who would like to buy cassettes to play over on their television receivers, and the other is the professional or semi-professional market. What we don't know is: will the public be interested in buying cassettes to replay film material, knowing that they can't record. There's no evidence at the moment to indicate that the public are terribly keen on this. Whereas you can take a favourite piece of music and play it over

and over again, there may not be a lot of incentive to play somebody else's material over and over again. There is if it's your own
children playing on the beach.

*What about actual home recordings of the television pictures?*

GORIOT: That's the other side of it. There's obviously an enormous
amount of money to be made if somebody can replace the home
movie with television camera and recording facilities. This alters
the whole thing, you see. I mean, people didn't buy many magnetic
tapes that somebody else had recorded, but they don't half like
their recorders when they can record anything they want to themselves. So the real market will come if they produce a cheap home
recorder, which can record off the air.

*We have been talking about future technical developments. But their
speed, I imagine, will be controlled on a political level. For instance,
colour was held up until after the change-over to 625 lines.*

MAURICE: Oh, yes. We would have been happy as a broadcasting
organization to start in 1960 on 405. If somebod yhad given the go-
ahead in the late 1950s we could have started colour then.

*Has it often been the case that you could do things technologically
and you have to wait for political decisions to go ahead on it?*

GORIOT: Oh, yes.
MAURICE: But I don't think one should necessarily assume that
politics is always holding things up. Without some restraint
scientists and engineers might go off the rails, put out things which
they'd regret five or ten years later, when it'd be a bit too late to
do anything about it. Perhaps it is a good thing at times to slow
things up a bit.

*Are developments being demanded by the programme-makers or do
you offer them?*

I think it's still true to say that an awful lot of the new developments – and here you'll say, 'Oh, it's an engineer talking' – come
from the engineering side. The programme people don't really
know their own struggle. They get used to it. I mean, in the studios
in the old days when the lighting had to be enormous and everybody perspired, well, it was accepted that that was television. I

think really it's the engineers saying, 'Look here, these cameras are damned insensitive. We ought to do something about it', rather than the programme people saying, 'Why should we perspire like this'. They regarded it as part of the act. It had to be suffered.

# 3 · Foundation of ITV

The first official proposals for commercial television were made in 1949 by Selwyn Lloyd. They were contained in his minority report to the Beveridge Committee of Broadcasting, and were suitably thorough. The development of television should be handed over to a commercially sponsored corporation licensed by a Commission for British Broadcasting which was to have watchdog powers over it. At a later date when the public demand for alternative programmes grew pressing, 'then it might be desirable to follow the same pattern as with sound broadcasting, a public service non-commercial programme financed by license fee, along with one or more commercially financed agencies'. This was a clear proposal to reverse the evolution of British broadcasting entirely: to take television from the BBC: to hand it over to commercial interests, in fact to structure our television like that in America.

This was probably the most extreme statement of the commercial case. In subsequent discussion, debate and proposals the commercial lobby recognized the need to modify its demands if it was to get anywhere at all.

The case made out by Selwyn Lloyd for his proposals was that only in this way could we right the evils of monopoly. Monopoly had great dangers – as indeed the Beveridge Report itself stated. It would tend towards centralization and bureaucracy; it would be afraid to take risks; as the only employer it would inhibit its employees from criticism or daring; and it might abuse the dangers of excessive power which might threaten a democracy. All this Selwyn Lloyd argued forcefully. He made little mention of the hope that commercial television might one day make enormous profits and enable people to get rich. Inhibited by a British reluctance to be seen to be in it for the money, the commercial lobby recognized they would have to seek a compromise. Reith's legacy of public service haunted them and eventually found its way into their structure.

The Beveridge Report, published in January 1951, rejected the suggestion of sponsored television or the idea of three separate public service corporations all supported by licence fees. It recommended that the BBC should continue to be responsible for all broadcasting in the United Kingdom including television and the overseas service. Its suggested safeguards against monopoly included the strengthening of the advisory committee, a five-year review of the BBC and the setting up of regional commissions for Scotland, Wales and Northern Ireland.

The government of the day accepted the majority recommendations of the Beveridge Report and issued a White Paper to that effect in July 1951. On 25 October 1951 they lost the election. The Tories came in and in May 1952 the Memorandum on the Report of the Broadcasting Committee 1949 stated their rejection of Beveridge and their intentions to permit some element of competition in television. In November 1953 these intentions became proposals, embodied in the Memorandum on Television Policy. The proposals were less extreme than Selwyn Lloyd's: they rejected the sponsoring of programmes. They were more guarded even than their own White Paper. They believed the controlling body over commercial companies should be a public corporation owning transmitting stations and being responsible for ensuring adequate standards of taste. The earlier memorandum issued by the Conservatives had said the new stations would not be permitted to engage in political or religious broadcasting. With the creation of a strong public corporation now proposed, this ban was no longer considered necessary. Similar controls to those adopted by the BBC would operate.

So, from the extreme proposals of Selwyn Lloyd, the whole case for commercial television had been progressively modified. The proposals of November 1953 were embodied in the Television Act of 1954. The first Independent Television (ITV) programmes were transmitted in September 1955, under the eye of the second and newest public service body in broadcasting – the Independent Television Authority (ITA).

The man who was most responsible for the conduct and success of the campaign for commercial television was a former Controller of Television at the BBC. His experiences with the Corporation, of the way in which television was regarded, convinced him that its potential was unrecognized and the monopoly should be broken.

# Norman Collins

1946-7, Controller, BBC Light Programme; 1947-50, Controller, BBC TV. Director, ATV.

If you have a total monopoly, as the BBC had, there has to be someone in charge of that monopoly. At one time it happened to be me. I remember that driving home late one night after I'd been going through a very much over-loaded tray of programme proposals all of which required decisions, the truth suddenly came to me. I realized that if I had given a reverse decision in pretty well every single one of the cases that had been put before me it would have made just as much sense as the decisions which I had very carefully arrived at. In other words, it lay in my decision, and my decision alone, whether the work of any particular artist or writer should be seen on the screen at all. Now that was a moment in my career – a moral decision on the basic iniquity of a monopoly. Another reason for leaving the BBC was that I think that I had failed to persuade the BBC that television was as important as I believed it to be and that the resources of the BBC should be diverted in the direction of television if it was to develop television properly.

Having left the BBC, I decided that I must certainly do what I could to see whether some form of Independent Television could be developed in this country, and at this point it's interesting to look back and find the number of people who were opposed to the idea. They included at one time virtually the whole of the House of Lords, and I would have thought, probably the majority of the Conservative Party, certainly the majority of the Labour Party, to which you have to add the Churches, the Headmasters' Conference, the Conference of Vice-Chancellors and the Oxford and Cambridge Unions. Now an interesting thing emerged. The interest of the public was growing very greatly and it was absolutely unpredictable which view any one of one's quite intimate friends would have. Indeed I remember being cut dead by some of my friends for upsetting what they thought was the sacred institution of the BBC, while equally being applauded by others whom I had no reason to believe had any interest in the matter.

I spent some two years gospelling up and down the country on the matter of independent television, and then there was a gradual change. One found that the bodies of representative opinion were coming round to the view that just as it would be bad if all the theatres were conducted by one corporation or the cinemas by one corporation, or the newspapers by one corporation or publishing by one corporation, or worse still, the whole lot of them together by a single corporation, then, as that was the position of the BBC in terms of broadcasting, that was bad. One found votes of confidence coming out for the idea of an alternative service conducted by other than the BBC.

I decided that to show my sincerity in this matter it would be necessary to form a group of people and make a declaration that we were ready, if the government allowed us, to operate a television service. The names there should certainly be remembered: they were Sir Alexander Korda who came from films, there was Mr C. O. Stanley who was then Chairman of Pye, there was Sir Alexander Eichman, then Chairman of EMI, there was a banker in the person of Viscount Duncannon, now the Earl of Bessborough, and above all there was Sir Robert Renwick, now Lord Renwick, who had been in charge of radar during the war.

We registered the company under the name of the Associated Broadcasting Development Company. The public recognized that there was a company and the City of London was involved; the whole project was then taken seriously.

*Has the present television system turned out as you originally envisaged?*

By no means. I certainly would not have fought so vigorous a campaign to break the BBC monopoly if I had thought for a moment that the result would be the creation of commercial

30

monopolies quite as rigid as the non-commercial monopoly of the BBC. Indeed, I am on record as having said many times that it is ridiculous to imagine that anyone broadcasting in Birmingham can conceivably be in competition with broadcasting in Edinburgh or Penzance or London. I had certainly hoped that there would be an alternative independent system. Indeed, I think that the Tory government is to blame, very considerably to blame, that when a second service became available they gave it to the BBC without the adequate means of financing the BBC service and denied it to independent television where it should properly have rested. Indeed, if you think of the very, very grave financial crisis operating in independent television at this moment as a result of the Turnover Levy, it must be remembered that the Levy itself was invented only as a means of redressing unduly high profits arising from a monopoly situation. Had there been competition there would not have been those unduly high profits and there would have been no Turnover Levy. I think also the Treasury probably would have been as well off in deriving corporation tax from two separate companies in any one area as it is at the moment in deriving its Turnover Levy plus corporation tax from single companies.

Now I think that in this country we've got a curiously inverted pattern of what would have been the normal development of television. Let's imagine for a start that television had begun with the commercial companies running it. Now, I've no doubt myself that the commercial companies would have put out a programme which was satisfying, fully satisfying, to the vast majority of the public. Even so, I believe that the serious minded people would have said that television would be capable of dealing with some things which the commercial companies were not providing, and would have invented a BBC to supplement the popular programmes. That is happening in the States where you find the educational stations are putting out a supplementary service. I think that just as you would not say that you want a large public library to have nothing but the most popular books, so you cannot look to the future in which television will not also have the specialized services.

There was a period when any event on television was regarded as the newcomer, as an oddity, resented by some, welcomed by others. By now it has become completely acceptable that the

British pattern of broadcasting happens to have the BBC and Independent Television. All I was suggesting was that the pattern of development might have been happier if it had been Independent Television that started first and the BBC had been invented later to supplement with the serious programmes which the commercial companies might, or might not, have ignored.

# Mark Chapman-Walker

Former Chairman, TWW.

When the Conservative Party was in opposition I was Director of Publicity of the Conservative Central Office under Lord Woolton. During the 1945–51 period the general feeling amongst Conservative MPs, and I think Conservative supporters in the country, was that there was a left-wing bias in the BBC and that a state-owned medium of communication was not in accordance with Conservative principles of free enterprise. I think that during that period a considerable head of steam of frustration built up, perhaps a little unfairly, against the BBC, because the government of the day always has the news and the opposition doesn't. Therefore, it was perhaps inevitable that the Attlee government should have more air time than the Conservative opposition. Nevertheless this was a hangover from the war, where the BBC had been directed very much by the government for obvious reasons and perhaps the BBC were less quick to realize that we were back in peacetime conditions. So from the frustration in practice and the motivation of principle, the Conservative Party felt that they should break the monopoly of the BBC.

Opinion was very much divided within the Conservative Party. I think you could say that at that time there were certain elements which were definitely hostile to any form of commercial television. The House of Lords was largely against and then there were considerable Conservative vested interests outside, such as Conservative newspapers, cinema owners; in fact most of the people who subsequently became participants. But there was a young group

32

who were very anxious to see the monopoly of the BBC broken and this young group found support in rather strange places.

But these people were mostly motivated by the principle of allowing free enterprise to have its head.

*What was the Popular Television Association?*

They were the group that proclaimed the concept of independent television. It was not connected with the Conservative Party; it didn't receive any funds from the Conservative Party although, of course, it was in fact implementing Conservative policy.

*From where did it receive its funds?*

I think it received its funds from vested interests in the makers of television sets, cable makers and quite a few individuals who were just against the monopoly of television being in the hands of the state.

*How did you build up the pressure for commercial television?*

The Conservative back-benchers who were anxious to break the monopoly of the BBC did a lot within their own constituencies, but certainly the Margate Conference, when the famous resolution was passed, did more than anything else because it was an expression of opinion of the grass roots of the party. The compromise was a fascinating one, because it was an entirely political compromise: that the ITA should own the transmitters and lay down rules of behaviour and give out the franchises and that companies should produce the programmes. This, I think, must be one of the few occasions where a political solution has been found for what after all has become a very big commercial venture.

*What sort of independent television would you have preferred to have had at that particular time?*

I think we really saw it more in terms of sponsorship rather than spot advertising. We thought this was in the end better for the programme content. We could well have been wrong, but we were then thinking more in terms of sponsorship.

Sir Winston turned down any form of sponsorship and Lord Delaware, who was then Postmaster General, was also against it, so one had to work rather quickly. I put up this compromise idea to Lord Woolton – and this was very largely accepted. Instead of calling it the Independent Television Corporation we called it the Authority to show that it was going to stop any abuses, and so the mere fact of setting up this Authority did nullify a large number of our critics at that time.

*You obviously played a major part in the creation of independent television. Is it something of which you are proud?*

Certainly. Well, let's put it at its very lowest reason. It has certainly improved the quality of BBC programmes without any doubt. And as I am a convinced Conservative I believe in the freedom of choice. There have been many critics of it, obviously, and I think another thing we did not fully realize was the voracious appetite that television has for talent. But overall it still remains that we gave the British people a choice.

*In the early days of ITV when it was making a loss, what was the mood at that time?*

When we were raising the money for TWW, which was eight months before we went on the air, was when ITV was really losing its money. That was the time when we found it very difficult to get participants on the station. By the time we actually got on the air, the corner had been turned and we hadn't made a really substantial loss out of it. I mean we made a profit in our first year of operations. When we were forming the consortium the mood was a very varied one. This was the time when Associated Newspapers sold out to Rediffusion and there was very little City support at that moment to form or finance the new operation. When we finally got on the air, as I say, we had turned the corner and it was by then a great adventure.

*Do you think too much money was taken out of the industry for diversification of one sort or another?*

Very few of the regional companies did diversify. They paid high dividends, but most of them put back into the companies themselves. It was only the major companies that could diversify. I'm not really competent to say whether too much was diversified in the big companies but I can see the reasons for their doing it. It was after all only a six-year licence and they had shareholders' interests to look after.

*Do you think the regional structure of ITV really is a viable structure?*

The structure was really the creation of the Authority and of Sir Rober Fraser but, being an ex-newspaperman, I think it's a perfectly feasible operation. Where the thing fell down a bit was the networking committee which dominated the programmes in my years anyway. It was set up by the big four television stations and it was very, very difficult for regional stations to get network because of the domination of talent – almost the monopoly of talent – by the big four.

I think the major thing, the major frustration was, certainly as regards the morale of people working in the region, that one was never able really to show what one could do in the regions, nationally. It's the national audience that every embryonic director wants to make his name with.

# Sir Lew Grade

Deputy Chairman and Managing Director, ATV.

I was the first man, when I was an agent, to book every type of British talent on television in the United States of America that was suitable for television in America. But I booked every singer that there was, every comedian, all the novelty acts; and that's how I started. I didn't really know anything about television. I was just an agent booking talent that I thought was suitable for people to see. Somebody said to me one day, 'Have you read *The Times*?' I said, 'I don't read *The Times*. I don't have time to read *The Times*. So what's in *The Times*?' 'There's an advertisement for applications for independent television.' So I said, 'What's that to do with me?' 'You must apply.' I didn't know anything about television. All I believed I knew was about talent suitable for television.

35

There was the thing about you require a capital of £3 million, which to me was astronomical. I said, 'Who have you got?' and they said, 'Warburg the bankers.' And then I collected a Board in about four hours. First of all I got Val Parnell, then Sid and Phil Hinds, Binky Beaumont and Stuart Cruickshank.

We applied for a licence and didn't get it. Norman Collins had formed a group which applied for a licence and got it for five days in the Midlands and two days in London, and we somehow felt that a combination of the two would be a good thing and we got together.

In September 1955, when we went on the air, I was still an agent. I didn't want to know about television. 'You want my advice, I'm part of the Management Committee, call me when you want to.' Val Parnell was in exactly the same situation. And by December there was disaster and they said, 'You must be full time.' I said, 'That's a nice time to come in, when we're facing disaster.' Anyway, Val Parnell and I came in and that was it. Eventually the two companies, ITC and ATV, amalgamated.

JOAN BAKEWELL

# 4 · Servicing

Television programmes originating within the BBC or the ITV companies require services beyond that of the drama or documentary group responsible for their production. The most important of these is Design, and the BBC has the biggest design department in the world. An army of about 750 working under Richard Levin is made up of scenic, graphics and costume designers as well as make-up and design services. The workshops which are under separate administration combine scene staff and construction staff amounting to another 800 or so. Together they spend something between £3½ and £4 million annually, of which drama and situation comedy account for some 80 per cent.

Richard Levin, who became head of design in 1953, had previously been a leading exhibition and industrial designer. His policy for the development of the department included employing designers other than those with stage or film experience. There was a large intake of graphic artists, painters, architects and industrial designers. Many were taken in on short-term contracts, and after two terms of five years, encouraged to go freelance. Today he has seventy-eight staff designers and sixty-eight assistant designers, also about fifteen freelance designers who had about 18 per cent of the output. The BBC workshops handle about one third of all construction work: two thirds is put to outside contractors. Richard Levin, who began when just twelve designers handled the total output, now heads a creative factory operation that is working at full stretch to keep up with the fantastic demands being made of it.

# Richard Levin

*Have the economic pressures on programmes affected your unit?*

Well, not seriously. I fight a constant rearguard action about this as I'm generally responsible for the artistic standards of all aspects of design and their development. So, wherever there are any pressures to cut costs or increase productivity, I have to keep a sharp watch out that standards are not affected. Everyone agrees that the one thing that mustn't suffer is the programmes. In practice, to achieve what we do is a great struggle. We never use expensive fabrics; what we do is not lavish, it never has been. It's just been adequate. We've never allowed too much gloss – there's a level after which you are wasting effort because of the size of the screen.

*The new total costing system means that every cost within a programme must be budgeted beforehand. Is this particularly difficult in design?*

This often can be so as there may be 700 bits of furniture in the drama and you've now got to quote a price for them before you've done your shopping. You know what the average hire charges are but you don't know whether the thing you have in mind will be there when you get there. You may have to get it somewhere else at a much higher price, and you can't put these prices in after you've done your shopping. All this really happens later in the designing cycle. You see, you've got to design the sets before you can specify the furniture, and the designer has to give a price for the settings and their furnishings and all the materials their sets are made of before they start. This is no easy job and it's also an extra job in a very tight schedule. There were no ecstasies of enthusiasm amongst the designers about this new system.

*Have you found disadvantages for your unit as the BBC has got larger?*

Yes, because a giant organization and individual creativity are unhappy bedfellows. Communication is much more difficult all round. In spite of the size, it's curious that the thing tends to break itself down again into smaller units. If one starts on a programme, and if it is a series, the series becomes a unit. But generally design

38

staff go from one show to another working with lighting people, different directors, different scene crews, nobody knows anybody and it's more difficult in those circumstances to build up the necessary rapport which makes the design realization team work at its best.

*Is there any way of avoiding this or is it really just a bureaucratic problem?*

This is just a planning problem – bureaucratic, if you like – and it's not solvable in the present circumstances.

*Could the whole system be more streamlined?*

I don't believe so at our present level of productivity. Although one chases everyone all the time to increase efficiency, this is still by miles the fastest turnover of any television service in the world. People who come here to look around are shaken rigid by the turnover in our studios. I mean, we are turning them over so fast now that we are caught in a bit of a trap. When colour came along, as we could not, for economic reasons, reduce our productivity, this naturally created pressures on the design team.

If television had never shown a film everything might have been fine. The day we started to show films was the day we had to start to match films with our own product, and professionally we couldn't do a second-class job alongside the super glossy Hollywood film. So gradually more filming came into our programmes, which added a tremendous complexity because people suddenly had to be in two places at once. The poor designer – he's out on location and he's doing his drawings at the same time. You know, it's very, very difficult and the planning departments are not prepared to do much about it. I know only too well that output departments and channel controllers have their problems, but I'm a designer myself and I tend to look after my own.

*In terms of attitudes to art and visual art in our society, do you think television has much impact?*

I think it's been the most influential medium of visual communication yet devised. It influences buying habits and popular decorative style up and down the country. All the local decorators, the do-it-yourself addicts, get their ideas from our settings. Any new

*Servicing*

style we introduce goes straight into the merchandizing pipeline. People see things on television and they seem to generate an instant 'want'. They ask their suppliers for it and manufacturers, not being stupid, are quick to supply it.

It is no part of our job to improve public taste in a 'do-gooding' kind of way, but trained as we are we are conscious that we have a responsibility here – whether we like it or not.


# Tony Abbott

BBC Staff Designer.

*What attracted you to TV?*

I think mostly the sense of urgency, the sense of designing something quickly and then finishing with it. In architecture, if you put up a building you take a comparatively short time to design it and maybe years of slogging away to see the thing materialize.

*In terms of a career in designing is the BBC a good place to be?*

I think it was very much more so for me, back in 1954. Things hadn't been done. We were experimenting. Every production that we did in those days, everybody would crowd round in the studio to see it and we'd be working on Saturdays, but just because we enjoyed working.

Now one could get the impression that everything has been done, and there's a feeling of repetition which has taken away a lot of the excitement of the experimental stage.

*Is it more difficult to get things done now?*

There are big administrative meetings about methods of working and the new forms of contract that you have to go through. What type of show yours is. How the designer budgets for his particular show. Now he has to think much more seriously about the whole concept and the total costing of a show than he used to. In the past you were given a certain number of man-hours, which were the hours spent to make your set, and on top of that you were given a certain amount of money which was for the material cost of the set and also for the props and things like that. Now you're given a total figure which must include many more items of costing than we ever had to think about previously. For example, now if you have one practical light on the set, a standard lamp or table lamp, you would be charged £3 for the electricians to come along and wire it up. That cost has got to be taken into a designer's budget and calculated by him. Therefore, he's got to work out how many lamps he can afford to have on a set, whereas in the past this cost was totally ignored; you could have as many lamps as you wanted. Now, we're total costing every single thing that goes into the studio. One spends much more time being an accountant than being a designer.

The director and the designer must now put forward a figure that they believe this production can be done for and once you've stated this figure you're more or less compelled to keep to it.

*Are directors realistic about it?*

Not yet. In six months they haven't really come down to realizing this new process and it's still a shock to them when you say: 'Well, I couldn't afford this because I've had to pay for all sorts of other things.' I think it would help them immensely to have talks on these total costings, so that they would understand it more. Often they think that they're given short measure because a designer hasn't bothered or hasn't set out to give them something, but it probably is that he just can't afford to do it.

*But has pressure on money reduced the standard?*

It shouldn't do. It's my contention that a lot of sets on television are overdressed and there are too many props used and that a certain amount of simplicity, if used the right way, is quite a good thing.

*What do you think makes people overdo it?*

Often designers think that there should be something to break up backgrounds on every picture that occurs on a television screen, whereas perhaps somebody against a very simple wall with nothing on it at all is equally or much more effective. I personally like rather bare sets. I think if you see a large bare set in a studio it's

41

very exhilarating, because we're used to small, rather over-dressed sets.

*Wouldn't it be possible to substitute cheap imitation props, cheap wallpaper, bargain basement fabric, but make it look good?*

I don't think it's possible to make these things look good. For instance, a reproduction piece of antique furniture never really looks as good on the screen as an old piece. If you're doing a classical play, you have to get the real thing, a thing of quality, because the richness of the wood, the colour, definitely shows on television. The cheaper stuff just won't do.

Cheap wallpapers, however you look upon them or however you like them, are cheap wallpapers and cheap fabrics are cheap fabrics however you see them, whether you use them in the home or you use them on television. They still look cheap. But in general the camera picks up every single detail and the quality stuff certainly shows.

I think the only economy, as I say, can be in terms of taking less of the good stuff rather than lots of rubbish.

The tendency, of course, in *Wednesday Plays* is to do a lot of them on film now and, like all location films ever seen in the cinema, the quality of the real thing is so much higher. The standard, the finishes of the paintwork and the doors, if you go into a real house and shoot your film there, this is absolutely for real and beautiful.

*What does the viewer really notice?*

The viewer does notice when something is exceptionally good and when something is very, very bad. If scenery isn't noticed that means it's pretty good.

You certainly get reactions if blatant mistakes are made, and you certainly get reactions if things are particularly good, either in the press or from letters and so forth. But the average programme, not very much so.

*Can I ask you about the turnover in studios – it seems to me that studios are tremendously utilized and there could hardly be any increased efficiency. What do you think?*

I can't help feeling that it's a pity studios aren't kept for specific types of programmes. All our studios are used for interviews, *Panorama*, *Grandstand*, big dramas, light entertainment. If a smaller studio was permanently equipped for interview sets it seems to me there would be more economic use of a studio than when you get a turnover in, say, TC8 where you might get one day *Grandstand* or *Panorama* and the next day a big drama and it all has to go in and out all the time. And then for light entertainment audience shows the seating has to be brought in, whereas if a studio had been designed so that permanent seating was always in a studio for light entertainment this would save a lot of effort.

*People work twenty-four hours a day, do they, on sets?*

On a night set there would perhaps be twenty-six men to change the night set of six major productions and this is an awful lot. The poor men are white in the face in the morning with tiredness.

This production of *Ross*, for example. You get four days in the studio altogether. We set up for the first two days and record. This will come off about half-past ten at night. The whole studio has to be cleared, everything out of the studio, all the floor painting done, all the lighting has to be re-rigged and then the new sets are built to start by two o'clock the next day. This is a very big turnover, extremely hard on everybody concerned.

\*

*Writers look upon television, quite rightly, as a vast publishing complex which offers the opportunity of publishing their work. Television itself is so voracious of words and ideas – 637 BBC drama productions planned last October for the subsequent twelve months – that it simply could not, even if it wished to, ignore the immense amount of unsolicited material that comes to it. The Script Department is the unit that deals with this influx, coming somewhere between a servicing department and a programme department.*

*The BBC's Script Department was set up in 1951: in 1955 it was enlarged into a bigger department: in 1963, under Sidney Newman, it was broken down again. Today, the script unit is staffed by twelve people with some half a dozen freelance readers to call on. Drama Departments now have their own script editors constantly on the look out for new material. But the script unit's brief is to handle scripts for the entire television service.*

# Robin Wade

Head of TV Script Unit, BBC.

We get about 6,000 scripts a year and we reckon in very broad terms that about 10 per cent are of interest. Ninety per cent, which is unfortunately very high, are going to get serious treatment in that they will be looked at by somebody or other for as long as they're worth it. But 10 per cent are going to be given serious consideration. They will be read at least twice in the script unit before being sent up to some editor and being read again. So there's really no stone unturned to try and find those 10 per cent. Nearly all that 10 per cent would be drama, the other would be of some interest perhaps to light entertainment or documentaries, religion, children and all the other departments put together.

*What proportion of that number will eventually reach the screen?*

Of that number, about 10 per cent again, which is down to about 1 per cent of your original total – the original 6,000. So that's one a week or one every other week which will reach the screen. A very exciting figure, I think, to find a new writer for drama or light entertainment every week or every other week: it's certainly more than you find in the cinema or anywhere in the theatre.

*How much are you prepared to teach someone to write a play for television?*

We expect him to have the basic tools of the craft which are to be be able to write dramatically and to construct a play. If a writer can do that well, but is not ripe for TV drama, then we would certainly sit down with him, pull his script to bits, send it away, come back, try again, try it on an editor, marry them up with an editor if possible – it's a mini television writing course. We don't believe in having general courses but individual encouragement. We spend a lot of time warning writers not to expect too many sets, too big a budget, particularly if they're trying to break into television. The best way of breaking in is to be practical, to write a play which is not going to make too great a demand on the film effort, the costume effort and on the production side.

We say these are the tips which apply to most television scripts.

But break them if you really feel you must. If you want to write a play that's burning inside you and breaks all the rules, then write it. This way you may get the odd runaway success, the odd weirdy, and perhaps start an entirely new trend or reveal an exciting new talent. But 90 per cent are coming in on the straight and narrow path, written by looking at the rules.

*Do you think television is able to pay new writers as much as you would like them to?*

I think it's a fair rate for the job. There's no doubt that the faster writer does very much better on television than anybody else, because if he can turn out three or four plays a year this is then getting into very decent figures for supporting a wife and children, whereas the slow builder-up of plays, who perhaps takes six months to write a script, is going to find it rather hard to make ends meet.

*Do you think the BBC is flexible enough in terms of time lengths?*

Again there is the fashion. There was one time when we used to have nothing but sixty minutes; then everybody wanted to write seventy-fives or ninetys. Now we seem to have a good range from *Thirty Minute Theatre* which is a very good nursery-slope length for us, to fifty minutes, seventy-five for the *Wednesday Play* and the occasional ninety for the BBC 2 plays.

On the whole, I think we get most of the types in that we like to see. The type we see least of is probably the type that's hardest to get and that is the well-made, middle of the road, middle-class play.

I would like to see more experimental drama. In fact I know that the Plays Department have plans for more experimental drama themselves but that's of the greatest interest to the very serious viewer. Most viewers are not really serious. They want to see something they all recognize and enjoy, and this tends to be series and serial.

I'm certainly torn between what I know the viewers do want and what I want the viewers to see and this is really the BBC Charter problem. You must do a bit of both. In fact you must have 90 per cent entertainment really and 10 per cent experiment in that the majority of drama slots are at peak time.

The writer for television tends to build up to the big scene and

*Servicing*

then when you are ready for the clash between, say, the generations or the opposing camps, suddenly the credits are rolling and you realize it's all over. Now there may be two reasons for this; one is that the author has been brought up on television plays which tend to funk the big scene and there's the old model of Paddy Chayevsky, the leading American television playwright who said you can't write a third act in a television play because life has got no third act. This is a very good excuse I suppose for rolling the credits when you get to the point where you have really built up to the climax. But nobody ever gets down to the real battle of the theme which is behind the whole play. The two big heads battling it out – that should be the real climax of a television play.

It's possible that this has become the problem of television economics from the playwright's point of view. Perhaps we ought to be paying them more in order to get that big scene, because they may need an extra three weeks' work in order to work it all out.

\*

*Because of their size the ITV companies on the whole do not have script departments. Certainly, the heads of drama in Yorkshire and Anglia, for example, deal with incoming scripts and selection within their own group. ATV, however, has set up a script department interested in a range, though not in an amount, similar to that of the BBC's.*

# Renée Goddard

Head of Script Department, ATV.

The Director of Programmes makes the first request. He will say – we're having a slot coming up from the network Planning Committee that will be six or eight anthology-type slots. Are there any ideas that came in from agents or from writers that we know, or from producers who may want to produce such a thing? And so

46

we work towards the taste and request of one producer. And at the end of the day, what's important is Cecil Clarke's taste [Head of Drama, ATV] and his ability to service his bosses with what they can actually get in on that air. In *Crossroads* we don't ask a writer to do one episode. We ask him for three months, contributing one month's worth of episodes. And we have a story-liner who goes on for a long time, maybe a year or more, to supervise the intake of story lines which may come from anywhere. I think that *Crossroads* is one of the most important drama series on the air.

*Why?*

Because of the family response to it. It is a thing that people watch together: they don't read it separately like a newspaper. It is the ritual of doing it together that is important. School teachers say, for instance, of children who come from homes where there are no books or no stimulation whatsoever, that the one thing they might have heard is Dad and Mum discuss a television programme such as this. In some cases it is the only kind of drama that people see.

*What do you think the pressures are in the whole of television writing?*

The single play is the one that in the end will influence the standard of writing. I think there should always be enough slots for single plays to keep up the standard of production in everything: producers, designers and cameramen, the lot. If you just let it go, look at America: they cannot even mount a big live entertainment show properly because there is a lack of experience in the single programme.

British television produces the most drama in the world that any country is doing. Now, out of that, I know, next year there will be ten marvellous plays. In the West End theatre, if you have two new plays that are really splendid, you're doing well.

*How can you keep up with supplying the enormous demands of television?*

Dramatists are passive people and will, in fact, come about only by request. It is the request that matters and it is the people who actually make the request who matter. It is they that will stamp television drama with their taste and it is the people who choose these people who will in the end stamp the look of the thing on our screens. The reason people are depressed is because the people who run drama and drama series are nineteenth-century men. I would like to see a Royal Court of the air, where once a month at midnight, you try out the new things, the new form, new facilities, new electronic hand-held cameras, new ways of editing, new anything. Anything like that can be tried out. The writer will always come after.

*

*Most countries outside America, Russia and the Eastern European countries buy more television programmes from elsewhere than they produce themselves. The situation in Britain is different: ITV have an imposed quota of 14 per cent of foreign material. The BBC have a self-imposed quota of something like 15 per cent from abroad, simply because they are equipped and staffed to produce 85 per cent of the output themselves. However, the availability of foreign markets for television programmes has made it worthwhile for the BBC to set up its own Sales Department: BBC Enterprises. It is virtually a limited company working within the BBC and paying its rent, overheads, running costs and travel out of the profits it makes abroad.*

# Dennis Scuse

General Manager, Radio and Television Enterprises, since 1 November 1963.

We've been in business now for ten years. After I took over, some six years ago, we spent the first five years working to establish the fact the BBC product was wanted, was acceptable and was saleable in world markets. We've proved the point in the last two years. Our total gross income in 1969–70 was £1,900,000 from television sales, and another £700,000 from other sources. We've built up from an income of £200,000, so we now know that people want our product. What we now have to do is to increase the profitability of the operation by being more selective in what we offer.

*Do you envisage much market expansion?*

It's very difficult to generalize about world television. The big market, of course, is America. We've worked very hard in our six years in the States to try and establish ourselves as a major distributor. One of the main problems, however, is that the product we have to offer for sale is electronically produced as opposed to the product which is produced on film – the sort of thing Lew Grade does or that which Hollywood is turning out. So by definition it is basically not a really commercial proposition because it is on tape and the action is much slower. The second point is that by and large BBC programmes are not made with the idea of selling a product, whereas commercial television is predicated upon this. The third aspect is the question of costs. I don't know what the figures are in 1970 but I would guess that to make a fifty-minute version of *The Avengers* or *The Saint* or whatever in colour on film costs in the order of £50,000. Now this, of course, is a budgetary situation which is way beyond the BBC's financial resources. So to that extent we've never really been successful in selling product – as we call it 'off the shelf' – in the States to network television. And that's where the money is.

The interesting thing developing in the States is the sudden explosion and requirement for educational programmes in what I call the non-theatric field. We've moved into this over the last year in a fairly big way, and the indications are that there's a great deal of money to be made there. If you take a series like *Civilization*, for example, which was incidentally the most marvellous series, we have been unable to sell it to network television, but it is selling widely to colleges, museums, etc. The networks wouldn't buy it because they couldn't clear the time; one network talked about a Sunday afternoon spot but *Civilization* was being weighed against football or tennis. It lost. It's too good a product. This is exactly it. It's far too good a product. I would hope that one day, just one network or one sponsor will have sufficient guts to stick their necks out and sponsor something like *Civilization* because the approval they'll get is enormous. We sold *The Age of Kings* to

Standard Oil some six years ago, and they sponsored it on four or five major stations in the States. They'd never had such a terrific response in the whole of their lives. *The Forsyte Saga* – currently on its second run on Education Television – also proves the point. Many networks and sponsors are looking rather ruefully at its enormous success and wondering how it got away. With this in mind, we're now pitching the *Six Wives of Henry VIII* very strongly. A pity he didn't have thirteen. But America isn't the world. Australia, Canada and the rest of the Commonwealth brought about £1 million altogether last year, and Europe about £500,000. But to answer the question: No, I don't see much expansion either in markets, or in hours. Top money comes from sales for 'prime time viewing hours' – these are now established – so it's a question of how many hours we can fill, at the expense of our competition. Certainly we're hurting the American distributors – or getting a bigger slice of the world cake. We hope to expand sales in some areas; for the rest it's a matter of running faster to stay in the same place. We're confident that with the BBC product we'll be able to do so.

My policy on this is that if the BBC has made it and transmitted it, then it is good enough to be offered overseas. There was an example with *Cathy Come Home*. One school of thought said we should not distribute this because it put Great Britain in a bad light. Well, the answer to that is that *Cathy Come Home* sold very widely, was widely acclaimed by almost every country in which it was shown. Most of the journalists who wrote about the showing of it used it as a stick to beat their own governments, saying, in effect, 'Well, why aren't you as frank about the conditions in this country?'

We're trading in eighty-two countries and we sold about 19,000 programmes last year.

*What image does the BBC have among television companies abroad?*

The BBC is still the BBC, and people are proud of their association with it. But there is a feeling abroad that the BBC producer as such can be a bit of an arrogant animal. He tends to feel that only the BBC know how to produce a programme. This is all right, of course, but it could create problems in a co-production situation. Since the middle of last year a new policy has been set, that we will now go out actively seeking co-productions. This is going to be one of the interesting developments. I mean, if somebody comes along with a great pot of gold, and you say, 'Thank you very much indeed, I'd love to have it', you must realize, going in, that there are strings attached to that money! I think this is, in a sense, where the whole thing may well come unstuck, unless we accept some form of production control by the partner or partners. We are also, of course, eventually going to have to invest in other people's ideas; there must be a two-way traffic.

# 5 · Light Entertainment

Historically light entertainment was off to a good start: it dominated the BBC output before the journalists had got themselves organized to compete. It profited by the reluctance of the BBC to recognize the importance and eventual supremacy of television over sound radio. Thus the early developments at Alexandra Palace were geared primarily to entertainment, while sound broadcasting carried the responsibility for Reith's imperative: to educate, inform and entertain.

Forces radio producers like Dennis Main Wilson and Brian Tesler took radio and music-hall talent on to the box. When ITV began, many of its first recruits were from light entertainment: Bill Ward, Francis Essex, Brian Tesler were already in television. Sir Lew Grade was an agent for variety stars. These men are now programme executives and their backgrounds naturally influence their choices today, most particularly in the conviction, held by many of those we talked to, that they are closer to the audience and more in tune with what it wants than the producers and executives from informative programmes.

This closeness to the audience is quite literal. The studio audience is the one factor common to almost all light entertainment programmes and absent from almost all others. *This is Your Life, Not in Front of the Children*, quiz shows, even *Jazz Scene*, all have a live audience there: in *Top of the Pops* they become part of the show. They are important for two reasons: the writers of sketches, jokes, half-hour comedy series all write to get laughs from that audience. They look for the tangible reactions of a group of 300 viewers present in the studio. The actors and entertainers likewise use this audience as a touchstone for the reactions of viewers at home. Without them the programme might be more or less entertaining: but it would be different.

The very existence of such a traditional audience indicates how much light entertainment is still reproducing for viewers the traditional shared entertainment of the music-hall, night-club or local rep. Television comedy is still shackled to the idea of people on a platform entertaining people in an auditorium. Feature films in the cinema do not have either real or canned laughter tracks: television comedy dies without it. We do not laugh so heartily it seems in twos and threes at home. It is in the nature of comedy and variety to be shared pleasures.

It is not surprising then that the people to whom we talked felt more in touch with mass public taste than other programme-makers. Yet the paradox is that although they claim to know what people want, they were all extremely hesitant to say they knew how to provide it. At least in one respect, however, they have an easier job than others: their brief is quite clearly and simply: to entertain. If they fail to entertain, they fail entirely. The other criterion of social responsibility, to inform, does not apply here.

Light entertainment shares with film series and old films the role of being what most people want most of the time from television. The evidence of the ratings is undeniable: eighteen million for *Till Death, Not in Front of the Children* played regularly to fourteen million, *This is Your Life* to an average of eighteen million and throughout the series was regularly in the top five programmes. But if popularity is the objective is it the only measure? If cheap and nasty shows get big ratings, is any further criticism invalid? The writers, the producers and the executives we talked to all held standards other than simple popularity. And they all offer different points of view as to what makes a show good in its own right. But popularity remains the goal and the measure of real success. Indeed, the concept of minority comedy is an elusive one: *That Was The Week* was intended as a late-night show for a sophisticated audience. It was funny: so it became very popular. *Monty Python's Flying Circus* gathered viewers once the word got round it was amusing. Comedy cuts across barriers of education, class and taste.

The most consistently mentioned factor in creating quality in light entertainment was the standard of the writing. The writer in the best of British television is not a hack: the structure of our comedy series allows for the individualist. It limits the number of programmes; it doesn't farm out ideas to teams of writers; it gives the writer freedom for his own ideas and his own style to emerge. If it ever ceases to do so we will have a system of characterless committee writing to a formula that makes most American comedy so repetitious and dull.

If comedy depends on its writers and its actor/comedians, variety depends on its stars. In both fields talent is short, and there is now more than ever a need to extend the search. Certain moves in that direction have paid off well: *That Was The Week* came from the *Tonight* camp and made journalists into entertainers. ATV is trying the idea of a religious revue on Sundays: jazz programmes have nurtured a steady following in what was thought to be a tiny minority interest. So far, so good. But lest Galton and Simpson ever run dry or Johnny Speight cracks under the strain, television now must make a forward investment in developing new writing talent.

Variety entertainment is probably the most internationalminded of all areas of television at the moment. Its annual Montreux festival has been going for ten years and now attracts delegates from about thirty countries. The market for spectacular shows is universal; Averti's spectaculars for ORTF win awards for their brilliance at exploiting television's potential and are shown throughout Europe. At a time when the trend in light entertainment is for big international spectaculars, British television looks remarkably insular. The American show built round Raquel Welch cost £150,000 to make: but it is expected to sell round the world and show a profit. The Averti show with Zizi Jeanmaire produced by ORTF is intended to do the same. There is an opportunity for the British lead in pop music and pop styles to be used by the broadcasting services to earn us a place in the big league: it is not being taken up. This is not to ask for more Tom Jones – Tom Jones is an American-styled hybrid tailored to a mid-Atlantic audience – it is to ask for a wider development of the sort of flair that currently goes into *Top of the Pops*. But while we remain content with Cilla Black, Val Doonican and *The Black and White Minstrel Show* alone then we will be left in the Stone Age of the variety musichalls.

Light entertainment comes under attack not primarily for its own standards but because it takes up so much prime time on the box. The ITA handbook classifies a third of its programme as serious, but the schedules show that ITV documentaries and serious plays are put out late. Comedy and variety get peak viewing. This is the second reason that the intrinsic quality of both comedy and variety is important: in terms of their responsibility within the pattern of programmes they must be seen as equalling in their own terms the quality of programmes around them. It is the programme controllers' role to nurse the heavyweight programmes by slotting them after a popular show where the audience may be persuaded to stay switched on. The possibility of viewers staying to see a documentary after *Wheel of Fortune* is less than after *Steptoe* because the one is trash and the other is among the best of its kind. If the standard of light entertainment were allowed to sink to the lower level of mass taste it would create a downward spiral that would take other programmes with it. It is the sheer awfulness and abundance of so many American 'entertainment' shows which makes intelligent viewers there despise television. It completely swamps in their minds the excellence of news coverage and reporting. They write off the entire medium. Were our light entertainment programmes to proliferate across the schedules with no regard for quality, then the same would happen here. Television as a whole would stand discredited.

# Billy Cotton, Jr

1967–70, Head of Variety, BBC Light Entertainment. Appointed, since this interview, Head of Light Entertainment, BBC.

I went on a training course for BBC 1 as a director for light entertainment. I remember Michael Elliott was on it, Stuart Burge was on it, I think I was the only philistine on it. I think it was a very high-powered intellectual course: I slept through most of it – but I also learnt a lot.

Now I'm responsible for nine shows a week, roughly. But each show is an entirely different operation and it depends on the experience of the producer of doing that type of show. So part of this

job is to put the right producer with the right type of variety, because variety is what it says it is, it is anything from a panel game
to Morecambe and Wise through Bobby Gentry, *Top of the Pops*,
Val Doonican, Rolf Harris; they are all actually as different as
chalk from cheese.

*Did television variety develop by simply taking the talent from the
halls and putting it in front of the cameras?*

Television had to adapt itself to dealing with people who were
stars on record, people who had been stars on radio and people
who had been stars on music-hall, people who had been stars on
films to a certain degree and it had to adapt itself each time. We
only recently got round to making what I call television animals:
I believe Val Doonican is a television animal and I think he would
admit to that, and Cilla Black. They are the beginning of the electronic age, so to speak. They are people that could adapt themselves to television. Television eats you, you've got to know how to
cope. Cilla Black knows how to cope because Cilla Black actually
was a big recording artist and then did a long stint on the stage.

People say, why don't you give more people a chance? What
they don't realize is that I've seen too many people literally be
over-exposed and fall by the wayside because they have been
brought on too quickly. Some have made a quick rating, a quick
few hundred pounds, a quick film and then they're dead. They've
got nothing to fall back on.

*I don't see why doing the halls teaches you anything about television.*

Because the training is tough and when you get to television you
are able to adapt yourself very quickly, even within a show. Subconsciously you probably know how to speed up an announce-
ment or two, or you know what reaction you're getting. It also
helps you in a series, when the first one is a flop, you've got something to fall back on.

*In terms of variety – is there any criterion other than popularity?*

Yes, there are standards of quality, but the trouble is you can get
bigger figures with bad shows than you get with good shows.

*Isn't there a case for saying Americans make variety programmes
very smoothly? Why not just buy their product?*

56

A lot of their product is bloody awful. All you ever see here are the top shows in America and even then they don't get very big viewing figures here. Andy Williams's show gets probably at its best, ten million. Val Doonican, Rolf Harris, Morecambe and Wise, and Cilla Black all get in the sixteen million class.

*Why don't we sell to them?*

We get £17 million to make programmes for a country that is one of the most advanced countries in the world. I see no reason whatsoever actually why the BBC should put too much emphasis on selling their programmes to anybody, if it means they've got to change their standard to do it. I would like to sell out of vanity rather than anything else, but under our terms, not their terms. I'll tell you exactly what happens in a variety American sale. They say we will give you $130,000 a show, we will send over a producer who will tell you what you put in it and we'll send over the writers and we know you'll do the rest. Well, what the rest is, is nothing.

*Why do you stay in public service television?*

I believe that television is a very important part of life, but it's not that important. I don't believe that you can twist people's minds with television. I believe too much in human intelligence. I believe that if a country has anything like the BBC and it's properly run, it is for good and I think it is not only good for the public but is good for the people who work in it. I feel better being here and knowing that I can go and argue with a man purely on the basis of the content of a programme and the one thing he can't say to me is, 'Look, I agree with you, but the sponsors or advertisers won't buy it', and you say, 'Well, look, how do I get to talk to them?' and he says, 'You don't'. Then you get in your car which is probably a Jaguar that you've been given and you go home and spend the £15-20,000 a year that you've been offered and you have all the fringe benefits. But you are really not a broadcaster, you're a commodity.

# Dennis Main Wilson

Producer: productions include *The Eric Sykes Show*, *Scott on Birds*, *The Roy Castle Show*, *The Rag Trade*, *Till Death Us Do Part*, *Marty*.

*Is television comedy a direct heritage from the variety halls and theatres?*

Up to and, I would say, including Ned Sherrin and that shower with its late day satire, it was all variety. This is where it gets tough today, because you never notice Peter Sellers doing a television series any more; he used to do a weekly radio show year in, year out. Yes, Spike, because you can't wear Spike out, he's made of granite. Robb Wilton, the day war broke out, did, I think, about forty years in the business, on probably a dozen acts, the magistrate's act, the fire-station sketch, etc. – they lasted him his lifetime, and today he would last exactly one television series.

They ran *Till Death* in three series. I fully expect that if they brought *Till Death* back we would destroy Johnny Speight as a writer because he would have to start repeating himself. There are not that many ideas in any one situation. Television writing, with due respect to Wodehouse, has to be sharper than Wodehouse. Great comedies, all the great comedy writers like Gilbert and Sullivan, the most prolific of all time, some are good and some are bad. In television you can't be bad. I don't think Alan and Ray ever wrote a bad comedy half hour. I don't think Johnny Speight ever wrote a bad *Till Death* but, my God, the pressure nearly killed him. You see there comes a time when the mind boggles and can't create any more. You have got to stop and rethink. Alan and Ray went into feature-film writing. Johnny, luckily, is rich enough at present to do what he likes. Speight will become one of the great playwrights of the British theatre, because it is there.

*What impact did the arrival of Sherrin and his group have?*

As my generation wrote themselves out, suddenly there was this super bunch of young new-thinking people, different-thinking people. But the only danger I think is that comedy takes years. The only way to learn comedy and the practice of comedy is to do it, and then look back on it and think, Christ, that was awful, or to do it and die a death. My gripe against Peter Cook and Ned Sherrin and John Cleese and Graham Chapman and Mike Palin and Terry Jones, John Bird, John Fortune, Eleanor Bron, all of whom I love and have worked with and shall be working with yet, is they have got about ten years to go to know when to shut up. They go too far – they destroy the most beautiful one line. The art is to write just one line and stop a show stone dead. They can't do that – yet.

*Where does comedy light entertainment fit into the total television picture?*

Well, all channels are excellent at these news documentaries, but I am sure 50 per cent of the nation don't understand them. They're not published in a language that they can understand. I think this is one of the reasons why *Till Death* became successful and in the end too successful, because people took him too seriously. By some peculiar quite non-intellectual circumstance he became some sort of voice of authority, because at least he spoke a language they could understand.

# Ned Sherrin

Producer: *That Was The Week That Was, Not So Much A Programme, BBC 3.*

*What made the whole series, starting with* That Was The Week, *such a success?*

The whole of *That Was The Week* was founded on good writing. I think that was my instinct, because it had always been galling to have only to work with light entertainment writers. A lot of good writers came and worked for *That Was The Week That Was*; they were much better because they were able to write up rather than down. It was nice to be able to coax something out of Peter Shaffer or get John Braine to write something, or John Arden.

Booker was frightfully inventive in those days and Kauffman and Quentin Crewe and Dennis Potter.

*Do you feel the standard declined badly towards the end?*

There was never the same feeling of surprise; but I thought the sketches were probably better on *BBC 3* than on any of the other shows. I think that the trouble towards the end was more the question of not being hard enough rather than of being too hard.

*When the BBC took it off did you feel they were taking it off under pressure?*

Well, we had done the first season which had been terribly successful and we had had a summer break and the nice thing about it was that the Tory Party didn't really know how to get at it because it was very popular, and they couldn't really get at it without appearing to be bad sorts. Stuart Hood made a speech in Blackpool saying 'Yes, it would be coming back, but all that nasty filth would be removed.' Nobody had ever used the word 'filth' about it before and suddenly there was a great rally, and all the people who wanted to get it off for various reasons were able to point to the sketches about fly buttons and things and say 'Oh, how filthy'. When we came back 'watch the filth' was the great cry. Fortunately for us it was announced that we were coming off after about the fourth or fifth week, and we got a sort of sympathetic award as a result. We went to receive it on the night Kennedy got shot. Then the Kennedy programme came up and we were the most favoured nation again.

*What do you think of the Kennedy programme?*

I think it was one of the programmes which most accurately did what we set out to do which was always to take apart or reflect the mood of the week as the people on the programme saw it. It was the only literate and eloquent piece of writing that the Kennedy death produced.

*How do you feel about television now?*

I feel very antediluvian watching the different techniques. Technically if you look at *That Was The Week*, it was hopelessly spotty and slack. It did seem the cat's whiskers at the time, but it doesn't now. The programmes look like early silent movies.

*Do you think there has been a reaction?*

I think that we loosened up what television felt it could do. People are always saying how much TW3 changed everything and I have begun to believe that by now because I have been told it so often. But I can't be sure. Apart from the odd extra 'bloody' I can't absolutely trace anything to it. I suppose it helped with things like the *Wednesday Play*, but the television I see now always seems to be technically in advance and from the programme point of view not frightfully exciting. The standard of the documentaries seems to get glossier and glossier but I don't know that we aren't waiting for another revolution.

# Barry Took

1967–8, comedy consultant, ABC; 1968–70, comedy consultant, BBC. Since the interview, he has joined London Weekend as Head of Light Entertainment.

I think the worst thing in the world is the people who have rules about comedy. I honestly think right now, speaking at the end of 1969, that we should aim at a period of anarchy in comedy, in television. We *should* be anarchistic, we *should* break the rules. We should employ writers and performers who look at things from a different point of view. We must reverse our perspectives. Or else we'll just die. We'll all die. We'll collapse and die of sheer inertia. Everybody will become fat and middle-aged. As soon as people get to a certain age with a certain ability they become powerful, and all the things that make them powerful make them want to prevent things. . . . They come up with rules, 'We must do this, we must do that'. There are guide lines, but there are no rules. OK if you want a success, yes. You can say if we have a series of programmes about a middle-class family who are poorish, but struggling through, and the daughter is engaged to a chap who works in Boots, and the husband is an assistant manager in a bank, and they have a fairly easy and happy cheerful life. And if that is written fairly amusingly, people will think it's a comedy. But it's dead. It's dead as *Coronation Street*.

*Are you saying that all the domestic kind of comedy writing like* Steptoe *and onwards is going to decline?*

Yes, I think *Steptoe* is the last situation comedy ever written of any value at all. *Till Death Us Do Part* was the chicken running around with its head cut off. It still seemed to exist, but it didn't really, because it didn't go anywhere.

*Why do you think that?*

*Steptoe* talked about neurosis, and about problems, psychological problems. . . . It saw the world in terms of psychology, of relationships. But *Till Death Us Do Part* acted out the psychotic things that were in the producer, and in the star, and in the writer. You couldn't get three more individual men than Dennis Main Wilson, Johnny Speight and Warren Mitchell. They came together like the three witches in *Macbeth*, shrieking with hatred and fear of the world, all in unison. That's what it was about. But *Steptoe* carefully observed the behaviour of the mind, and was helpful. A very gently therapeutic show. But *Till Death Us Do Part* wasn't.

*Do you think* Till Death Us Do Part *really misfired seriously then?*

I'm not knocking its success, or its credibility. But it was destructive. It was a destructive force. It didn't attempt to teach. It pretended at times it was rationalized . . . but it was a real shriek of hatred and fear. And as such, it was . . . it was like propaganda. My guess is that, in the long run, it won't have any effect, because it's unreasonable. *Steptoe and Son* was as funny, was literate, and yet it taught gently. 'We're all in the same boat,' it said. 'This failure to communicate, this inability to understand – we are all in the same boat.' It was a teaching show, rather than a propaganda show, and I think that reason wins.

*That means that you see comedy on television as in some way philosophically educational?*

Yes, indeed I do. I see it as the great reassurance. I mean all comedy reassures us. It reassures us of our own survival. The whole point of a joke, the whole point of laughter is that it reminds us that we survive. That's what comedy does. That's its function.

*But you could be reassuring people about a state of society which isn't worthy to be reassured.*

You're not really reassuring them about the society but about their own individual life. This is why comedians are individuals, not groups. You name them – Frankie Howerd, Marty Feldman, Tony Hancock, Alfie Bass, Warren Mitchell. These are individuals expressing themselves. You only get success when the writer is giving the comedian what the comedian wishes to express. Then it's so powerful that it's noticeable and it becomes a hit.

The audience will seek us out if they want us. We don't provide a service. Now *Newsroom* provides a service, which, whatever your beliefs or views, is a group of facts assembled and presented properly. But a comic or a comedy writer, or a comedy administrator, is throwing it up in the air. Nobody needs it, really. You throw it up in the air, and anybody who wants to catch, catches it. And sometimes it's twenty million and sometimes it's none at all.

*Television is such a monster, eating up scripts and jokes. Is there a limit to comedy?*

No, never! Scripts come in every day and everyone thinks they've written their idea for the first time. The hardest thing to tell people is, 'I've had five ideas like this, this week', and I can remember doing the same thing ten years ago. . . . And it was done twenty years ago . . . and old comedians will say, 'And I remember doing it fifty years ago, and seeing Harry Tate doing it seventy years ago', and so on. Comedy constantly repeats itself because all it's concerned with is people.

*But in terms of hard television, is there a shortage or is there plenty?*

In terms of hard planning there is more than enough. I mean there is a great queue of able writers whose work I can't get on. I can't get them a higher priority than next June, or maybe never. If you look, if you ask, there's tons of it. All you've got to do is ask.

63

*Isn't there anything new in comedy then?*

Well, the philosophy is changing. The whole conception of comedy writing is changing. For example, the cast and writers of *Monty Python's Flying Circus* boast one, two, three, four, five, six degrees among them, and there's what, five MAS and a PhD or something or Doctor of MD, or something. In *Broaden Your Mind* the two principals have got three degrees between them. This isn't talking from a snob point of view, but I would say that nowadays people with tremendous intelligence are writing a lot of comedy. It's no longer the boozy fool with his page of jokes, in a public bar of a pub saying, 'Here's a joke. I'll take a Guinness for it.'

*Do you intend to stay in television?*

Of course I do. I like the people in television. It's exciting. This is where it's happening. It's happening in this building. It's not happening anywhere else. This is where show business is now. It's not at anywhere else. Don't tell me it's at Shepperton or in, saving their presence, in Broadcasting House or the Aeolian Hall, or the Working Men's Club, Wigan, or the Dolce Vita, Hull, or whatever. It isn't. It's here. This is where it is. It's certainly not much in evidence in commercial TV. They're making money, of course, and they will make money. They're nice people. They're decent people. They're good technicians and they're good administrators, and they're making money, like the Westminster Bank. We're making show business.

# Eamonn Andrews

TV compère and interviewer. BBC: *What's My Line, This Is Your Life, Crackerjack*; ABC: *Eamonn Andrews Show, World of Sport*; Thames: *Today.*

*A lot of the programmes you have done,* This Is Your Life *and* The Eamonn Andrews Show, *are regarded as being the bland end of the product. What do you feel about that yourself?*

I have always thought that *This Is Your Life* was one of the best ideas that ever happened. I know it has been criticized, mostly by people who didn't know what we were about. I think this is a thing that people can look at. It doesn't strain them and yet we salute people in the public eye and learn something more about them and discover people we never *would* have learnt about. People underestimate how much people love surprises. I always say how can we surprise the person, because the central figures must enjoy it. If they don't, we are wasting your time, but, if they do, we think the viewer enjoys it too.

I think there are some superb people in television who are so frightened of the bland end or the light end that they get television out of perspective. I have an absolute view that the greater portion of television must be entertainment. I am terrified of clever people getting control of television, and giving us day-long superb programmes of world affairs, current affairs, literature and ballet. It's the kind of argument I have occasionally on *Today*. I look at the context for an edition and say it's too heavy. The producer may, quite rightly, say I'm scared. That you mustn't be afraid of serious topics. I'm not, in fact. But I always think of the switch-off point. If the housewife does switch off – what a waste of effort.

Then, of course, there's the old-boy section that people used to think was the sole property of the BBC. In fact, they're everywhere, bless 'em. The 'intellectuals'.

'Well, did you see what I did on Stradivarius last night?'

'Great. Great.'

And they are happy, and they are broadcasting to each other.

*Is that the situation now?*

I don't think it's too bad. You must have the minority programmes. The eagerness to do good, thorough, tough, informative television is a desirable object. But you must have the other stuff or eventually you are talking to yourself in a wilderness.

*Why did you move into* Today? *Did you feel you were too flimsy as a television artist?*

No. Simply when Thames opened they wanted to do this kind of programme and I was very flattered to be approached by Brian Tesler and Jeremy Isaacs who thought I could do this kind of

65

programme. So I suppose they didn't think I was flimsy! They invited me to front this programme which they regarded as one of their most important on Thames. Although at my stage in television life I wasn't exactly jumping to do a five-day-week programme, I was so intrigued with the thought that I said yes.

*Would you say it's very important that your personal opinions on central issues are kept very much to yourself?*

No, I don't think so. I used to think so, but not any more. I made a point for too long of subscribing to that. As an interviewer I thought it wasn't my business to project my views: but I think I went too far with that. I think I became faceless in a way or whatever the various accusations were. So I let my views come out a little more now, but not too far. I tend to be irritated by linkmen who suddenly hit out with strong views, more especially when I suspect some of them are views on the prompter from the editor and not from themselves.

# Frank Muir

1965–7, Assistant Head of Light Entertainment, BBC; 1967–9, Head of Entertainment, London Weekend. Scriptwriter: *Whacko, 7 Faces of Jim, Brothers in Law, Mr Justice Ducannon, How to Be an Alien.*

I first worked for television as a performer. I introduced programmes – one was called *New to You* in which Norman Wisdom was the young comic who did that falling about in the piano. It was watched at that time by about four hundred dealers and old Queen Mary, who for some curious reason was besotted with telly.

*Television must have been very strange in those days; was it considered the coming thing or was it just considered a very minor part of broadcasting?*

No – a leafy backwater. Dennis Norden and I wrote for radio for thirteen years, and in most of that time television wasn't a threat to radio. It took radio a long, long time to find its own sense of humour and to find its own drama, and its own feature programmes. And it'll take television quite a while. There's a long, long way to go yet before you get, as it were, true television comedy.

*You were two and a half years as Head of Comedy at the BBC, you then moved to London Weekend as an executive. Why doesn't television recruit its managers from the business managerial class?*

I don't think you can. When you get people without experience of the television industry in a position of control, then things tend to come unstuck, because television at the moment doesn't obey the rules of business. It's doubtful whether it ever will because it's making entertainment, and that is a wasteful process. In a sense you can construct a wild paradox that the more wasteful it is the more efficient it is, the better the result. In that, say, you've got eight producers, of whom four are idle. Now on paper that looks very wasteful, but in effect it means that for the four programmes you've got to produce you've been able to select exactly the right producer for that programme.

*What would you say are the specific problems of television?*

Well, this question that it is on paper a wasteful operation, is the trickiest one. It's about handling creative talent. It's managing people with different responsibilities from the people you manage in other industries. Managing people who probably owe their fourth allegiance to the company that employs them, not their first. And creating a climate in which creative people can create – that is so vitally important and difficult.

*Do the same things still make people laugh?*

Yes. Oh, yes. The same things do. The way they're expressed changes, changes quite quickly, and fashions come and go. But you cannot be dogmatic about comedy. Comedy fulfils a need. It's a thing that they need in this country – and the sort of comedy they need changes according to the mood of the country. Again this is a rationalization, but it's a crude theory which seems to hold a bit of water. A few years ago when there'd been a Conservative government in for about nine hundred years and one

67

had the feeling there was a Texas colonel with a red neck whose finger was on the button of the hydrogen bomb, there seemed to be no future, and a very sort of bitchy comedy proved to be successful, which was called satire. It was a kind of malicious entertainment. But now you see the situation has changed entirely: we've got a different sort of government, different sort of problems. This thing of 'annihilation might be Thursday' has gone. And that kind of malicious entertainment doesn't work any more, it seems vaguely old hat. Because it doesn't fit the mood. At the moment it seems to be a sort of John Cleese kind of humour. But there's comedy in the air all the time.

*Then how important is comedy in our lives?*

You can look on comedy as an aspirin – a half-hour comedy show is an aspirin tablet and for half an hour if you like it, it makes you laugh, obscures your symptoms of worry and depression and stress. It's a kind of escapism – laughing is the second best to the orgasm as a complete release. And if you look upon a half-hour show as an aspirin tablet which does that, the aspirin is needed for different things. There's all sorts of comedy around all the time – there are still people wandering around with satire shows in their pockets and farcical shows and fantasy shows, and dialogue shows and hard-hitting social-comment shows. But they don't work – the public rejects them. Now they're taking the sort of John Cleese fantasy – not that John Cleese is suddenly writing better, he's always like this, but suddenly they need that sort of aspirin. Now in about two years' time it might change again and suddenly the social comment, the Johnny Speight thing, will suddenly find touch again.

*Looking at situation comedy like Steptoe, Alf Garnett – do you think it's had any social impact?*

I don't think so, no. I think it's a particularly effective aspirin tablet with residual benefits. Those shows were so good that people have enjoyed them and are grateful to the people who have given them the enjoyment.

*Is it the job of a Head of Comedy to know what people will want next?*

You can't, because you don't know what's going to happen in the world. You don't know what's going to happen to the country, what the mood's going to be. You don't know what writers are going to think and people are going to think. You can't gauge this. And it's all made much more subtle than I said because there is quality of product, and this is also terribly important. And in fact if a product is of a sufficiently high quality, the script is sufficiently brilliant or the casting is just right, that thing can break through on its own merits. And what happens is that the influence of the feelings, the political feelings of the country, affect the writer. So the product is that much better if it's in line and does that much better with the audience because they need that kind of reassurance. It is reassurance against what one's frightened about usually – I mean it's reassuring when you laugh against people who are better off than you are or more powerful, you laugh to cut them down to size. Which is why you're always against whoever's in power, because you can chop them down to size, you can laugh at them. You also laugh at people less fortunate than yourself, because that gives you a feeling of superiority.

*Is television giving people a wide enough spectrum to choose from?*

Well, most of the work is mediocre, and most of the work is un-inspired – in other words it's hack work. It's 'How about a show about people running a travel agency?' And quite a lot of this gets on. They're not significant shows but they make up quite a bulk of what's on at any given time.

I've always thought that my mission – when I was in any position of command for a brief period – was to raise the standard of mediocrity a notch. Because the big ones you can never foretell, you never know it's going to be a big one, they always creep up on you. Nobody was more surprised than Galton and Simpson at *Steptoe*, nobody more surprised than Johnny Speight at *Till Death* – but when you're set up for a big one like *Curry and Chips* it doesn't work. It's a small one. Because you can break the thing down with a slide-rule and a computer and you can rearrange it – and the second time it just doesn't work, or it does. It does not obey the rules.

*So the big ones are going to take care of themselves?*

The big ones will take care of themselves. And the flops you should

69

be able to avoid in the main – you shouldn't have a run of disasters. You should have one resounding flop, one really big one, and you should legislate for this. Because if you legislate for having a really big flop – not a grey, dreary lack of success, but a big wild failure – it means that you stand a chance of having a big wild success. You've opened your mind to having a big success as well. If you play cautious all the time, you can reduce flops. You could quite easily reduce your big flops, but you're severely reducing any chance of a big success.

*What did you hope to get out of belonging to the London Weekend experiment?*

The two and a half years at the BBC was really very successful. I say that because it's not strictly true: what is strictly true was that in the two and a half years I was there I was able to protect the producers to a certain extent and to encourage them to a certain extent, and there happened to be a run of successful shows, which I got the entire credit for! With the BBC you've got the marvellous machine, it's a programme-making machine. You've got all the facilities and resources and libraries and whatever, and the idea of at the age of forty-eight starting something absolutely from scratch with nothing going for you at all – you've got to start by sending out for a ballpoint pen – that was just a marvellous opportunity.

*What did you hope to carve out of the schedules for yourself?*

What I hoped to do was to alter the face of ITV comedy, which until then was virtually non-existent. It was situation comedy of relationships and so forth – most ITV comedies were vehicles for stars on the books. Which were good or bad, but they weren't writers' ideas. So I wanted to start that up in ITV, which I think worked, which happened.

# David Frost

1962–3, *That Was The Week That Was;* 1964–5, *Not So Much A Programme;* 1966–7, *The Frost Report;* 1967, *Frost Over England;* 1969, *The David Frost Show.*

*How do you deal with a combination of light entertainment and current affairs? Isn't there a conflict?*

Well, it's never been a problem. All along, my basic, most passionate feeling about television was that the public are much brighter than they are taken for, and people do not need to be given uni-tonal – to make up a new word – programmes. When you do a programme that is serious most of the while and has a light passage in it, they don't need huge flashing signs to say 'solemnity'; people adjust very quickly. In fact, the one thing complements the other and the lighter thing makes the serious thing more interesting and the serious thing makes the lighter more diverting.

*Do you think if you were interviewing for the press you would conduct the level of debate more thoroughly in terms of the subtlety of argument than you are able to do on the screen?*

No, I wouldn't say it would be either deeper or shallower. It would be different. I think that there *is* a slight difference. I think there is an extent to which you can reveal more of a real person on television, and maybe more of a lengthy dialectic in the press. That's not necessarily always true. But I think the point of an interview is to turn it into a conversation or a dialogue as fast as possible. I think you are more concerned with what the real person is like. That doesn't mean that you can't discuss issues; obviously you can and you can discuss policies. You can discuss policies on television and personalities in the press, obviously. One is only talking of the shading.

*But the shading suggests that television is going to give an exposition of personality better than an exposition of argument?*

No, I think that's making the shading too definite. All I am saying is that in general probably you can do a lengthy dialectical argument better on paper and you can do a lengthy character study better on television.

71

## Light Entertainment

*How would you react yourself when people say television is constantly trivializing the issues of the day?*

Well, the point is that because television coverage is different that doesn't necessarily mean that it is more trivial. Twenty reports from, say, Julian Pettifer in Vietnam, six minutes each in duration, are not less trivial than one two-hour slog through a book. It is a different medium and because it makes its impact with a series of short pieces over a long period, it doesn't mean that it is necessarily any more trivial than a long book.

Obviously any medium is partially guilty of most of the things it is accused of. No medium is perfect. But I think a lot of the criticism of television in trivializing the subject comes from the resentment of an *élite* at finding subjects which they had regarded as élitist subjects, élitist subjects no more. If an *élite* subject is suddenly made available to a mass the *élite* has lost something and may resent it.

*Do you think the élite has any justification in suspecting that in making their subject available to the mass you in some sense distort it?*

It is obviously possible; but it implies that the British public responds solely to distortion and ludicrous simplification. I was talking to the National Viewers' and Listeners' Association and someone there said television brainwashes people and I said: 'Are you saying that television has brainwashed you into believing what you really do not believe in?' 'Oh, no, no. Of course not,' she said, 'but it does brainwash people.' And so I then said to the entire room: 'Is there anyone in this room who would say that television has brainwashed them into believing what they do not really believe?' And of course no one puts their hand up. Most of their arguments depend on an assumption that other people are more stupid than one is oneself.

*Do you feel that you have, at any point, really changed and affected public opinion?*

I don't think that you can ever give people a Damascus experience by television and turn them round in the reverse direction to the direction they were going in before.

72

What television can do is to articulate something maybe eighteen months before the individual person would have done and he will think 'That's true. Yes, yes I suppose I feel that.' You can edge them in a direction they were already intending to go. For instance, take *Cathy Come Home*. If everybody in the country secretly felt 'Homelessness is the just deserts for lazy layabouts, and it's a good thing to see these lazy out-of-work so-and-so's homeless,' then the programme couldn't have turned them right around. The reason it had an impact was that people's possibly not yet articulated feeling was that, in an allegedly affluent society, there was something shameful or immoral about homelessness. And it articulated it, edged people in the direction they would probably eventually have gone.

Where my programmes have had any impact, I think it is in terms of articulating something people probably would have articulated later or edging them in a direction they were already going maybe subconsciously. For instance, the realization that there was something that could be done about the spread of heroin addiction through over-prescribing or that there were certain dangers about the pill that hadn't been discussed, those things had a great impact because they were in the area in which people were thinking, moving, feeling already.

In the end you come to the decision that if one's feeling about the audience means anything, people can cope with the truth, can cope with facts, can analyse them for themselves, and that the one thing that you cannot do really is to deny them facts allegedly on your better judgement.

*Do you think the battle for the ratings might bring the standard of British television down a level?*

Well, I think it all depends on how intelligently people are competitive. In fact, if you are going to be truly competitive and smash the opposition you do that by actually being as creative as possible. Now you could be as imitative as possible and that would be very bad for British television.

But, let's face it, ratings are also people and the fight for a large audience is a very good thing as well as potentially a bad thing. If you actually believe that in a democracy each man's vote is equal, there is no reason, when you turn to television, to sud-

73

denly assume that each member of an audience is not equally valuable. If they are important as an equal voting electorate, then they don't suddenly lose those powers of discernment when they turn to television.

I found with *Frost Report* three or four years ago at the BBC that the audience appreciation surveys would give it two or three points higher on a cracking edition than it would on a not quite so cracking edition.

Now I am not saying that they all prefer a documentary to entertainment, but if you look at which entertainment shows tend to prosper as opposed to those which fall by the wayside and which drama series prosper as opposed to those which tend to fall by the wayside – I think the public make a pretty good judgement.

*Do you think it's probable that television will get better?*

My main hope is that in searching for new adventures and new challenges television doesn't slip back into the élitist view. I think some of the reforming pressures on television now are in fact élitist pressures – to do with reinstating the dominance of the minority documentary, for instance, which I am not opposed to. But I think the whole pressure needs to be most of all in terms of lifting and continuing to lift the value and the quality of the mass appeal programmes because those are the ones that have the most profound effect and impact.

One of the most formative experiences in my television life was when Ned Sherrin and I were cooking up *That Was The Week That Was.* We went into the *Tonight* hospitality room after a very good show and everyone was very happy about it, and Donald Baverstock, who was by then Czar of BBC 1, strolled over as spiritual father to join the group, and there were lots of 'genuine experts' about television in that room. Suddenly in all the euphoria, someone who had just joined the show – the fourth production secretary, started that Monday – said : 'I didn't quite understand that item about Madagascar.' And immediately Donald switched off everyone else in the room and concentrated on her, to see if there was some way in which everyone else in the room could have enjoyed it as much but *she* could also have understood the whole thing about Madagascar.

*David Frost*

It is always worth analysing, because sometimes there is just a little extra something you could have done that wouldn't have spoiled it for anyone else but would have made it live for those who didn't understand.

# 6 · Drama

The BBC Drama Department consists of three creative groups: series, serials and single plays. Series provides at the last count (April 1969 to March 1970) 133 hours of television a year (all hours quoted exclude repeats) and under Andrew Osborne has a staff of about half a dozen directors and eleven producers. Serials, providing 146 hours, is headed by Ronnie Marsh with some six directors and eight producers. Single plays come under Gerald Savory who has on his staff about five directors, twelve producers; and uses many freelance directors: there are around 116 hours of single plays in a current year. Each group also calls on upwards of 100 freelance directors. Within each group there are also script editors whose job includes finding authors and plays, and then preparing those plays for the screen. The producer – the impresario figure – selects the plays he wants to do, and is responsible for casting, budgeting, rehearsal and recording arrangements; he works closely with the director who rehearses the actors and directs the cameraman. The look of the play on the screen is his achievement.

ITV is served by an entirely different drama structure. There are five separate and autonomous drama departments in the five networking companies. Beyond that, other companies – especially Anglia – make a contribution to the network drama. The smaller regions simply cannot afford to. Within ITV as a whole there are five heads of drama.

These, then, are the two structural systems of television drama that stand between the playwright and his written words and the pictures on the screen. Together they are the largest television drama complex in the world.

Whether or not critics are important they have certainly been unanimous in recent months in their complaints about the level of television drama. And this is certainly an area of television that feels itself threatened in different ways: the executives feel threatened by high costs, lack of material and scheduling pressures; the writers feel worried that the range of their opportunities might be reduced; the producers and directors, caught between both, feel a balance of unease in all directions. We talked to executives, producers, directors and writers, who all shared a sense of anxiety. Yet there are important reasons why this should not be interpreted as a dilemma internal to BBC and ITV politics or a case of professional bickering.

Television plays, series and serials are the major form in which the majority of people experience drama today. The theatre must always count its audiences in thousands rather than millions; the cinema's comeback after its major decline has been to particular audiences in fewer and often smaller houses. So in considering the nature of television drama, it must be seen as the inheritor of the role theatre has played in society heretofore. It is that important.

Why then do we need drama? Some sort of theatrical ritual has existed and exists in most societies: all of them have certain characteristics in common. They are performed publicly before an audience, they are of a repeatable nature, they evoke a strong emotional response and, dealing as they do in fiction or historical myth, they consciously or unconsciously play out the themes of that society. The themes may be patriotism, ancestor worship, death, honour, fertility – but the drama explores areas which its society can be expected to feel strongly about. It can alarm, allay, reassure: the effect is called cathartic.

Now examine television drama: many of these conditions it does not fulfil. It is seen by the public in private groups at home, it is not a repeatable or repeated experience, and very often it aims at gentle satisfaction rather than strong emotion. But in other areas, in its content and audience response, it fulfils the old traditional needs. Television drama lives out for its audience in fictional form the themes that concern it. And in so doing it often explores areas that rouse, provoke and disturb.

Confusion then arises because television itself – the very existence and power of the medium – is now one of the most talked of themes of our society, and a disturbing one at that. The whole

77

school of documentary drama has offered one of the most vigorous attempts so far to deal with the transition from theatre to television drama. The argument that follows a documentary drama production is not about the content of the play, but about whether it confuses documentary with fiction. A play that looks at violence in our society provokes a debate about violence on television. A playwright who examines, say, the breakdown of a marriage investigates our social and sexual neuroses. The argument will be about sex on television. People worry about sex and violence on television; it is easier than worrying about sex and violence. This feeling then becomes a pressure upon television in fulfilling the very role that traditionally was that of drama.

Television drama as discussed here with directors and executives is seen to be under threat from various pressures: most of them relate to cost. The financial problems of ITV and the BBC are reaching the programmes even if no actual schedule budgets have been cut. The BBC, for example, has passed its current programme budgets, but requested a cut back in the extra allowed beyond that to take account of rising costs. The amount of money is not reduced. In real terms there is less available. This represents a threat of a uniformity of output, an over-concern with ratings and majority audiences. In justifying their high costs, drama executives hold a strong card if they can say the programmes pleased a large number of people. In cost-per-thousand terms, therefore, a popular play gives better value for money. A popular play is often a play that gives no offence, causes no protests, creates no argument; it can also give delight, pleasure and insight. There is certainly a need for such plays. The danger that they may become the *only* kind of television play, is one that preoccupies writers and directors at the moment. The feeling is strong that television drama is in retreat from the place it once held in the exchange of contemporary ideas.

The high cost of drama is already damaging in one area: the commissioning of enough new and untried playwrights to allow a percentage to fail and another percentage to learn the craft. The natural temptation – and indeed responsible temptation within solely economic terms – is to cut such obvious risks. But in fact this failure to invest in the future could result in a downwards spiral of the level of drama.

Many directors and writers also feel that the single play is in danger. The fashion for bunching plays under umbrella titles that has recently grown up is entirely an expedient for building audience interest. It is legitimate only if it leaves writers genuinely free from pressures to conform. The other side of the coin, of course, is that the drama output is threatened by lack of material. The classical plays have probably all been done at least once. The novels of the eigtheenth, nineteenth and twentieth centuries have been ransacked for serial potential; the boom of contemporary writing that began in the mid 1950s has dwindled in amount and quality. So where is the new drama to come from? The problem is likely to get more and more difficult – and to deal with it some more thorough search-and-find operations need to be mounted. Which is where the vicious circle began : the need for money to finance such a project.

Finally the threat is a scheduling one. If home-produced drama is prohibitively expensive, why not buy the American film drama series or put out feature films? The idea has certainly been advanced that if the audience want conflict, clash of personality, or a good story why need we have such a thing as native television drama, when the serious feature film deals in such subjects? The answer is simple : the feature film, however much concerned with contemporary story-telling when it was made, is out of date when it reaches the small screen. Drama on television, to have any continuing impact, must be as contemporary in its attitudes as a newspaper. Television drama must reflect life in this country with immediacy : yesterday's cinema sensation won't do.

Scheduling of drama on ITV with any single drama policy for that channel as a whole is prevented by the nature of the ITV structure. The five network companies all have drama departments. The network scheduling committee is responsible for fair shares all round so that each gets a slice of network time. This is a bargaining operation between the big five, with occasional favours bestowed on the rest in the interests of inter-company harmony. The ITA which insisted on *News at Ten* being in peak viewing has never made any criticism or insisted on any change in the scheduling of plays. What results is not a thought-out policy for ITV drama as a whole. It is wasteful, too, in that it supports the existence of separate drama departments, facilities and personnel at a time when ITV claims to be in a chronic economic plight.

Some streamlining of structure is urgently needed without stifling the variety of approach to drama expressed by Cecil Clarke, Lloyd Shirley and Peter Willes. Television drama means different things to different producers and different audiences. It's right that it should: only then will it be the successful inheritor of drama in our society. Otherwise it will be an attractively packaged, highly marketable commodity: and dead.

# WRITERS

# John Hopkins

Playwright. 1953, *Z Cars*. Plays include: *Horror of Darkness, Fable, A Game Like Only A Game, Walk a Tight Circle, Talking to a Stranger, Beyond the Sunrise.*

*Why do you feel television drama was so strong in the early 1960s?*

Look at the quality of the people who were actually there, intimately involved with television, people like McCarthy, Kennedy-Martin, Plater, Dewhurst, David Mercer, Alun Owen. These people who were actually serious writers were almost totally involved with television, and had to produce something quite remarkable. That happened because three years before it happened, there was a script department which gradually drew into it all these people who later did all this work.

*Would you say that you really learned the craft of your business while working on* Z Cars?

But, of course. Complete dedication to that programme that we all had over two and a half years, stretched you far beyond what you thought you could do. One could write an hour's play every week for four weeks and then take a couple of weeks off.

Elwyn Jones took me on as the story editor of *Z Cars*: I knew the day after he gave it to me, that this was *the* chance, not just a chance, that you took and you made it work. This is still the same. It happens. At the moment it is not happening with anything of any

great merit. But a writer can create a series and that is the chance
of a lifetime. And nowadays when they've got themselves even
better organized in terms of residual credits and the 'created by'
situation you can also make a fortune out of it. No one made a
fortune out of *Z Cars*.

*Where did it begin to lose this enormous impetus?*

Well, inevitably, as happened in America, when people began to
leave television. We all, perhaps, got greedy, because there is no
question but that there are greater rewards financially outside television. This has always been one of the great problems. First of all
it is not easy to write twelve plays a year, or even six, and you need
to write at that amount upwards if you are to make a good living.
When you compare what you can be paid to write a film, you begin
to look a bit askance. I do not think it began to lose impetus
necessarily in the way of running out of steam. What should have
happened is, there ought to have been a whole bunch of people
saying 'Get out of the way and let us have a go', and the ground
had not been prepared.

The BBC was turning from paternalism which does produce
some good effects and was swinging violently in the opposite
direction, to a really almost frighteningly winner-take-all attitude.
The paternalism of Donald Wilson, Michael Barrie, was very important in my life, because they created a climate in which it was
possible to work and to learn. Donald and I as writers could hardly
be more different, but Donald as the head of the Script Department was a very important man in my growth because of the
quality that he gave us as writers. I do not think that the one or
two surviving good people involved in the Script Department at
the moment have the scope for training.

*How important is the survival of the single play?*

Without drama you have no series, because you have no one
trained to write. You cannot write a series unless you can write a
good play, it seems to me, and many series are bad because there
is a whole new breed of often very good writers who are specifically
series writers. But that leaves out the one whole aspect of craft, the
creation of character, because you are always arriving with a
whole group of people readily created.

*Drama*

Drama has always been the most difficult bit of television to fit into a programme and necessarily, because plays should be disturbing. Plays should make you think. Plays should do all sorts of things that a certain attitude towards television finds very disturbing. Every time you see a David Mercer play – a very disturbing writer – you reach the end and you think, 'Well, that's it. I'm not going to stay here and watch *24 Hours*. I've got enough to think about', or 'I'm unhappy enough. I don't need that in my life.' I would like to think that was true of my plays too.

It is very difficult for drama to survive in the way that it should be – radical, exciting, demanding – certainly if it is sandwiched between commercials, because commercials are anti-drama. The commercials are a confirmation of all the things you want to believe; that if you drive the right car and drink the right drink and eat After Eight Mints, everything will be absolutely sublime and beautiful. And then you go into another segment of a play which says, look, this is what life is about and it is wrong. If television is not simply to destroy itself by its own banality and glorification of the mediocre the only way is to set up some kind of recognition of the need for quality as well as quantity. This is why the medium is so demanding.

# Dennis Potter

Playwright: *Vote, Vote, Vote for Nigel Barton, Stand Up Nigel Barton, Son of Man, A Beast With Two Backs.*

*As a playwright how well do you think television has served your needs?*

I think better than any other medium could have done. One, just in terms of sheer numbers; two, in terms of what technically you can do. (You couldn't have a worse audience and, as a paradox of that, you couldn't have a better one either. You really do make an effect.) The main criticism with television is that it just seems an endlessly grinding thing – a burning monk, an advertisement, and Harold Wilson, and a pop show, and Jimmy Savile, all seem the same sort of experience. How do you make people sit up suddenly and say 'Shouldn't have thought of that; I didn't feel that, I knew it but I didn't know I knew that'? Drama seems to be one of the few things left which has the kind of flexibility which can just about do that. The theatre is a kind of middle-class privilege, a dying, sort of minority thing, despite various attempts to inject new life into it. But only television is classless, multiple, and, of course, people will switch on and people will choose. On the whole I suppose I'm very pessimistic. People will tend to choose crap rather than not. But on the other hand, you do just have the chance to grab them. It's the biggest platform in the world's history, and writers who don't want to kick and elbow their way on to it must be disowning something in themselves.

*How well has the structure of television served the production of your plays?*

There's scarcely a single play which has gone through without some sort of fuss or bother. But I think this is inevitable. You have this huge organization with people under pressures that you, yourself, are not aware of, so you get these comic twists of policy; one moment going through a script taking out all the 'bloodies' and 'buggers' and things and then another moment saying that as a subject this is too complex or too way out or too whatever. But once a play has been scheduled, once it's got under way as it were, once one is in the studio, once it's been cast, then I think it's solely between the writer and director. Now, the BBC is a marvellous anachronism, you know. It's like one of those English bits that's survived. It's a lump: it has no logic to it: and it's our safeguard, in a way. Plays that I've done on BBC I could never even have submitted to ITV. I know this. And my experience of ITV – the things that you can dare to question or bring into question are so much less, because it is a commercial organization. Whereas the BBC is weird, an anachronism: I mean unique in the world. It does genuinely give one this chance to create . . . I think it's a federation, really, of various pressure groups. The *Wednesday Play* as a unit became, as it were, its own little force within this huge stadium called the BBC. And that does give one a sense of greater freedom and it doesn't seem so anonymous and huge and technocratic.

*What is your actual experience of ITV?*

I've written a few plays for them. I've gone along to a few story editors and talked to them. I've always been aware that I was in a different world, different atmosphere. It was no use, for example, talking about a play in terms of abstraction, or it was no use me saying 'I'm trying here to show the collision between reality and myth.' What happens? – they wanted to know 'How does it work out? Is that the end of act two?' It's much more brutal and to the point and much more like Fleet Street, which I hated. And so really it's only because one is aware that one ought not always to put all one's eggs in the same basket – that you go across to them.

*But have they served you less efficiently, the creative people there? I mean, are there built-in disadvantages?*

There's a play now waiting to be shown on ITV. It's directed by Christopher Morahan, a very good director, and I like the play. But they suddenly whipped away our filming allocation. After some filming had been done in the street, you suddenly had to have an encounter in the studio, and it looks like it. Whereas I think that's the thing the BBC would not allow. I mean, I think they made a mistake in putting *Son of Man*, for example, in a plastic and polythene Holy Land, but they decided in advance it was a studio production and that was the end. But at least you knew where you were. I've only done a few ITV plays, and I'm never quite sure what budget is going to be cut, what is going to be taken away, what is going to be censored. So you have these weird memos. For example, one from Humphrey Burton before he resigned, which said 'I really must draw the line at "bollocks". May I suggest "knackers"?'

# David Mercer

Playwright: *Where the Difference Begins, A Climate of Fear, The Birth of a Private Man, A Suitable Case for Treatment, The Buried Man, For Tea on Sunday, And Did Those Feet, The Parachute, On the Eve of Publication, The Cellar and the Almond Tree, Emma's Time.*

*Your first play* Where the Difference Begins *was done by the BBC in 1960. This was your first encounter with the BBC as an institution and with drama production on television. What did you think of it all?*

I think at the time I was slightly overawed by the kind of benign, paternalistic civil service temperament, not only of people but the whole atmosphere. What I thought were very posh people, Cambridge and Oxford degrees, being kind of, you know, free and liberal and gentle and all that, rigorously sticking within the meaning of the Charter. But when I look back on that period, in a way it seems to me that those people had virtues which have possibly disappeared in fact from the set-ups all over the place, not only the BBC.

*What were the virtues?*

I think they were the virtues of a genuine sense of responsibility towards the meaning of the Charter. A sense of responsibility towards the virtue of art if you like, the right and the necessity of art. And the idea that what writers write is not something to be turned into a product, but it was something that it was their business to see was presented to the world on its own terms for what it was, not as part of a competitive consumer sort of attitude towards television.

*Were your subsequent plays written very much for television?*

Well, yes. But it was a slow process of discovering what I felt writing a television play meant and it is not something I can intellectualize for you. I think it's basically a question of discovering where words, where only words can do what you want to do and where pictures can do it anyway. If pictures can do it anyway, then in television you keep out the words. It took me a long time.

Let's Murder Vivaldi *ran into censorship problems. What do you make of the attitudes taken towards censorship?*

The thing I've never been able to find a way of refuting in myself is the argument that television is seen commonly by family groups of varying ages and sizes and temperaments and inclinations and educations and so on. And that the feelings or the responses

aroused by the play may be so different in this viewing group that
it could create embarrassment or shame or humiliation or anger
in a family, simply because they'd all seen the same thing together.
Now why I can never answer that one is because in fact there's
quite a few of my own plays that I wouldn't have liked to have
sat down and watched with my own mother and father. So I have
to kind of accept that sort of argument. I think that the people,
the executive people in television, are understandably preoccupied
with that as a problem and I think one has to take some account
of that.

*Do you feel that television drama is now highly competitive and
geared as a consumer product?*

I can't remember the last time I saw a play I admired on commercial television. And I am increasingly finding that the switch-
off potential for BBC drama is coming down all the time – I
think it's down to about five or six minutes by now. Most of it.
But this is not because I can say that these plays are bad or
mediocre or shouldn't have been done, it's just that, on the whole,
the plays exist to a level of creative standards which I have no
respect for. If I were to ask myself 'Is this process going to continue until finally even work that one can respect is engulfed as
well, or eliminated rather than engulfed?', I wouldn't say that
there's a real danger of it at the BBC, but there's certainly a smell
of danger about it all.

*Under what pressures would you say?*

We'll really just have to face the fact about the BBC at the moment
– its pressures are awful and basically financial. It's starved of
money, and naturally in an enterprise if you start looking round
for things to chop, you rationalize this by chopping the things
which you can arguably say are becoming less relevant to public
need. I think what people are worried about – writers, directors
and, I hope, actors and producers too – is that they don't seem
to have any role in the process by which the decisions are made at
the top which they have to carry out. In any case there is no
debate about the first principle of the argument. I think this is a
disgusting state of affairs and one has to attempt to rectify it.

# Irene Shubik

Joint co-producer The *Wednesday Play*.

*You first came into television drama as a story editor on* Armchair Theatre – *what was it like?*

Peter Luke and I were story editors on it together and we got all the scripts and all the ideas and all the writers in, and then we had a monthly meeting with Sydney Newman and presented him with all the people we'd seen and ideas we'd like to commission. We'd discuss them all and he'd say 'OK. Go ahead on this – go ahead on that.' And he never saw the script again until it was in a shape that we considered was absolutely produceable. The minute you got a script, you know, you talked to the director and the designer. It was all little conferences. Unfortunately, you just about never can get this sort of early discussion here because it's so big.

*Is that the snag about the way the BBC operates?*

Very, very much so. You know, it's a perpetual frustration as far as I'm concerned. I can just about never get together the sort of package deal where I've got everybody I want – the right designer, the right make-up, the right camera-man. They're all separate departments and are all frightened you're interfering with their authority. One says 'I want so and so for this play', and they say 'No, you can't have him, we think you should have so and so.' You end up having a fight with them. This is especially true with the design department.

*Do you look back on the* Armchair Theatre *days with a certain nostalgia?*

Very, very much. And all the people I know who worked together do. Everybody says they've never had that feeling again of a whole unit of people who had the same ideas and approach to production and tremendous enthusiasm. It may have been because it was early days, but the plays we did we really believed in, and we seemed to have much more fun out of every production because of the general group enthusiasm. When you got a script, the designer came in and said 'Wouldn't it be more interesting if we set this scene here and changed that set to shoot it more imaginatively', and everything was sort of re-jigged, in that way. I've never yet experienced that approach here. It's like doing things by computer here. You just feed the script in and out comes the system's answer. There are some good designers here, but they just can't overcome the system. Nobody has time to talk to anybody. All the designers are up to their ears in one show, at the time you most want to talk to them. By the time they're on your show, they've got to get the plans in the next day, so it's a perpetual struggle against time. That to me is the big disappointment in it – and the same thing with make-up and wardrobe. The good things about the BBC are that you have a tremendous number of technical resources and facilities available – like all the film units which you don't have in most commercial companies – and also you are more or less left alone.

*There is a great deal of talk that the BBC drama generally has been tamed recently.*

I think what has happened, which is a very unhappy situation for us, is that one's trapped into having to produce too many plays. You just can't keep up a high standard; often you've got to sling into the studio a play with which you are unhappy and you know is not going to be any good. Inevitably, you're going to get mediocrity and there are not that many good writers or directors to make a lot of work really worth watching.

*But there are the people who'll say there's always a lot of untapped talent about.*

Well, there isn't. Again it may sound arrogant, but I really think I'm in a position to know about original talent and there really isn't. There's no reason there should be. You couldn't fill a West End theatre almost every night of the week with a new marvellous play. I would much rather produce far fewer plays with much more time to plan – we never have time to think. You know, things go on and then afterwards you think, 'Oh, my God, how could I have let that happen.' But you just couldn't think about it at the time. It's the same with everybody. And you know, for instance, with the plays that we have done on film – in a film company the producer looks at the rushes and if there's something wrong, he says, 'You've got to reshoot that.' Our looking at rushes is almost academic because our schedule is so tight we haven't got time to reshoot anything.

*Does making things on film compare economically with doing them in the studio?*

Well, it is still more expensive, mainly because of the Equity agreement. You see when you're in a studio you pay the actors a category fee and that's it: but on filming you have to pay more – on top of the category fee, you have to pay £10 a day for every day's filming and if you go over the schedule, they go into new categories. You may go one day over schedule and they go into a brand new category and you pay them another quarter or half fee. When you run into overtime and going over schedule, that's where the money goes.

*Do you hanker after directing yourself?*

Yes, but not studio; only film. I'd hate to direct in a studio. In fact I'm beginning to hate working in a studio altogether, mainly because of the time pressure which, I find, is unbearable. There's a perpetual anxiety that you've got three hours in which to record a play and if you don't get through in three hours there's some poor director going mad, and you've got to be there telling him 'For Christ's sake, get on with it.' You end up with everybody hating you.

*Do you think that the single play as such is under pressure at the moment? Is there a tendency to package things in series and serials?*

Well, we haven't really been affected yet, but I've got a horrible feeling it's coming. It is basically due, I think, to the fact that BBC Enterprises don't seem to be able to sell plays properly. I know that they find it difficult to sell any single plays.

*Drama*

*Do you think also there's a sense in which you've got to educate your audience to writers?*

I think one of the most disappointing things is that if you try to do anything at all off the beaten track nobody seems to want to understand or know. I hate to say it, but after a while – the only thing to do is forget about them, otherwise you'd never do anything.

# Philip Saville

Director: *Afternoon of a Nymph, A Night Out, Prisoner and Escort, In Camera, Hamlet at Elsinore, Rise and Fall of the City of Mahagonny.* Wrote and directed *Exit 19.*

*What sort of preference do you have for television direction now over films and theatre?*

I look upon them as the same – the process of creating a television project of any kind today is not unlike anything you would do in the cinema. In the early periods of television, of course, it was completely different. The major periods of *Armchair Theatre* were interesting because it meant, for the first time in England, a new creative surge of writing talent, and as a director, this was very exciting. And also working with Sydney Newman was very exciting because Sydney had the ability to be able to give a free hand to people that he could trust, and he surrounded himself with a group, a handful or so of people, who were bold enough to cause him to have to be bold, to excite his sort of dreams, even though he may not directly be able to do them. He felt that through these other people he was living out a kind of dream, and because of that a great style of television presentation was evolved, greatly organized by his abilities.

*Did you run into censorship problems?*

Well, I'm probably the only director who has three productions that have never been seen.

*Are they recent?*

No, over five years ago. I have been working in television for about ten years now, and the change in censorship is incredible. There was one production I did called *Three on a Gas Ring* – about three girls who lived together. Two of the girls are in love with the same man, and it is the ultimate scene which caused the rejection by the Board. One of the girls finds she's pregnant, says 'No, I'm not going to marry; I'm going to have the child out of wedlock.' This was untenable by the Bishop of Birmingham, by this and that, the Aldermen, the Mayor, even the Board of Directors of ABC Television themselves. They asked me 'Would you please do an alternative ending.' I said, categorically, 'No, this is the reason I am doing it this way, because I believe it is serious. I don't think the play is a masterpiece, but I think it is a very good piece of television, and I think it must be seen. It must go out as it is.' But it never went out. Now you cannot believe it. The other one was a very brutal, very savage piece. An American play which at the time they felt was too much even at eleven o'clock at night. And the third one was a beautiful play by Michael Campton, called *Bandstand*. This was banned because the authorities thought that it would be indecent to show people above the age of fifty-five involved in acts of love. When I say acts of love, there was some degree of horse-play but there was no act of love as we know it. Not at all. It was remote. There was nothing hot about the scene.

*Would you have no censorship?*

Well, you see, I believe that unless people are seriously ill – where their actions cannot be accounted for, which is not usually the bulk of people working in television or working in responsible areas – they have their own sense of values. Now some people's values are very much more fluid, much looser, wilder than others. But if we're human beings, whatever we're doing, or creating, or showing, is about other human beings. And if we can't show it, then we're denouncing, rejecting human behaviour. Some things shown on the screen now are remarkable. For example, the film about Warrendale, tracking down traumatic mental disturbances in children in Canada. And there were scenes in this film of a boy aggressively swearing. The fact that it went on television is fantastic, and the fact that it did not cause such a disturbance is remarkable.

*Did you find life more difficult in ITV?*

Yes, tremendously, in the early period. Everything I did, and everything my colleagues and friends who worked there did, was a tremendous battle. It even became a personal battle. Sometimes as directors we would have to literally appear outside the board room and say, 'Look, I've got to have money for this.' And I remember saying once, 'Look, do you realize that with the money you are spending on this cocktail party I could erect a whole set in the studio?', and Mr Howard Thomas laughed and offered me a drink. But points were made that way, and gradually they saw what the considerations of directors, who were interested in their work, were, and meetings were held to give us more money. But, at that time, you had to be a very individual person to overcome their prejudice against any form of anarchy.

*You were interested in experimental work, and all that you've done has been pushing techniques, ideas, further. Where is the frontier now?*

I suppose television drama has got to a point where technique is in the hands of so many different people. It's so easy now – a new man or machine pushing a new button there, and full works, loud voices, on a tape. But that's not what it's all about. No, it's what the technique reveals, what the camera contains in our complex life – a life of survival. I think television drama now is probably going to become less theatrical and more where it is almost impossible to see where the drama is. There's more violence, more brutality; the demolition of any one of us is so imminent that it almost becomes impossible, dangerous to wake up in the morning. Television drama now is covering these areas, is covering the everyday lives of lots of different people. In particular I am a great fan of drama that Ken Loach and Tony Garnett and that group has done. I like the drama where you can't tell it's drama, where it's just happening. It doesn't mean to say that it's not very dramatic or very strange or very horrific, or even very funny, but I don't like 'The Play' on television, and never have.

*Is the drama on television good enough to survive and do people want it that much?*

I think people, in England anyway, still like it, providing it becomes technically smooth, proficient and swift and ingratiating. You can only do this with subjects that a large section of the community will be interested in, but unfortunately these dramas become watered down and packaged in a series, umbrella or generic, *Boy Meets Girl*. People are interested in drama, but they're not interested in the one-off drama.

It is paradoxical because the best of the *Wednesday Plays* have been about things which a cross-section of the public identify with, can involve with. But all the eccentric ones are usually dismissed by the critics, some quite rightly, some wrongly, and not reviewed at all by the audience. I would say the play in the drama is not finished, because to use the word 'finished' doesn't allow for the odd genius lurking around the corner, who's going to upset and change everything. I would say that as we know it 'The Play' has changed into something else, and we would all be foolish working in drama to even continue this.

# Peter Hammond

Director: Armchair Theatre productions, *The White Rabbit*, *The Count of Monte Cristo*, *Hereward the Wake*, *Cold Comfort Farm*.

The 5.30 spot in television to which I've contributed over a number of years was always what we called the classic serials and they've always done stories which were relatively elegant, like Jane Austen. Then they started to get stories that were more muscular in structure and had battles in and all this type of thing. They suddenly found themselves faced with the cliché of doing classical serials in the kind of Hollywood way, where everybody was beautiful and fights weren't really fights and people never got ill and it was all – just a little bit – arch. And I – by the people I chose – the actors I chose and by my own nature – started to make them maybe a bit more complicated. And I think I made a mistake.

93

*Drama*

I tried to put ideas into them. I tried to have a point of view about them and that I think was perhaps a mistake because I think television is at its best when it's straightforward, vivid – inviting comment.

*Did the ideas that you were injecting into them spoil programmes?*

Well, it didn't spoil them for me but I think they started asking their own questions. When somebody was hurt, they were in pain: somebody that was frightened showed their fear in a stronger, dramatic sense. In other words, I asked people to examine the stories and maybe read the books again and realize that, for example, maybe Dumas is not for children after all. I always worked on the basis – that parents were always watching with the children, so that if ever anything awful happened the kids could always turn to their parents and ask why.

*Was this generally accepted when you debated it in the BBC?*

It was never debated at all. I just took it for granted and communicated to my producer that if we do this story certain things are going to happen. I had this with *The Three Musketeers*, which had stark undertones. I played D'Artagnan as an anti-romantic, a non-comic, and everybody was quite rightly cross about it. And I'm quite sure, for example, if you saw my *Monte Cristo* you'd find it more complicated in production than the Robert Donat one. Very often, of course, as you get tired, you put too many ideas into the thing and it explodes. I mean, *Cold Comfort Farm* was an interesting kind of failure for the simple reason that there were too many ideas for a family audience to assimilate easily – all the ideas then came up half-baked. Incidentally, the main idea – it was intended to be a 'micky-take' on television techniques – brought no comment. The demands of television couldn't meet it. And as such it's just an enormous explosion of nothing. The result is that I was offered hundreds of pounds of work in advertising. Because they like explosions of nothing.

# Alan Bridges

Staff Director with BBC: *The Father, Dial M for Murder, The Brothers Karamazov, The Idiot, On the Eve of Publication, The Cellar and the Almond Tree, Emma's Time.*

*How does television compare with the theatre in the satisfaction it gives you?*

I think it's much more a director's medium in the sense that you can invest your own ego a little more into it; the end result is a bit more you and to do with you. The theatre is definitely, I mean quite definitely, the writer's medium. If you feel that, as a director, you want to communicate very subjective things, then television or films is the medium for that.

*Are you interested in the fact that you have an audience of ten million at a throw?*

I never think of the audience. I do it for me, really. The theatre is done much more by committees, whereas there are committees in the background in television and films. But the actual doing is really the work, the actor and the director, and what the director can do with the camera.

*You're in a very happy position, aren't you, to choose the plays you do, to be able to select the authors with whom you work?*

Not entirely, but I am in a happy position in that I work for two or three producers who I know quite well and who are, in themselves, in a happy position to be able to commission good and marvellous writers.

*Do you think that works best – that the same producer should have the same director constantly who would then work with the same writers?*

No, I don't think it does. I don't think necessarily the same producer is a bad thing, but I certainly think there ought to be many more young directors and writers doing freer and bigger plays, as I'm able to do. Somewhere or other there is economic pressure

95

*Drama*

which, I feel, is growing up to make it more unlikely that these things are going to go on happening.

*Do you have budget pressures at the moment on you?*

Yes. I think the pressures are getting greater, even on the *Wednesday Play*. What I mean by greater is that there's not so much freedom.

*What do you mean by freedom?*

Well, I mean with McKinsey one has got to make out a most complicated and elaborate Programme Budget Estimate form now. Not me, but my producer has to, and has to account in a very elaborate way for artistic decisions, whereas before, the artistic decisions came first. Now you have to make artistic decisions ahead of time to fill in the PBE form and then play around with that later on, to shift one sum of money from, say, make-up to props or something like that.

*So you're making decisions as you fill in the budget?*

Now if you're lucky, as we are with major plays, you get enough time to do them and a reasonable budget; but if you're not in that position, you really haven't got quite enough money or quite enough man-hours or quite enough time. You're making artistic decisions on things before you've even thought about it.

*You suggest that all the plums of drama productions are going to the old-established directors, like yourself?*

They seem to, yes.

*And it's also you who get the most generous budgetary treatment. So really you feel the pressure applies to the young director and the new writers?*

I think a lot of young directors feel that they are now, for budgetary reasons again, having less time to work on the script with the writer, less say in the actual commissioning of the writers.

*You held a meeting of people concerned about television drama.*

The brief of the meeting was 'Are we really satisfied with things as they are and are we satisfied with what seems to be now the future of television drama in the country, not just the BBC?' And the reaction was a general fear for the future. Very conservative, very reactionary in a way, in that we were desperately keen to keep what we've got in this country. Some of us expressed the views that it's less possible now to be adventurous, it's less possible now to have the *Armchair Theatre* as Sidney Newman introduced it, the *Wednesday Play* as it was first introduced, the Ken Russell ideas. We're certainly having much more economic pressure here. The *Wednesday Play* is only possible if you have a certain sort of artistic freedom. Once we have other pressures, then it will become like any other spot, it will have a definite umbrella title, it will have a form, it'll have to be a certain length, we'll have to stay within a certain budget.

*But you feel that your umbrella title is a threat, do you?*

Yes, I do. Maybe we're really very reactionary, very successful reactionary people who want to keep things as they are, and perhaps project it into an altruism which we don't really feel about young directors and young writers; that is possible.

I would like to talk to Paul Fox and to Attenborough. They are the men who are in charge of our art – at its best it is an art. You know we don't get to them. We don't talk to them. I don't see why we shouldn't sometimes.

*In the best of all possible worlds then, how would you like to see the structure shifted?*

Let us make sure that we are not going to go the American way, to give in totally to the economics and make the fortune that can be made out of television, completely disregarding the content of it.

I think that the artists, the creative people in it, would like to know why certain things are done. They're going to dock eight ninety-minute plays off BBC 2. Why? I mean it's not good enough to say economics. We would like to know a little bit more about where all the money is going.

# Peter Willes

Head of Drama, Yorkshire TV.

*Is the future of the single-shot play very much in the balance?*

I don't believe it is because I think the Independent Television Authority will always demand a certain number of single-shot plays on the television network, and I think companies are not prejudiced and realize that the public want the single-shot play once in a while.

*What do you base that on?*

On certain ratings of plays recently, for instance, Margaret Lockwood in *Justice is a Woman* – there it was in the top ten. It was jolly good and gave many people a lot of enjoyment. We'll see how *The Root of all Evil* goes. The last series went like a bomb, because if you can put an umbrella title over plays like *The Root of all Evil*, the audiences aren't so suspicious and they think they know what it's going to be like.

*Do you feel that the audiences are keeping pace with the sort of things directors and writers are trying to do on television?*

I think the audience is much more sophisticated than people think. Don't forget how much they look in. If they don't understand, that's our fault. It's indulgence if you do a play you understand and they don't. They must understand, they must get enough out of it.

*What are the main themes that writers want to write about today?*

Things people don't want to look at. That's the trouble. If I wanted to do the plays people wanted to look at I'd have to write them myself, and I can't. I know what the audience want, they want romance and a good story. The writer wants to get them into all sorts of terrible social situations.

*Do you feel under any obligation to try and balance plays on your schedules?*

I try to do that. But by the time it gets to the public, with all the other stuff coming in, this just doesn't work. But I worry about my overall output.

*Couldn't it be thought that if drama output on television was so terribly depressing the public would say no?*

Yes, I think that must be watched. I'm very conscious of it: whether the other boys are I don't know, but I'm very conscious of not depressing my audience too much. For instance last night, *The Root of all Evil*, I did put out a gloomy play. Next week it's a farce. That's all right.

*How have the teething troubles in the companies affected your budgets?*

My budgets have been affected because of the Levy and all that sort of thing. The cost has gone way up – it costs about £2,000 more to do a play now than it did when I was in London.

*But you're not depressed in the long term?*

I think economy is a worry. It's just the question of the awful thing of choosing more intimate plays, less filming and smaller casts, but I'm frightened of this because I hate to put limitations on writers.

*What are the limitations of censorship on television?*

Only personal standards and what affects your audience. I think you've got to be more particular if you are going into people's homes than if they come to you. Taste, really, which it is your job to maintain and not offend; in other words the better something is the less likely it is to offend. If it's bad then it's offensive.

*You maintain that responsibility yourself? You don't delegate it?*

I maintain it entirely and am responsible to my company. If I have any doubts I go to my bosses and say, 'Are you prepared to stand by me over this particular play, because it's dicey. I think it may affect the public.'

*How would you advise someone who wanted to go into television?*

I mean this whole-heartedly – I'd say, 'Don't touch it, it's a destroyer.'

*Why?*

Because it's a monster. It's destroyed me.

*Why do you dislike it so much when you are in a happy position to do something?*

Because I'm always worried about tomorrow and keeping up the standard as one creates it. One can never relax: it's too much, there's too much of it. If I could just do my fifteen plays a year and nothing else then I'd be happy. I'm always worried about these series and the output and getting the right people and enough producers and people to work under me who have the same dedication as I demand from myself. It's all too much.

# Shaun Sutton

Head of Drama, BBC TV.

*What would you consider the big technical changes that have made the most difference in the last fifteen years or so?*

In 1953–5 I think the pace was much slower, the shows were all live and so they had to be very much more simple. The camera would seem to be very far back, and I think there would be a lot of group shots that we wouldn't accept nowadays, close-ups would appear to be very much farther away, and the amount of incidental music would be so irritating. *Z Cars* stopped all that, you know. Sort of overnight, link shots disappeared in drama.

*You're now Head of Drama. Do you think that the complexity is becoming a hindrance?*

No, because it isn't all that complex really, you know. There are three hundred people in drama and the actual number of administrators is very small indeed. In the hierarchy, we have two controllers, a director of programmes and managing director and beneath those four are group heads. But when you get to the group head thing you are really at contact with studio level.

*How are plays chosen for television?*

Writers and directors bring in ideas, producers bring in ideas, Heads of Departments add ideas and we form a big pattern of offers: Plays have, say, a page full of offers, and Series and Serials have a page full of offers and we put them together and we go up to the controllers of 1 and 2 respectively and say, 'This is what we are offering you for the coming year.' Then it has to be examined from the point of view of money and point of view of effort (which is the same thing) and the controller will pass what he can afford. And there is a great deal of trust and a great deal of understanding. We know that there is a shortage of money now, and that the controller isn't being beastly to us when he says we can only do nine Plays of the Month instead of twelve Plays of the Month. Then we regret it and we'll go on fighting for ten Plays of the Month, trading for one more as one does. But it's quite informal.

*Has the code on language, sex and violence changed?*

Yes, it has changed and we do swear more. I wish we didn't really because it is very rarely a play is any better because people are swearing all the way through. I think one can be quite plain about violence – where violence and sex do not grow out of the story, they are wrong. They are not there for a true reason. The man who sits down to write a kinky play because he thinks it will succeed probably writes a lousy play.

*Are there particular rules?*

Not really. There is a sort of code of violence, but I think again it becomes an emotional thing, a matter of our own taste. It works awfully well. We have coming up now a pretty broad permissive classic serial* – now at the end of the third part, is a castration scene. . . . We had to be awfully careful with that and we really had to be careful in the shooting of it, and careful about the distance of the shots and all the rest. We shot it in such a way that

* *Germinal*, now transmitted.

those who know about such things will understand and those who don't will merely think that the man's being killed by the mob, so we used taste. How can you write down rules about how to handle a castration scene: it would look slightly odd wouldn't it?

*Whose is the responsibility?*

Technically it is the responsibility of the particular Head of the Drama Department, Series, Serials or Plays, but it's a collective responsibility and it's one that works surprisingly well. Producers are aware that they've got to watch the moral content or the swearing content or the violent content of the play, especially in relationship to where it's going on. It goes wrong sometimes and you switch on and to your horror you see somebody in a children's production cutting off the cat's head with a rusty sword or something like that and you realize the system has slipped but it is the exceptions that prove there is a system.

*How would you define what type of drama we have now?*

I think the concern with social problems still remains with writers just as it remains with students because most students are serious about social problems. It isn't only a question of having demonstrations and riots on the streets, they really care about political and social problems and this obviously is the same with writers. Therefore, I think we've got a rather serious drama picture at the moment which is reflected in the fact that we write very few comedies. The social content, the social aspect, is still very much to the fore. On the other hand, the competition to adapt classics is enormous amongst writers now. There is a feeling of wanting to get in amongst these works of great stature and grace and something more than kitchen sink.

*In terms of viewing, the* Wednesday Play *has lost over this period. Does that concern you very much?*

It is a matter of concern, indeed. I wonder how much the name, the *Wednesday Play*, has slightly outrun its usefulness. If you go to a mass meeting on drama with, say, the press or television writers, or, indeed, with any organization, the first thing that people talk about and attack is the *Wednesday Play*, and yet it's a tiny little part, about 5 per cent of the drama output. To the public the title *Wednesday Play* seems to guarantee that they're going to get something either very permissive or very kinky or very much in the realms of fantasy or very obscure, anything but a straight play, and it becomes a strait-jacket after a while. Many an excellent play is missed by a public partly put off by the reputation of the title alone.

*Do you think there might in the future be less drama?*

Yes, you've got to fight for it all the time. You know, you really have got to fight – not just for the amount of drama, but the quality of drama. And it's going to be a great fight because drama is the most expensive item in television; nothing costs more than drama. Light entertainment sometimes costs as much because of the large fees of single artists, but nothing overall costs as much as drama. You can go out and you can buy a marvellous film drama from America or an old film for a few thousand pounds, and it gets the most marvellous figures; it has a tremendous edge in many ways as a film product and the greatest edge of all is the fact that it costs a tenth of the price.

*Why don't they have less?*

You mean less and better? Well, one of the points about BBC is that they present every single sort of drama. In fact, there are still one or two places we are not presenting enough. It's the only television service in the world which presents drama at all levels. The moment you knock out something you are taking away one of these assets: it's not a question of empire building, it's not a question of having a big department just to have it big: it's a question of supplying all the needs of drama. You know the BBC is the only organization in the world which put on dramas which they know will not be of top popularity, and they know from the start they won't be of top popularity.

*Do you think, under economic pressure, the single plays might go?*

Well, it would be a tragedy if they disappeared, for they are the life-blood of drama. The alternative is to have established series and serials, and in the end just established series. This becomes mechanical. If you have a total output of series only, crime series, social series and all the rest of it, however good they are, you would be seeing one sort of drama all the same length, all very careful not to offend or overstep any social barriers, all these non-offence dramas, and I can't believe that this is good. For one thing, if we get into this state, the brains of drama, the best writers and the best directors, will go back to the theatre, which is very healthy in this country at the moment.

*Are you aware of competing with the output of ITV?*

Of course, we are competing. We want the writers, above all we want the best writers. It all begins there. That's another reason for doing proper productions and not any sort of old rubbish. Writers like Alan Plater and John Hopkins are not going to be content just to come in and do routine work. We've got to offer them things like the *Quartet* and the *Plater Trilogy*.

*If the BBC is under pressure to economize does that mean that the whole tendency for drama to put up its film ratio is going to be limited now?*

Not necessarily, because it is still possible for us to film an episode as cheaply as we would have done it electronically. This has been proved several times recently – I've just done a four-part *Dr Who* and this has turned out cheaper than had we done it electronically. A *Softly, Softly* has been done which compares very favourably with the electronic product so it may well be possible, especially using 16 mm film, to film things at least with a comparable sort of price.

*Do you find that the budgeting of film for drama is in a way dictated by the massive investment that the BBC made in its very big electronic studios?*

Well, yes. We've gone a long way down the electronic road and this has got to be respected. But no one is suggesting that we go and film all drama. It will remain a very modest percentage of our output for some years yet.

*Do you think today, in this generation, theatre is the place to recruit for people in television drama?*

Yes, I do. I think that the theatre is the cradle of it all; I know it

104

sounds very pompous, it's an awful phrase. I think you'll find that practically all the assistant floor managers, all the production assistants, all the directors, have come at some time through the theatre and very few have come straight from university backgrounds, or straight from films. Most of us began in the theatre. The important thing about being a director or a producer is the emotional thing, knowing how to direct actors and to manipulate the script. The best way of learning that is in the theatre, where you are in live contact with the audience the whole time, and you see your thing working in contact with the actual public.

# Lloyd Shirley

Controller of Drama, Thames.

*To what extent do you think the advertising industry influences the product of commercial television in this country?*

An independent television company has to achieve high ratings in order to justify high advertising rates. A high rating means that it is possible for the company involved, be it Thames or whoever, to charge a very high rate for the advertisements they need to live on. So in an indirect way, there is a pressure to achieve rating targets. But that pressure is not defined. In other words, if it were your problem, as it is mine, to make drama productions, nobody is telling you what drama productions to make, but they are saying, 'Please, bear in mind that we must achieve a certain rating target in order to earn the income which we need to finance not only your programme but the entire company operation', which is a valid commercial point. There is no machinery for conversation between independent television makers and advertising interests. This is legislated by Act of Parliament, and, in theory and in practice, it's strictly observed. I know of no instance where advertising has brought direct pressure.

*Do you find, as Controller of Drama, that writers and directors are irritated by having to set their plays around natural breaks?*

No, I don't. We've a lot of elbow room in this way. You know, a first act can be anywhere from about eight minutes to fifteen. So with that latitude, I don't think they're worried at all. You could get the odd scenario where it could really bug you and indeed we've had instances in the last few months where we had such a play. We went to our own company and said we would like to play this one without a commercial break – they said yes, go ahead. But if you think about the structure of television drama, the majority of the stories as told by playwrights have a time-lapse factor, and it is where you have the time-lapse that a commercial break is enormously easy to accommodate.

*Do you think there's a tendency to lose your audience every time there's a break?*

Well, the minute-by-minute reading graphs don't bear this out. Theoretically I would have thought so, but there is no evidence to suggest a dropping off in commercial breaks.

*Can you assess roughly within what audience range a thing will come before you put it on the floor?*

No, I think if you could do this, you would have the key to show-business. The only thing you can do is to hope that your own instincts about entertainment and communication run parallel to the public's. I tend to go for stuff that I believe in personally and I just hope that the public'll like it too. If they don't we're both in trouble. They're bored and I'm fired.

*What sort of things are you looking for in scripts?*

Humanity. An instinct for human beings as they are. Provocation. Stimulation. Originality. You know, a writer that has that flair – a writer that can make you look again, that can tell you something fundamentally truthful about yourself or other people. You can't legislate for it. You don't know where it's going to come. That's what you're constantly hoping for, looking for. Because oddly enough, given that, you find often all the other desirable things about technique fall into place.

*Do you have censorship rules – the feeling of an audience out there that has to be protected from certain things?*

No, I don't. I think perhaps they should have more of an early-warning system. You see, there's a curious thing about the self-consciousness of television audiences, which is in its own way rather tragic and rather poignant. Often letters, complaints, take the same tone of voice. It's something like this: 'I was watching with my teenage daughter/son and I was embarrassed.' And so, in other words, the embarrassment has taken place within that family circle and there's not a thing you or I or anybody else can do about that. If there are tensions between the generations, which of course there always must be, and those are shown in bold relief in that family, all one can say is 'I'm sorry if I've offended you, but your own family problems are your family problems.' It's part of the condition.

*Is there too much violence on television?*

I hate violence, as an individual. It's maybe my own hang-up, I don't know. Well, to equivocate once again, I think there are two sorts of violence and I'm very torn on this one. I would guess if you've got to show violence then it should be truthful violence. The 'bang, bang, you're dead' stuff worries me. I still feel the most immoral fiction series that was ever offered in the UK was *77 Sunset Strip*, because the message of that series seemed to be written large that you solved problems by bashing somebody on the head or, if that failed, shooting them, that all women were there as quick lays. Frankly, I almost got around to writing letters to television companies about *77 Sunset Strip* when they used to put it out at 7.25 on Sundays when a lot of youngsters are viewing. Because I thought that was just plain bloody immorality.

*Is the Levy really beginning to affect you at departmental level?*

Oh, yes. No cuts – it's just that we can't expand and in that sense cut. Actually my budgets have been increased by 15 per cent in this last year. But what is not there is the residue of cash on the part of the management to chase hares, to chase the unlikelies. There's also a natural tendency not to be prepared to write off so much money in script commissions. You see, it's a well-known factor in this business, to get say twenty effective single plays on the air, you'd probably have to commission thirty-five. Out of that thirty-five, you probably cut off five at the first draft – ten more you probably pay for completely which you won't use – the other twenty you finally get around to using. So in a way this is an oblique form of patronage. Now clearly, as money becomes tighter, there's a desire not to take that many chances, which is unfortunate.

*Can you see any changes in the present system of commercial television which would make your job easier or the product better?*

There should be more faith in British domestic products, and the British viewer. I still feel that not only independent television, but the BBC as well, is dominated in too many peak hours by imported material. There's still too great a tendency to worship at the shrine of the Americans. The ratings will prove often that British domestic products will outrun them all over the spot and yet we constantly feel that too much prime time in British television gets taken up with American products. They don't do it to us. We do it to ourselves. You know, they're not coming around cap in hand, asking you to buy it. The Americans don't need any overseas sales, they've got their money back in the States. But I think we still, putting it bluntly, suck around American ideas and American standards too much. I think anything they can do we can do better. And finally we've got to pursue our own cultural destiny, whatever that may be, irrespective of theirs. What they do is right for themselves, but it's not necessarily right for us.

*Do you feel that there is a television aesthetic which is separate from the theatre on one hand and separate from cinema on the other?*

I think there's a very big difference. The television viewers watch in their own home, in their own controlled environment among their own familiar objects, amid their own familiar routine. So there isn't that conspiratorial suspension of disbelief working for you, that works in the theatre and cinema. Secondly, the cinema is working, to state the obvious, on a much bigger canvas, therefore in actual story-telling and minute-by-minute technique terms, the cinema is much more about environment than we can afford to be. The most spectacular films can be screened on television and that spectacle reduced to miniature by the size of our screen. When we try and make our drama hinge on an environmental flavour, there's a very strong chance we'll fail. But with cinema, they might well pull it off. In fact, very frequently do.

# Cecil Clarke

Executive Producer, Plays, ATV.

Hugh Beaumont of H. M. Tennent said 'What about coming and organizing television productions because I've been asked to do twenty-six plays a year under contract to ATV?' I knew very little about television, but I said I'd have a bash, and I set to. I organized a little unit, a completely independent television play-producing unit with freelance directors, and we did twenty-six plays a year for ATV – and very exciting it was, because one was in a little creative world of one's own. Eventually after a time doing mainly West End stage successes, I was able to get down and start finding my own writers. Then at the end of just over nine years ATV decided they should do plays themselves, I came over into ATV to carry on doing twenty-six plays a year, and that's what I'm doing now.

*What impression did you have of television as a theatre man and at the beginning of television?*

I found it completely impersonal : terrifyingly technical, a machine-like medium which worried me intensely at the start. I'd been used in the theatre to working with a handful of people who, somehow or other, were much more responsive to the director's authority than one found in television. I found that no one seemed to have any time to discuss anything in detail. One went into rehearsal, and come what may in a fortnight's time you did it. And in those days you did it live which was even more terrifying. The hardest thing in the world in a big studio and a big complex was to mould a team.

*When you look at television drama today, do you think that the theatre is necessarily the right place to be recruiting people from?*

Yes. Particularly directors. I think that probably television drama is going to go back to where we need the writer more than ever, the writer who will give us things to say, rather than give us things to do. Television drama has drifted, possibly through the influence of television films and the film series, into plays of action rather

109

than plays of words with good acting possibilities. It's going back soon to the stage where people will again have to act, and the directors will have to know how to direct actors much more than quite a number of them do now. The writer will write dialogue as opposed to stage directions.

*What do you look for in writers as regards potential material for television programmes, what qualities?*

I think basically a jolly good idea and then secondly an ability to translate that idea into terms of dialogue. Dialogue is the most important thing because through the dialogue one creates the characters. So by the dialogue a good imaginative director will find the way to make the play live – to give it its action.

*That's almost heresy, isn't it?*

Yes. I think so many directors are apt to read the scripts looking for the shots – and they expect a writer to be able to write shot potential! To me it's the wrong way round, I would like to be able to give a director a script with dialogue and the minimum of stage directions and then for him to use his creative ability to translate it on to the screen as something which moves, breathes and talks.

I try to cast the director to the play in exactly the same way as the actors. It's very important to get the right director for a play.

*For nine years you had this situation of supplying all these plays to ATV but being as you said a group on your own. That in a way seems an ideal situation.*

It was the most perfect way to do it, for I had a very small team: I just had myself, a good assistant, a secretary, a script typist, and two PAs to work with the directors, and, as we had two or three plays on the go, two teams of floor managers and stage managers. I had a scenery and property workshop, a wardrobe supervisor and we were able to cut down paper work to an absolute minimum. The easiest and quickest way to get things started was to all sit round and say, 'We're going to do this, that and the other', and discuss the thing in detail. People got on and did what they had to do.

*Do you think that television in the future might revert to a lot more of that kind of situation? It seems to be what creative people want.*

I think the creative people want it more and more, and I would like to see within the larger companies much more specialized creative groups. I think the smaller the group the better the result, although one can see that one of the objections from people above is that people create their own personal empires. But if you've got the right people, then I think you create a team not one man's personal empire.

*Do you have to choose plays that are going to be highly rated?*

I have to be sensible and, obviously, in holding down my job I have to respect the wishes of the management, but I am never hammered or anything like that about 'You must do more popular plays'. Of course I must produce certain rating results on them but I get marvellous understanding and co-operation, when I produce a play which achieves critical success, but a minority audience appeal.

*What do you think of the state of television drama today? Is it healthy?*

Not terribly. We're desperately trying to find new writers. So many of the old ones that we've all used have moved on to other fields, mainly to films, and we're trying to fill up that blank. And until we fill that blank I think that television drama will remain on an even keel – with every now and again the odd interesting and exciting production.

*Your programmes are networked. If they weren't, could you do a much more* avant-garde *or exclusive piece?*

No. I think it would be far more difficult if we were not networked because then all our plays would have to be regional in outlook and I don't think that one can be completely regional in television drama. The scope would be too narrow.

*Are your budgets under pressure of the Levy?*

No, not particularly. I have a set budget and if I want any more money for a particular production I present my case.

*But how much do you see ITV companies having some sort of patronage role?*

I think it's very difficult for a commercial organization to become patrons of the arts, because it's difficult to know where to draw the line. Once one starts everyone wants help. What I would like to see more than anything in independent television is an 'ITN' of drama. I've been a sort of advocate of it for years – that all the drama resources of all the companies are pooled and you have an independent television drama unit with its own pool of directors and producers. Pool what we have in order that Independent Television drama can really present the best possible. At the moment it's too diversified, with no overall style, or look, or feeling of presentation or anything really. It's just a hotch-potch of the four or five or six major companies' idea of presenting television drama. I think that if we had a unified front we could make a strong impact as Independent Television drama. The public will then accept two sources of plays – ITV and the BBC. Not the BBC and a collection of plays under an assortment of 'umbrella' titles from ITV, as now. We could do 'specials' and afford to do them well, we could find a style – an identity, which we have not now as a Network. Individual companies obviously have their own style and would wish to preserve it, but it would, I am certain, be worthwhile, exciting and rewarding to both sides of the fence – the public's and ours.

*Do you think you have any hope?*

A few of us who produce plays have talked among ourselves, but none of us are policy makers. We are not network policy makers, we are not company policy makers, we are not planners, we are doers. So individually we have to sell our ideas for doing certain types of plays to our own particular programme company, and then get on and do them as well as we can.

NICHOLAS GARNHAM

# 7 · Arts Programmes

It is all too easy to confuse arts programmes with art and so measure the cultural state of television by the quantity and quality of its art programmes. But television is continually transmitting what would be commonly accepted as works of art. To say commonly accepted as works of art is not to imply any judgement of quality. A work of art is an artefact in a form in which the possibilities of quality are present. Daily television transmits plays, films, documentaries, comedy shows and it is here very probably that much of our contemporary art is being created. And in television drama the art of the past is preserved and refurbished by performances of the world's theatrical repertoire. Now some arts programmes are art in that sense, transmissions of performances that have come to be regarded as artistic experiences, concerts, ballet or opera. About such programmes two questions need to be asked. Are they efficient transmissions and do they justify their use of scarce air-time in terms of audience?

When you ask are they efficient transmissions, you are asking a set of related questions. If a concert, you are asking whether, as the quality of sound on television receivers is so poor, it wouldn't be better to leave the job to radio. How important is the visual aspect of a musical performance? Is it merely an accidental by-product of the need, before radio or gramophone, to gather people into a hall in order to hear music at all? When asked of opera and ballet performances the question becomes more complicated. Because the characteristics of a television camera differ so markedly from those of the human eye should you attempt to record ballet and opera performances at Covent Garden or should you re-stage them in a studio for the camera? If you are going to re-stage them in a studio wouldn't it be better to concentrate scarce talent and resources on creating new works specifically for the new medium rather than perpetrating the restrictive conventions and social overtones of the opera-house?

If the social overtones of the opera-house are restrictive, television's are the exact opposite. Covent Garden, with its gilt and plush, its audiences in evening dress and, because of its limited capacity, its necessarily expensive seats, reinforces the idea of minority culture for aristocrats and plutocrats. The enjoyment of television, on the other hand, is inhibited by no economic or social barriers. Even the most minority television transmission, such as *Review* on BBC 2, is watched by 550,000 people and its audience spans all ages and classes. The difficulty with all arts programmes, both those that are straight performances and those that seek to elucidate and criticize, is to find the right relationship with their audience. There are those who say that below a certain audience figure a television programme is not viable; that it would be more efficient to publish a book or hire the Albert Hall. Certainly for any work that couldn't be expressed in print this figure must be very low. Television has the immense advantage that you don't have to leave home for it, so that there is that large audience of the housebound who can only be reached in this way.

Television's audience can also be made up of individuals scattered throughout the country. If there are only ten music-lovers in a given town, they cannot financially support even a touring opera company. But if these ten are multiplied by the number of towns in the whole country they become a viable television audience. It is for this reason that a television performance of an opera is probably watched not by the Covent Garden audience but by those who cannot get to Covent Garden. For this audience television opera is extremely cheap. *Billy Budd* was watched by 1½ million on BBC 1, considered a dangerously low audience and yet at £100,000 that only comes to 1s. 6d. per head. Very high in television terms, but ludicrously low compared with prices at Covent Garden which is subsidized by the Arts Council to the tune of half a million. If we really believe in the social value of opera, perhaps it is on television that our subsidies should be spent. What is clear is that if video-cassettes catch on anywhere outside the field of education it will be in this specialized field.

But art is a restricted minority interest in this country. It is so

114

for a variety of historical reasons. What we call art was produced for those who held political and economic power, an upper and middle class. In spite of political and economic reforms, this still remains largely true. In so far as traditional art embodies enduring values, they do not embody these values self-evidently. Works of art are a language. To understand what they are saying requires education. Until very recently education in Britain, especially higher education, was restricted to a minority. If art is ever to become more than a minority interest, it will be education that transforms the situation not television. Until that inevitably slow transformation takes place, the maker of critical arts programmes is faced by a dilemma – how to talk to a mass audience in a language only the minority understand or want to understand.

Huw Wheldon in a BBC Lunch Time Lecture on 'Television and the Arts' said that the television producer 'serves three masters. The masters are the subject, his craft and the audience. The service required is absolute. The imperatives are categorical', and he went on to examine this conflict facing the producer between his subject and his audience. 'If a producer can only achieve a programme by making it so complex that only a hundred people can follow it, he is sacrificing the audience to the complexity. If he can only make the programme by over-simplifying a complex situation, he is sacrificing the artist to the audience. Neither sacrifice is tolerable.'

But are the three masters really equal, and indeed can one serve the three masters with equal fervour? As the artist or art object pre-exists the programme its mastery must be absolute. As long as you serve the subject faithfully, the audience must be irrelevant. Indeed, it is only by serving the subject faithfully that you can serve the audience, for the artist and his work will not be harmed by television. But if the critic lowers his standards it is the audience who will suffer. The options open to them become narrower. If words are not used for fear of misunderstanding, those words die, the language is impoverished and the future possibilities of understanding are diminished.

The critical arts programme is involved in a process of education or it is involved in nothing. Such processes are long-term. In television, with its rapid rate of turn-over in programmes and the fleeting nature of its continuous flow, it is dangerously easy to disregard tomorrow let alone the next ten or twenty years. I believe it is very doubtful whether it matters one way or another that there should be arts programmes on television. But if it matters it matters over that sort of time span. They must be there for the audience to grow towards, not vice-versa.

As to the craft, it is not master but slave. It is the producer who should be total master of his craft so that it can serve both him and his subject. The ever-present danger in arts programmes is to hide the betrayal of the subject behind an excessive servility to one's craft. So in film after film never an idea stirs, but every prospect pleases. The sun glints through the trees, the music throbs, couples row in boats or run through trees. Increasingly for art and the authentic artist a cliché world has been substituted which originally sprang full grown from the imagination of Ken Russell. On BBC television Elgar and Lenin, George Eliot and Schumann all inhabit the same improbable world. As fantasies they are as harmless as the Val Doonican show and have as strong a justification in their role of popular entertainment. Their connection with the arts, beneath whose prestige they shelter, is purely imaginary.

# Humphrey Burton

1962–3, Editor, *Monitor*; 1963–5, Executive Producer, Music Programmes, BBC TV; 1965–7, Head of Music and Arts, BBC TV; 1967–9, Head of Drama, Arts and Music Unit, London Weekend; 1969, freelance.

*Humphrey Burton is directly involved with the current art output on ITV. He was one of a group of BBC producers who joined London Weekend with the idea of transplanting public service values to commercial television. In the light of the experience did he feel the failure was the result of naïvety or cynicism?*

I'm quite convinced that it was naïvety rather than cynicism. I mean I know about this from the inside, and whatever one may feel about ex-colleagues at LWT, I do not doubt their sincerity, both in the writing of the franchise bid, and the desire to change

ITV for the better. What I doubt, and I think everybody does now, is their actual understanding of how commercial television works. Not only how the system works but also how you make good programmes. I remember I went on record in a magazine interview saying, 'Please don't expect any great changes, it's not going to be all *that* different. You know, all you can do is to make little revolutions which take a long time to sink in.' But despite the poor-mouthing (as my show-biz colleagues might call it) of our programmes, LWT *did* produce twenty-five specials in the first year, we did things which had never been done before on commercial television and did them regularly – concerts with Bernstein and Davis and Previn and *The Beggar's Opera* and *The Soldier's Tale* and Cleo Laine and Kurt Weill and Gershwin – good programmes!

*Do you think it is possible to do good work in ITV as at present structured?*

I know it is possible. I am not disillusioned with the system, I am only disillusioned with the people operating the system, both in the individual companies and at the ITA. I'm quite sure that the checks and balances in the Television Act are such that, given a different person in command, the new order wouldn't have fallen to bits in the way it has. ITV only needs somebody with immense drive to say, 'Well, I'm sorry you *can't* run Michael Miles at seven o'clock on Friday, the Authority will not permit you to.'

*But aren't arts programmes, inevitably minority programmes, under particular pressures in a commercial system?*

Well, I can't answer that in a generalized way, I can only answer it so far as my own experience is concerned. Even though LWT was doing programmes which were not likely to attract a majority audience, London Weekend continued to make specials for a year. Now, it is true, both London Weekend and the other companies are making cultural programmes of a less ambitious kind, with lower budgets. But with that I have to sympathize, given the shortage of cash. Now this isn't a question of sacrificing programmes to shareholders, because LWT, for example, is not paying any dividends. One trouble with ITV is that ten years ago somebody in the ITA should have said to them, 'You've got lots of money, boys; you should be putting far more into programmes

than you are.' Whereas the companies tended, through bad conscience, to put the money into cultural concerns which actually
weren't on television. I always remember the ironical situation of
being in the Festival Hall for a concert sponsored by Rediffusion.
They had an advert in the programme notes saying, 'We do lots of
cultural things, but music isn't really suitable for television.' But
the concert was being televised – by the BBC. Nowadays that
doesn't hold any more – even ATV now does concerts. I'm not
saying necessarily that those were good programmes because I
didn't see them, but I certainly don't think it's impossible for the
commercial set-up to make good programmes. On the contrary,
the evidence shows they can make just as good programmes as the
BBC – particularly now that the BBC seems to be determined to
get ratings at all costs, almost all of the time.

*What do you think your responsibilities are then as a broadcaster?*

I have an academic training in the discipline of music, one of the
four medieval disciplines. The subject I did for post-graduate study
in France was the development of public concerts, public music-
making, when music was no longer a privileged thing, when it was
taken out of the Church and out of the Court to the people – at
least to the bourgeoisie. In other words, my subject was the breaking down of the barriers, the spreading of the good word. And as
a television producer I see myself as a proselytizer seeking con-
verts for that substitute religion known as 'Art'. That sounds
fantastically pompous when it's put like that, but I think everybody who works in arts television knows that they are spreading
the good word. The best definition I suppose is taken from that
poem of Keats – at the end of *Ode to a Nightingale* – 'charmed
magic casements opening on the foam of perilous seas in faery
lands forlorn', No one quite understands what is meant by 'faery
lands forlorn'. except that they are something out of this world;
the crucial thing for me is the phrase 'magic casements' and that's
what the screen can be – a magic window. So I think that as a
producer my role is to share my own enthusiasms, pleasures,
excitements, and I believe that enjoyment is very much in proportion to the amount you understand about something.

I see my producing role as a pushing-back of frontiers. Again I
know it's a cliché phrase, but we are, in a sense, frontiersmen and

in the exploration business. We're trying to deal with a mass audience, we're trying to lead a mass audience. I believe that almost everybody is born with an innate sensibility towards the finer things in life. These sensibilities are blunted by the dreadful education that most people receive, but one can go some way towards restoring and reawakening those sensibilities if one goes about it in the right way.

My job, when I make a programme, is to provide insight, either into the creative processes if I'm doing a documentary about a composer or a painter (and I've done both) or to provide insight into human nature, if I'm producing a play. I think television is not a very good medium for the transmission of art, but a very good medium indeed for the transmission of human involvement with art. This is our most successful area. I think our role is to educate as well as to entertain.

*Do you ever feel that in the process of proselytizing you begin to undermine your subject?*

I think I am by nature a middle-brow. I'm not actually interested in putting across extremely esoteric subjects. Surprisingly, there are people who would say that I am extremely intellectual! Different people have different vantage points, and one person's intellectual is another person's idiot. On that subject, I remember very well ten years ago having to persuade my colleagues in *Monitor* that it was worthwhile making a film about a string quartet. Nowadays, they're two-a-penny on BBC 2 but then, well, twenty minutes about a string quartet – it was crazy, you know, caviar for the general. But if you make the film in a certain way, it's got human interest which you can emphasize. So that perhaps there are some subjects which seem to be esoteric and yet *can* be tackled.

I don't think you ever need to compromise the subject of a television programme. You simply have to believe in what you are doing and have that gift of wanting to explain things to other people in terms that they can understand, of wanting to share an enthusiasm with them. I thought that Huw Wheldon had that gift in *Monitor* – although some critics felt that he was being too much the heavy-handed uncle and schoolmaster figure. In *Monitor* we were very conscious that we did *not* want to be condescending, although we were quite proud to be didactic.

119

*Monitor is still the most famous of all arts programmes. What did its reputation rest on?*

I think it was a very good programme; and I think this was because we put a great premium on *creativity* – and it wasn't only films that people remember. We wanted 'high-density' programming, where everything that was done – the mildest interview or serious discussion – was really thought about and worked on. That's what I'm trying to do now as I work on this new programme of mine, *Aquarius*. I am trying to remember what it was like, how we could spend three months preparing one edition, several of us, not just one person. How David Jones would go away for a month to work on a film about R. S. Thomas. You don't see films about R. S. Thomas any more, or if you do they've been done by some chap just out of university: researched for a day, and shot in a couple of days, and if the poems are spoken or read by somebody then they're not really *worked on*. When I say 'read', I mean that the actor is actually reading off a clip board, and he hasn't really worked for a couple of days in the way he should have done. That's an extreme example, but on the whole I find that production these days is rather more careless than it used to be; not more philistine but less thoughtful. People don't spend as much time as they did on programmes.

# Melvyn Bragg

Producer/Editor, *New Release, Writers' World*. Co-scriptwriter with Ken Russell, *Debussy* and *Isadora Duncan*. Novelist.

When I worked for the BBC the first thing that I wanted to do was to make arts programmes current. It seemed to me that television was a thing which was reflecting and refracting the whole of national life, or a great deal of national life, more than any other medium had ever done, more than novels had ever done, more than plays had ever done. And one thing that I was interested in at that time, to put it very crudely and portray me very naïvely, was culture. It seemed to me that making it part of the currency was important. I have slightly perhaps changed and revised my ideas about the arts since then – I mean, they can very well take care of themselves in most cases and television doesn't have to take care of them.

If I went back now it would be to put the arts on because I think that it's the only way that People, with a capital P, are going to find out about the things that I particularly like. Missionary is too big a word for it and propaganda is the wrong word – but it's certainly to do with the fact that the people I was born and brought up among very rarely read books but all of them look at television. They would never go to the pictures that I quite like and don't ever go to the theatre, but they will watch plays on television and will watch films on television. And being able to put that on for them and make it interesting is as clear an idea of what I want to do with my life as I've ever had. That's why I like the BBC and the public service notion it is tied up with – giving back to them what in a sense I've taken from them. Or what they've never had.

*Do you think the audience, in fact, watches arts programmes?*

I think it's surprising who does watch arts programmes. I'm sorry to go on with old wives' tales, but my father has a pub in an area which has a lot of Irish. It's a big working-class pub where they sell beer and they sell spirits mainly ten to eleven on a Saturday night. It's not rough, it's not nasty, it's not violent, it's just a respectable big working-class pub. Now, a great number of people in that pub watch *Omnibus*. Now, that's a fact. It tends to be in the saloon bar and they tend to be the guys who are working nine hours a day in the plastics factory instead of twelve hours a day in the biscuit factory, but nevertheless they do. So there are a few people there who actually watch *Omnibus*.

I was always surprised by the people who had seen the shows, the people who had actually caught things that I'd done. You have a great number of chances, you see, because you get all sorts of sectional interests prepared to watch one programme. I'm sure, for example, when they did that programme about the music-makers in Harlow New Town – about how every kid could play an instrument – that the whole of Harlow New Town watched. Maybe a lot of them watched the next *Omnibus*.

121

The point about broadcasting is that it's very much like throwing your seed all over the place, and that's the nice thing about it. The television is there, in the corner of the room. It hasn't been ordered like the *Sunday Times* or the book from Faber & Faber or whatever. It is available like water or like electricity and that's the enormous advantage of it. You are always in with a chance.

*Is there a barrier beyond which you can't go in order to get it over to an audience?*

Certainly, certainly, without any question. And that's what's wrong with a hell of a lot that is going on now. I mean, it's just like, if you're doing a football match, you can't say we don't want it in two forty-five minute sections, we've got an audience who prefers it in a twenty-minute section, do you mind folks? Similarly with a poem – you can go as far as you can or you dare with it, depending on how clever you are and how good you are as a television producer, but if you start to bugger about with it then don't do it. But once you have begun to do it you have taken on the challenge of doing it.

People outside television don't realize that those inside are quite aware they're taking on challenges and they have thought these things through. They're not just saying, 'Well, I'd like to get a bit of Eliot on.' They really know it's probably going to be beyond them. Nearly everybody I have met who has had anything to do with the arts has thought long-term, very intelligently and hard about whether they should do it, and how far they can go. Once you have decided to do it then you are working in television and you are not writing for *Scrutiny*, and there is a difference, and I think you can discern that difference. So what you decide to do you must do as well as you can in terms of yourself and also remember your audience. What remembering your audience means God only knows. I think it's very difficult to work it out abstractly. You can't talk about good writing, you can talk about good writers. Who defines what good writing is? You say 'Read that. That's good writing.' It starts from there. All I can say is that people have done it. It's a difficult field, but it's also a thankless field. It's a thankless field because you are dealing with somebody else's material, in a respectful rather than a dramatic way. I mean it's different from dealing with somebody else's material as a play because as a director you charge the play, whereas the poems are already charged. You represent them. So it's ultimately a sad field to be in. And you've got to be very strong-minded about your duty to keep on doing it again and again and again.

# John Culshaw

Head of Music, BBC TV.

I had been very excited by the good things I'd seen in music on television, made by my predecessors here, and very very disappointed by the bad things. So, clinging to the good things, I thought they could perhaps be developed and extended. But, of course, when you get inside you find how terribly complicated it is and how much more difficult as a medium than, say, the gramophone record.

The documentaries, as applied to music, seemed to me to be on the whole very successful. The magazine-type programme, exemplified I suppose by *Monitor*, seemed an excellent form of communication, without too much teaching. I was disturbed about much that was happening in opera, and I thought maybe I had something to contribute to that. But I had no illusions at all about presenting symphonic music on television. As a public service we have to do it, but I think it's a problem without a solution at present.

*Is a straight presentation of an orchestra playing the best solution?*

Well, I think so. You can try to vary it by putting pretty pictures to the music, and we do occasionally, but straight concerts are straight concerts. You can't leave the camera in one position, as some people say, for obvious reasons. The minute you start moving the camera about, showing horns, clarinets, bassoons, 'cellos, it is distracting, there's no denying it. Equally, I don't believe it's a solution to leave the camera on the conductor all the time. You're simply caught by this. There's no solution.

*So you feel that the expanding areas are in a sense education about music rather than straight presentation of music on television?*

Straight presentation can be fine if it's, let us say, a recital. All right, you can say it's dull television – I don't necessarily think it is. A beautifully set piano recital, with the minimum camera enhancements, can be very agreeable and relaxing and can communicate music. A Lieder recital can work. A string quartet can work. But when you go into the larger fields of orchestras and choruses you're stuck visually, if you are concentrating on the performers, and you're certainly stuck in terms of sound. The fact is that people who are interested at all in so-called serious music in this country have invested in hi-fi equipment of one sort or another. They have trained their ears over the last ten to fifteen years. They've got acute hearing perception and judgement. And they simply are bored to death by the lousy sound that comes out of television sets, and the picture doesn't compensate, most of the time.

*Wouldn't it be possible therefore just to do these performances on radio and concentrate your money and effort in other areas?*

I've though about that and even recommended something a bit like it. But I think the BBC feels that it has to represent all sorts of activity through its various departments, and so we are obliged to do so many concerts a year. Now, of course, if a major international conductor is doing his single London appearance, then it is perhaps immensely valuable for people in the provinces to be able to join in on that event, and have a look at the guy, as well as listen to him. But that's about the only justification I can see.

*What influence do you feel television has, or could have, on the musical life of the nation?*

I'm very sceptical about its actual musical influence, and, indeed, even gloomy about the future. It seems to me that there is a more or less fixed audience for what we have to call serious music. And that goes right through to, say, jazz and so on. Now, I think we can put a figure to this audience. It is, at its smallest, half a million to a million. At its highest, which will be for something like the last day of the Proms, which is a dubious musical event, it can be seven, eight or nine million. Now between those two figures, if you do, as we did, say, a documentary on a well-loved figure, like Kathleen Ferrier, you get a big viewer audience up in the North of England and your figures will hover around five, six million, but if you do a programme with Pierre Boulez trying to talk seriously about music, or you do a very distinguished jazz programme, your figures go rocketing down. And the depressing thing about that is that it doesn't show any sign of going up. In other words, your low figure is not actually gaining at all. After a year or two here, it's possible to pick up the schedules of projected programmes for the next two years, and almost put a figure to them.

*You are obviously very keen to move into opera. What do you think television's contribution to opera can be?*

I have very personal views about this and they're not shared by many other people in the Corporation. I'm quite unrepentant about them. I think that most opera is a strong theatrical form, and I think it's no darn use to pretend it's anything else. The theory that used to apply here is that the only way you can produce opera in the studio is to make it, in the word they use, naturalistic. I just don't think that's on. There may be a few operas that would come into that definition but the bulk of the repertoire has to be done in an operatic way.

People are always ready to put up ideas for advanced television operas, which – without being too Irish about this – if presented on the stage would get an audience of 300 for three performances at Sadlers Wells. If you put this on television it would be the biggest switch-off of all time. The fact is that we haven't really built up an audience on the box for *Bohème*, for *Aïda*, for *Traviata* yet. Those are the things we ought to get across before we start doing too much experimentation.

*Would it be better if television were creating its own musical forms?*

Your suggestion, of course, is a splendid one, and one that we are constantly thinking about. That is, we are trying to find the man who is going to create a new musical dramatic form conceived entirely in television terms. I have spent quite a lot of time in the last year talking to some of our younger composers about this and the frightening thing is that they're all too busy at present to think about it. Which is a bit distressing. And, of course, if you go to the older ones, they're probably now too formally cast in the theatrical mould. It remains to be seen what will emerge next year when Benjamin Britten does his first television opera.

*There are a lot of people who say, 'Ah, but the best way to do both ballet and opera is just go along to Covent Garden and show it.' What do you feel about that?*

Well, I think they may have a case, I'm depressed to say. It does tend to work awfully well and it fulfils two things. Generally, if it's a good performance, it's faithful to the music in a theatrical context. And, of course, something is added. We're back to thinking of people outside London – they like the idea of going to Covent Garden for an evening. All that plush and a sense of the theatre. I feel a very strong case could be made out for doing opera and ballet almost entirely as outside broadcasts from the theatre, and not trying to pretend that they can be something else.

*Do you think the proportion of the total budget allotted to music might be cut back?*

It's my private theory that, in fact, we do too much at present. I would like to do fewer, better programmes and make music more of an event that people would, I hope, look forward to. But this would demand a whole new structure, because what I'm really saying is that I would like the same amout of money to do less programmes and make them very very special indeed. But, as you know, television is geared to output, to filling slots, and you'll find Programme Heads view that argument with considerable horror.

# John Drummond

Executive Producer, Arts Features, BBC2.

You know, I'm all for knocking the arts. What I dislike is the holy reverence, the holier than thou attitude to the arts. I don't want anybody to put on their church-going clothes to talk about arts. This is one of the worst handicaps we have to live with. I don't want the arts to be taken without seriousness, but I do want them to be taken perfectly naturally. I have an enthusiasm and a care and a concern for them and I want other people to share that. And yet I don't think we're here in a teaching, preaching situation. I certainly don't think we're here primarily as educationalists, didactic educationalists. We're here as enthusiasts to share that enthusiasm. And the fact is it works.

People talk about minority audiences. You know, Maggie Dale does *Coppélia* and gets seven million. We do *Rigoletto* and get four million viewers. When I put on Ferrier last year – six million viewers. Ken Russell's films – six or seven million viewers. If we can say that one in eight people in this country watched a ballet or one in fifteen people in this country watched an opera right through, what's the minority? Where is the minority?

*George Melly said that it's very important that people in the arts programmes of the BBC realize that they are not art, they are substitutes for the real thing.*

I don't think it matters that our coverage of an art exhibition or our review of a novel isn't an artefact in its own right, provided, in fact, it is a channel for connecting the audience with the reality of the artistic experience. We know in music that the sound is awful. It doesn't alter the fact that more people watch opera on television than ever go to it at the opera house in this country and, therefore, you can't really say that television isn't relevant to the question of opera. The Arts Council Report devotes pages to television because here is the biggest audience ever for those artistic manifestations.

*I don't think that would be contested. But do you think that your film-makers in your department tend to feel this dilemma about presenting their programme as an artefact? They want it to be a part of the art?*

Current Affairs, if they were doing art subjects (and ideally I would welcome this), would provide reportage and we would provide comment. Maybe this is the difference, in the sense that we are trying to provide interpretative comment, which stands as more than a day-to-day reportage. We're not merely saying that an exhibition opened at the Tate yesterday morning and they collected

127

together some interesting paintings and let's look at a few of them. When John Read does his films on painters and sculptors, I know he has a feeling, a strong feeling, that he wants to make a statement which isn't really relevant for a television audience for forty-five minutes of time, but may well stand as a kind of evidence in the whole business of accumulating information and documentation on the arts. When he makes a film on Henry Moore I think he hopes that this film will stand the test of at least two or three years' time.

Most producers over here feel that there is more to making an arts documentary than merely stringing together the facts of the artistic manifestation. In other words, it calls for some kind of criticism, some kind of interpretation, some kind of analysis, transmuting this experience somehow into another experience. Now I'm not going to suggest that any film I've ever made is as valuable as the real thing, but when it comes to a programme like the ones I did on Diaghilev – I mean the Diaghilev Ballet doesn't exist any more. Nothing of this kind exists and it will gradually be forgotten. It seemed to me a valuable thing to try and examine this while there were still eye-witnesses and still people around. It's a different kind of programme, if you like. It wasn't a work of art, but at least it called attention to something which was extremely important in our time. We will throw up programmes, maybe it's only one a year, but it's enough. Everyone talks about the Russell *Elgar* film. I don't know when the tide turned for Elgar. It's very hard to know, but I know the people who were also involved, like Colin Davis and the record companies, believe that Ken Russell's film absolutely crystallized a feeling that was around in society that here was music that had been undervalued for twenty-five or thirty years and which we wanted to hear again. In that extraordinary flood tide of interest in Elgar which happened in the early 1960s, Russell's film stands as a beacon light and it still bears looking at today. Maybe in another twenty-five years when we've forgotten about Elgar we should look at it again and see whether it was wrong, or something. I mean, its amazing achievement is that it's not a catalogue, that film. This is what we must never be. We must never feel that to document a painter or a writer we must show everything they ever did, that the whole field must be covered. Humphrey Burton never ceases to point out that with

Ken Russell's Elgar film there was very little music! But, you know, it caught the tide.

*There is a sense that there's just general cosy approval of all art.*

The cosiness I want to get rid of. The cosiness is what I don't like. It's an unpleasant thing and it's a thing which belongs in *Miss World.* It doesn't belong in the arts programmes. One of the things which worries me about our work – we set certain levels of interviewing, for instance, when it comes to politicians or to economists. If you watch *The Money Programme* or something like this you get a level of interviewing which is pretty hard or pretty tough. The arts we don't produce like this. We produce softies. Now why can't we have the same toughness? I believe the arts are just as valid as economics. Therefore, why can't we have just as tough interviewers? I, for one, am jolly glad to see someone like Jim Mossman in this field, because I don't see why a novelist shouldn't stand up to a tough political interview. And people turn round and say to me what are Mossman's credentials for doing this kind of thing? God help us! He's an intelligent man. He's a novelist in his own right. He is a member of the community who is intelligent, involved with these things, and he cares about it. Why shouldn't he have the right to talk to a novelist just as he has the right to talk to the Prime Minister? You know, I think what the arts can't do is make special pleading. We can't say we're marvellous and everybody must accept this. Therefore, you must give us prime time. We can't do that.

Current Affairs is a thing which I don't want to get too deep in, because I have worked with them a great deal. I've never been in the department but there is universal feeling in television and newspapers that Current Affairs is OK and must be there. Everybody agrees, and we can put as many economists, as many politicians and as many planners as you can get on the screen, without questioning why they're there. Yet we are made to question every programme we do. We never get access to the prime time in the evening, we never get access to the big audience.

It isn't any good them putting us on at 10.50 at night and then saying, 'You get small audiences, dear.' What the hell do they expect at 10.50 at night when people have sat through five or six other programmes? It has been proved, occasionally, that by putting

129

arts programmes out nearer nine o'clock in the evening that we can, in fact, pick up a respectable audience. It's not as big an audience, I know. An arts documentary spot would probably pick up six or seven million viewers, whereas a social documentary or science documentary might well pick up eleven or twelve. Well, all right. I still don't feel seven million viewers for the arts programme rules it out of consideration for that spot. I would like to see arts documentaries in that *Tuesday Documentary* spot. The fact is now that for a family living in a part of the country where there is no BBC 2 coverage there is no single arts programme that a child under the age of fifteen can watch. None. They won't stay up until 10.30 on Sunday nights when they've got school the following morning. You've got to think about this.

# Jonathan Miller

1964–5, Editor, *Monitor*. Freelance director, Arts Features, BBC.

*What were the main difficulties confronting you when you took over* Monitor *?*

Well, my main difficulties were divided into two groups: one, as it were, purely institutional, and the other technical. The institutional difficulty was associated with the fact that I inherited a programme which already had a reputation, and therefore had an expectation of a certain sort on the part of its audience, and I violated that expectation. Secondly in terms of pure technique, there were things I thought could be done on that medium, and they could not be done.

*What were these things that you found could not be done?*

Well, relatively complicated ideas could not be put across. This is something which print will always have over television, until television is, in fact, simply a private viewing box with private controls which allows you, simply, to run the tape backwards and forwards the same way that you run the tape backwards and forwards with a book.

There is also the dogma within television, that it is boring to transmit ideas. This is partly to do with the determination on the part of those who work in television to set themselves up as a distinct profession with a quality and a skill and expertise of their own. Therefore, they talk about things being television or not. If someone simply sits in front of a camera and talks and tells you things and points things out with his finger, it is somehow not television. It is as if they had in their mind that somewhere, by common consent, there was a platonic ideal of television from which all other actual practical forms of television are, more or less, deviations, of which they are replicas. And this again is an absurd idea, because there is no standard. I mean, television is simply a hole, through which you push various communications. I rather like to see people sitting in front of a television camera and talking. As you no doubt know, the idea of the talking head is anathema to most television people. It seems to me that the talking head is the best sort of head there is, and the head, in general, is the most interesting thing we have really, and it is best to talk through it. It is, very often, very good and very instructive to place a head and fill the box up with the head and let it gabble on with its ideas. I do not believe that this violates some platonic ideal of television.

I actually hate the idea of arts programmes. It seems to me that there is only the ongoing work of the human intelligence, and to somehow separate these things off into the arts implies that awful dilettantish connoisseurship. It's an idea that art is to do with improving and life-enhancing values, with relish and pleasure. Relish and pleasure are the most inevitable outcome of intelligence properly applied. Nevertheless the first and primary function of these human initiatives is just simply enlightenment and truth, and therefore, I think it's a mistake to run too many things about artists.

*As though they were a sort of freak show?*

Not a freak show – as if one was visiting stars in their homes, that slight feeling of *Movie-Go-Round*. It's to do with a rather awful bourgeois idea of the artist as a privileged exponent of inspiration, from the experience of which comes a luminous and valuable object, rather than a series of propositions which may or may not be true and may or may not be enlightening. In this sense, I am commonly thought of as one who tries to bring the arts and the sciences together. I cannot conceive why anyone ever thought they were apart. They are both examples of imaginative initiative. That's all they are: they are proposals about the way in which experience seems to hang together and it seems that if arts or science programmes are to be any good they just simply advertise the fact that what is generally believed by scientists and artists is that life is a coherent business.

Arts programmes and educational programmes are not intended for a very large mass of people, they are intended for people who are going to exploit them and use them profitably and, therefore, people who are equipped to understand them. This is, in fact, a small minority. But because it is a small minority, to undernourish it is exactly like chopping off the head because it monopolizes so much food, in proportion to its size with respect to the other parts of the body. And the head is simply the most important part of the body and, therefore, so is the intellectual body of the country. One of the dogmas of the administrative levels of broadcasting is that in some strange way intellectual broadcasting or cultural broadcasting is a strange luxury which we allow ourselves to afford. This seems to me to be a very dangerous and ridiculous idea.

# Stephen Hearst

Head of Arts Features, BBC TV.

*How do you relate the decisions you make about arts programmes to the BBC's responsibility to lead?*

I feel an arts producer has duties towards his public, towards his employer, towards his subject, towards himself. If he cannot reconcile his duty to his audience and his duty towards his conscience and say 'Here I stand, this is what I have to say', then he ought to go. No arts producer on television ought ever to forget that 80 per cent of his audience left school roughly at fourteen to fifteen years of age and that only 5–7 per cent ever went to university, and that the subject matter he is treating may be relatively strange and certainly the terms that are being used may be relatively strange to an audience that left school at that age.

We operate on a flat licence, and the social effect of the flat licence fee is a cultural redistribution effect from the less well endowed to the more well endowed. Somebody who by and large does not need or does not think he needs a Rembrandt, but wants Steptoe and entertainment all the time, is actually subsidizing programmes that, if he were asked whether he wanted them, he would not know or may say that he does not want them. We are doing a cultural redistribution by the very fact that we have an arts features programme, by the very fact that we produce 250 programmes. Now when somebody in such a department, who has been chosen on a competitive basis, who has a great deal of education, then uses terms that literally require a university education, then I think he's failing in that particular duty.

# Brian Tesler

*Brian Tesler started the first ITV art magazine* Tempo. *Why did he do it?*

Well, it was something that I wanted to do, personally. It used to be forty-five minutes a week, and I got Ken Tynan to be the editor. I remember writing to him originally that I wanted it to be a swinging *Monitor*, and that's what we started out to do. Unfortunately, the BBC, rather piqued at the idea of some upstart at ITV doing an arts programme to rival *Monitor*, scheduled against its very opening edition the first Western that they'd ever played on Sunday afternoon, *Bronco*. I'd deliberately picked Sunday afternoon, I only had two afternoons at my disposal after all, Saturday and Sunday, and at no time on Saturday is it appropriate. I didn't want Sunday night because that's when *Monitor* was on and I thought Sunday afternoon would give an alternative to the children's programmes: an alternative that also gave it a chance of getting an audience. So we put it on Sunday afternoon and bang! *Bronco*, which, of course, destroyed the audience.

*It's a very small audience spot, though, Sunday afternoon.*

No, no. This was 5.15 on a Sunday afternoon. The audience is enormous at that time.

*I thought it came earlier?*

It went to 2.15. It got chased about the schedule by the BBC's highly competitive programming. You'd have thought, incidentally, that they would have been quite happy about that. I mean, an arts programme would never have had an enormous audience. You know, I think it's unfair perhaps to attribute this to them, but since it's either Donald Baverstock or Michael Peacock, each of whom is now in ITV, who must have done this, then I can't be considered too unfair. But it was personal pride, almost, on the part of the BBC. They were going to destroy *Tempo* because it was a potential rival to *Monitor*. So they chased it about the Sunday afternoon schedule.

*Why did you bother to try to do culture when you were being successful as a popular channel?*

Well, in the first place, as I say, I wanted to do it. The original title for it was *The Seven Lively Arts* because it always seemed to me that the arts aren't dull. You know the arts aren't dull and I know they aren't dull, but most audiences think they're dull as hell. It seemed to me a very real chance – because we had a fairly natural and fairly pronounced tendency on the part of the audience to prefer ITV. What better reason?

# Ken Russell

Film director for *Monitor*. Films include *Elgar, Bartok, Debussy, Rousseau, Isadora, Delius: A Song of Summer*.

The BBC took me on my enthusiasm and the amateur films I had made. I showed them to Norman Swallow and he showed them to three people: he showed them to *Panorama, Tonight* and to *Monitor*, about the only people one could show them to. John Schlesinger, fortunately, was just leaving to make feature films and they were looking for another film director. Huw Wheldon said, 'Give me half a dozen ideas on paper and we shall see if it will suit our programme.' Well, I gave him this list: one was a film on Albert Schweitzer in the jungle, one was on teddy boys' fashions, but he thought that a bit too much like *Tonight* and hadn't enough art in it. And then one was on John Betjeman's London. It was four short poems and would be only a ten-minute film which really cost £100. He thought it was worth a gamble. So there I had it, I was very fortunate in Betjeman because he was a natural personality and he lived the films and introduced them and read them. It was a marvellous script. It was concise and you had to make your images count very quickly.

Of all the thirty-six programmes that I did for television only one was in electronic media, the rest were all films. We came under BBC Talks Department and they hated films, they were always talking about television. Grace Wyndham Goldie always said she didn't want any film directors *manqué* on *Monitor*: they had to be television people. I think in retrospect she probably had a point there; when one sees some of the things today – she must writhe in her seat. But I don't blame her because I writhe in my seat quite often at the banality of a lot of stuff. It is almost too easy now to dress someone up in a cloak and have them wandering on top of a mountain. It's got rather ridiculous, I think.

*You must take some of the blame for that . . .*

I know. It's a terrible cliché. That was one of the reasons why I did the Strauss film in that way – to send it all up.

*How has television changed since your days on* Monitor*?*

I think if people are given a chance to do a film now they can do it, either good or bad. But in those days you had to convince Huw Wheldon that it was the way to do it and that the script was very curt and would make a terrific impact. This all came from making very short items: they were all fifteen minutes to start with, gradually we made them longer and longer until they filled whole programmes. But it was still very concise and nothing could get

135

by him that was second-rate. Because it was a fortnightly thing and we rushed it all out, and didn't have much time, we had to make a point very quickly.

Jonathan Miller when he edited *Monitor* was mostly just intellectual: he didn't care what the picture looked like, the spoken word was the important thing. And he did seem to be jumping on the bandwagon of all new things. Huw Wheldon was marvellous – he'd take anything, he had a very wide view. But Jonathan Miller, I think, was more specialized. Also, he didn't believe in inspiration in art. He had strange ideas about nineteenth-century art. I just felt that his ideas were totally alien to the audience, which would have been fine if he could have communicated them successfully, but more often than not he didn't. The point for me is that artists are ordinary people with fantastic imaginations that border on mysticism, magic, God, all sorts of things. The imagination, I think, is utterly fantastic. Bring this before people: if it touches a chord in them, it gives them a kick, they think it's great. I think it probably stretches their mind. At the moment I think they're too reverential and art can't be reverential: it's got to be tough and explosive, not Fischer-Dieskau in evening dress singing Lieder in a studio drawing-room.

*Your film about Elgar was widely popular . . .*

I suppose I was surprised at the reaction to Elgar but then in retrospect I can see why. I think it contains actually some of the worst aspects of popularization. I mean it's too corny now; it's too romantic. It's schmaltzy and it just shows that the public likes that. I suppose it was a good introduction for them and for me in a sense and one could go on from there to dig a bit deeper and be a little less fragile, less obvious and sentimental. And I think that's what I've tried to do. I think quite a few people have gone along with it but obviously it's reached a point where the outrage of a reactionary minority has, for the moment, brought the development to a stop.

*What do you feel about art on television generally?*

It seems to me it's not involved in everyday experience as it should be. It does seem that it's in a ghetto – it's in a class by itself, it's separate. And it's always treated like this: a slight hush still falls as

*Release* comes up in a slightly reverential way. I think the trouble is the BBC share the public's awe of somebody who puts themselves forward as an artist or an innovator and instead of attacking some of these new things, which I think are absolute tripe, they take them dead seriously. All right so let it be done, but let's laugh while it's being played or clap or shout and have the equivalent on a programme. Instead you might get four people sitting round discussing it afterwards: but that's purely academic. People should jump up while it's going on, should react. And that's what I mean about bringing it into everyday life.

*Is television responsible for that?*

I think in a large degree it is totally responsible. Certainly it might have brought art to millions, and lots of people realize that there's great fun to be had out of it. But as long as it is given a special little niche – two of the programmes are on BBC 2 and the one that is on BBC 1 is late at night – as long as this goes on so it will continue. If it can be brought in earlier and not categorized or pigeonholed, it might change. If a *Wednesday Play* can be about an esoteric subject and a lot of them are anyway, why not an arts subject at that same hour? You see the trouble with 'art' is that it was only at best tolerated under the old regime. Whereas there were plays before there were any arts programmes. If they had been bold enough to start it off at seven in the evening it wouldn't be in that position now. And the reason why they don't, it seems to me, is because the *Wednesday Play* people are very jealous of their niche and why shouldn't they be? They don't want to be ousted, and it would create the greatest precedent of all time and there's no machinery to bring it about anyway.

# Tony Palmer

Film director: *Benjamin Britten and his Festival, Corbusier, All My Loving.* Series: *Twice A Fortnight, How It Is.*

*You started in television as Ken Russell's assistant on* Isadora, *didn't you?*

Yes, I was still a general trainee and was therefore paid 2*s*. 1*d*. per hour during the film. There was a famous remark of Ken Russell's when we were coming towards the end of *Isadora*, which I think was his best television film. Something went wrong and he threw up his hands in despair and said, 'Why is it within the BBC, although I've made eight prize-winning films, I'm always given trainees?' It was perfectly true. I was his only other help and I was a general trainee, his secretary was a trainee secretary, he had a trainee designer with him and he had an assistant cameraman who, I think, had only just ceased to be a trainee cameraman. And this was astonishing. That was the first insight I had into the BBC.

*But you were there, at your request, to learn from him, that's why he had trainees.*

Well, yes. But, it was odd that, even so, no one else seemed to be available. I would have thought, from a distance, Ken Russell would have nine full-time assistants all searching the world for interesting subjects and I would just tag along at the bottom and move the tea around. But when I arrived I found that I was choosing the locations, finding the music, fixing up the artists, doing absolutely everything, simply because there wasn't anybody else. Which I loved. It was the best possible way to learn. I was forever grateful to Ken.

*What would you say you did learn from him?*

The two things stylistically I learned from him were the need for pacing film; that doesn't mean the film must go too fast, but that the fast bit is followed by a slow bit, is followed by a medium fast bit, or whatever. Also the pace of the film must have an overall shape. I sit in despair and watch – when I used to watch television – eleven films out of ten on television have no sense of pace at all. I think my films err on the side of pace. The other thing that I learned from him was the use of music. That music is foreground, not background, in that an idea comes with sound and picture. It doesn't come with picture and then you try and find record No. X346 called *Exciting Music* to go with it. You sometimes start with the music and sometimes start with the picture, but certainly, after the initial blow, you work on both at the same time. The soundtrack is just as important as the pictures.

*Out of* Isadora *to what? Where did you go then?*

After *Isadora* I did a comedy series called *Twice a Fortnight*. It
came from the Arts Department. The first week wasn't very good,
so Light Entertainment congratulated us saying, 'What a lovely
programme.' The second week was rather good; suddenly the
audience doubled overnight. Then we became a sort of vogue, and
everybody started watching. Light Entertainment said, 'What a
terrible programme. Isn't it monstrous that the Arts Department
should be doing Light Entertainment programmes? And why are
the Arts Department involved in Pop music? What is this Pop
music stuff? That's Light Entertainment. Get it off!' Again, through
the protection of one man, Paul Fox in this case, and only through
his protection, we survived for a while, but the pressures from
Light Entertainment were so great that eventually we got taken
off.

*Is this something you were aware of all the time, this great over-
lapping and rivalry?*

There is not only great overlapping and great rivalry but different
departments actually assume that different subject matter is their
*property*. You find this consideration dominant inside the BBC.
'This is my church – get out', Desmond Wilcox was heard to shout
at a *Panorama* team who were filming in the same location. The
property-orientated view of *Civilization* was sponsored by Stephen
Hearst who said of it, 'This [Arts Features] will be more popular
than *The Forsyte Saga*' [Drama Department]. And I think it's
also a great danger to what we call culture.

*What do you call culture?*

Things that happen around us. The way we live. And the way we
live is being segmented and, therefore, destroyed by the BBC
more than by anyone else. I think the BBC is the single biggest
cause of the steady destruction of there being in any real sense, a
contemporary culture. I don't want to go on at all about Pop
music, but the BBC has come to believe and is busy putting out
that belief to the public that Pop music is just Light Entertainment. The music that exists in the charts would never survive in
the open commercial world, if it were not for the biggest plugger

of all time, the BBC. The BBC is Tin Pan Alley with bells on. It's run by the same kind of people.

*Do you think that the BBC should put out everything that it commissions you to make?*

Once you accept the responsibility of commissioning someone, you commission them. You employ them, because you believe them to be of some talent and integrity and that's as far as it goes. You can give them whatever technical help you can. You can explain to them that there are certain limitations to what the BBC can put out because of its charter, its policy, its understanding of public taste. They cannot put out a programme in which there is 'fuck' every other word. But over and above that, it should have no editorial control whatsoever.

NICHOLAS GARNHAM

# 8 · Information

The history of television can be seen as a struggle between its two central functions, entertainment and information. When TV started here in 1936 entertainment was clearly its prime function. It opened with a revue and thereafter the policy was a play a day. Its slow development as an important news medium can be explained by the slow spread of its audience. It was not until 1949 that audiences outside London could see television, and efficient and powerful media depend upon the numbers reached. Until TV achieved something approaching full national coverage it could not hope to compete with the established news media, newspapers and radio.

TV news and information was for a long time, like the rest of television, a second-hand medium. The development of TV news suffered from the immense prestige of BBC radio news. Right up until 1955 the news on television was sound only. It was then followed by a newsreel directly copied in format from the cinema newsreels. So from the start there was a tension in television journalism, which still worries its practitioners, between words which are seen as the real business of journalism, and pictures, which are clearly a necessity of the medium, but are in some way tarred with the show-biz brush of the movies.

Many of the arguments about public service television, about whether the ITA is failing in its duty, about whether there is enough 'serious' television, are really arguments about whether there is enough informational television. Serious television means news, current affairs and documentaries. The traditions of the theatre, the music-hall and the cinema are very different from those of Fleet Street, in spite of the development of the popular 'yellow press' in this century. But on television they have to co-exist and fight for scarce resources and air-time. When a journalist writes a feature on Vietnam for *The Times* it does not stop someone else putting on a cabaret act in a northern club. On television you must choose between *This Week* and Tom Jones, and so inevitably the categories of show-business and journalism have become mixed and the form begins to dictate the content.

It starts with the news bulletin where the dramatic pictures of earthquake or plane-crash take precedence over Common Market negotiations or new pension plans, but, more insidious perhaps, competition for audiences means that people are told what they want to hear, not what those in a position to know think is important. To take a simple example. How many times does television news report a crash on the M1, between a lorry and a saloon-car? As news this can be of no interest to anyone except the relations of the injured. It happens to someone, somewhere, every hour, every day. Its only purpose on a news bulletin is to appeal to our sense of the ghoulish.

The stresses between information and entertainment are seen at their clearest in sports presentation. A sporting event is a fact which television is supremely equipped to enable millions to witness. Its job as a medium of information is to present that event as clearly as possible, so enabling the viewer to draw his own emotional or factual conclusion. This is a job that television does brilliantly, but they will not rest on that brilliance. They demonstrate a constant lack of confidence in the medium by indulging in the big sell. Football matches are now surrounded by acres of presentation in which David Coleman uses ranks of almost speechless football experts as an excuse to cue in clips from previous matches or the match just seen. The real is made as synthetic as possible in order to vaunt television. Television is no longer enabling the viewer to be present at a football match, the football match is being used as an ingredient in a television event.

When it is only a football match involved it does not matter that much, but unfortunately this ethos is catching, until now Apollo missions are presented like football matches. This aspect was seen at its worst on the near disastrous Apollo 13 mission. The routine nature of the moon-flights was making them increasingly difficult to televise; for between blast-off and splash-down there is very little to see apart from occasional TV transmissions from space and transmissions from the moon itself. Otherwise all one can do is listen to the talk between Mission Control and the space-craft, talk which with its bare, unemotional efficiency repeatedly shows up the false chat in the space studio with its attempts to whip up a spurious excitement. When things went wrong on Apollo 13 almost unconsciously a ghoulish relish spread over the whole performance. One began to understand the insidious attraction of a public execution. At last the coverage seemed justified, and the presenters began to assume an arrogant identification with those in space, as if they believed that not only were they too part of the enterprise, but the enterprise was given added significance and poignancy by their reporting of it. The audience was never allowed to make up its own mind about what was happening. The image of the great American heroes was relentlessly battered out of the screen. The nadir of the whole performance was the re-run of the splash-down. One expected to find David Coleman on the aircraft carrier asking the astronauts to 'talk us through it'.

Ironically, while the intervention of television in events is becoming increasingly accepted, the traditional concept of current affairs television is one of complete neutrality. Both the BBC and ITV are required by the Charter and Act to be free of political bias. But inevitably those who make current affairs programmes are intelligent and responsive human beings. Every creative decision they make must betray their bias, which is to say their personality, unless one asks them to be totally cynical and hypocritical which would be more dangerous than bias. Over the years TV journalism has increasingly faced up to this reality under pressure from its practitioners who found the maintenance of an artificial balance quite intolerable. We now accept an outspokenness from our current affairs programmes that would have been unthinkable fifteen years ago. Our attitude to this trend depends on what influence we think television has on its audience. Do television journalists reflect or create and lead public opinion? Are the biases those of a minority liberal *élite* and, if so, is this harmful or could the range of views expressed be widened? How far in fact should the editorializing trend be carried? Censorship of news in a free society is abhorrent, but does repeated showing of Vietnam war footage or violent student demonstrations encourage violent tendencies in society? Now that TV is established as a central medium of news and information questions like these are being asked with increasing force and urgency in all democratic societies. How do those responsible, the practitioners of informational television, respond?

## NEWS

*The whole field of informational television grew from television's possibilities as a medium for the straight reportage of news. The decisive influence in the transformation of TV news into journalism in its own right, with its own characteristics, rather than a copy of the cinema or radio, was the creation of ITN.*

# Sir Geoffrey Cox

1956–67, Editor, ITN; Managing Director, Yorkshire TV, since 1967.

ITN had a great advantage in the early days in starting from scratch, in being a brand new organization in what, so far as news was concerned, was still a brand new medium. We had no prestigious radio service alongside us, whose reputation we might damage by rash experiments or zany ideas. We were free to experiment with new techniques and new people. And experiment we did. We had Arthur Clifford, who came to us from the BBC as News Editor, bursting with the desire to use this new medium in new ways. We had Robin Day and Ludovic Kennedy as newscasters. All we needed was time on the air and money, the two categorical imperatives of good TV. The time was assured when the ITA decided there must be a minimum of twenty minutes of news per day. Winning the money was the big difficulty in the early months. The companies were losing thousands of pounds a day and they were staggered – as I was, coming out of Fleet

Street – at the costs involved in making TV news, but by the autumn of 1956 the corner had been turned. First the advertising revenue swept up, and in the autumn of 1956 we had one of perhaps the greatest news periods in any time except 1963 – we had Suez and Hungary. That reinforced beyond doubt the value of television as a news service. Thirdly, in 1956, ITN suddenly leapt forward and became a tremendous element in television. By the end of the year, the programme companies were also convinced that this was not only costly programming, but good programming and the corner was turned.

*None the less, has there remained a tension between ITN and the companies?*

A healthy tension. I will put it this way: television is journalism plus entertainment, therefore you get a natural tension between the entertainment side and the journalistic side. But I don't think that tension is as great as the tension that exists in all journalistic enterprises between the reporting side and the interpretative side. This is one of the built-in natural tensions of journalism, and in television this tends to become institutionalized, so that you get struggles between the hard news and the news in depth programmes with a treatment of subjects. I think it was a great pity that in 1957 Independent Television did not exploit success and say to ITN, 'You've got a superb operation here, widen it out into the news magazine field.' Instead of that we were given a tiny and inadequate area to make *Roving Reports*, and we had the bitter experience of seeing *Tonight* move in and make a major programme out of the same kind of programming that ITN had pioneered.

# Nigel Ryan

Editor, ITN.

*When you first came into TV journalism what difference did you find between that and newspaper journalism?*

The strongest impression was that it was very hard to express a subtlety. If you are not careful, you tend to come back with a film which is reduced to all the old clichés. I think you have to be a considerable master of the television camera before you can express anything other than the obvious.

*You, as a reporter, were responsible for the story that got into the news. Did you yourself have to learn to have an eye for the image on the screen, or did you leave that to your directors?*

In ITN we don't have a director: there is a cameraman, sound recordist and yourself. I think I learnt quickly. Occasionally I came back with the film, and was faced with cutting it myself. And I found that the script I originally had in mind gradually disintegrated as the film progressed. I realized that I was not going to be able to talk about death because I had not got pictures to cover it, and I was not going to be able to talk about what the Opposition man said because he was out of focus, and I was not going to be able to talk about some other matter which I thought was of enormous importance because I had not filmed it properly. I did gradually learn that it is tremendously important to be able to use the camera to illustrate what you want to say and not to let the tail wag the dog.

The other thing you cannot do as a television man that you can do as a newspaper journalist is to use information collected on the telephone. You have got to be there, whereas a journalist can actually collect information from his colleagues: or he can ring up the embassy and find out and it can become the lead of his story. A television man has got to be there when it happens and it is just that much more difficult. I think the thing really about television is that when you get there nobody can beat the camera. Nothing is more dramatic than the assassination of the alleged killer of President Kennedy watched instantaneously. No journalist can catch this. It is, equally, several times more difficult to be there. The great asset of television is that it can tell very effectively a simple truth. Truth is not always simple, and things that are simple are not always true. So when the two come together, then television is a marvellous means of communication.

# Gerald Priestland

BBC correspondent since 1949. Tried an experiment as a columnist on BBC TV News in 1969. Now presenting *Newsdesk* on radio.

*To what extent do you think the way a camera reports at a political meeting slants that reporting?*

Oh, well, the camera cannot lie, but my golly the film editor can. This is something which is very worrying. I don't think myself that television is the ideal medium for news. In fact what I do believe about news is that one should, as it were, take a balanced diet – it's a mistake to rely solely on television, solely on radio or solely on the press for one's news diet. I almost said television is the worst possible medium for news. There is no medium which is so hamstrung by technical complications. Covering a story for television is a matter of continuous compromise. You have got to be thinking of when you have got to ship the film in order to get it through processing in order to get it edited in order to get it on the air on time. By the time you have coped with all that, there is not a lot of time or energy left to cover the news.

*Does that mean, as a television reporter, that when you are gathering information for your story you have got to work within half the time of a press man?*

Oh, yes, I would say so. You see, the easiest medium is in a way the press. What you need is a notebook. Radio is relatively simple – a tape recorder. Television – camera crew, cameraman, sound man, all the things that can go wrong. If the film is exposed right it will probably miss the flight; if it does not miss the flight it will probably be fouled up in processing; if it is not fouled up in processing, someone may scratch it in the editing. I have offended a lot of good friends by saying this, but any of these things can happen. This is a constant nightmare, particularly if you are working abroad.

On the other hand, there is no substitute for seeing it, seeing it now. Think of the moon landing – television wiped out everything else. That is the way to cover a story like that, to see it. Television is also a tremendously powerful medium for conveying emotion.

147

If it is right that we should grieve for starving Biafrans, nobody can make us grieve like television. But it concerns me that television may be creating a world rather than reporting one. Creating a tiny, rowdy, rather incestuous sort of news world. I think perhaps the biggest crime of which British journalism is guilty is that of over-simplification: the tendency to present stories like sketches in review, the plot, the middle, the end, a nice snap curtain. Life is not like that, things are interrelated. It is not the real world at all, but it fools a lot of people that it is.

This is a personal thing, I suppose, and I correct myself immediately, but if we could be more scholarly! However, we must qualify that. For every one of us high-minded people reading this book, there are lots of people who could not care less why the Italian government is in a mess, and for them it's a real public service to present a bathing beauty with their bacon and eggs. But all journalism, particularly television journalism, is bound to partake to a certain extent of entertainment. My greatest anti-motto is drawn from words whispered in my ear by a distinguished BBC news man when I first joined. 'There is no harm in being dull,' he said. I think this is appalling. If it's worth being there at all, it's interesting; so it cannot be dull, it must not be dull.

# CURRENT AFFAIRS

*Current affairs television grew out of TV's news reporting function. It is the equivalent of the leader and feature pages of a newspaper. It has been one of the explosive growth areas of television. Indeed many (even of its practitioners) will argue that there is now too much. Moving, as it must, into the area of idea and opinion, it faces the same dilemmas as news, but more acutely. It is in this area that TV works out its relationship to society. It is here that the real sensitivity to political and social pressures is felt. For this reason, as Tony Jay, an ex-editor of* Tonight *points out, most of the television executives have come from this battleground. In talking to those now doing the job we see some of the considerations and pressures moulding those who will probably run television in the future.*

# Rowan Ayers

Assistant Head of Presentation, BBC TV. Editor, *Line-Up*.

I'm a journalist as opposed to a member of show-biz. We are running *Line Up* as a kind of nightly newspaper which looks at all sorts of things, including television. If that is our brief, which I believe it is, then we must be free in what we say. It's no good the show-biz element coming up saying, 'Come on, you should be selling us.' They have not actually bought advertising space on our programme.

*The general standard of television has been heavily criticized of late. Do you think this criticism is fair?*

I think TV is either too good at the moment or too bad. I'll explain that. I think there could be a case for saying that television ought to be much worse. It ought to be nothing significant at all, it ought to be home movies, films endlessly running through the night and have no effect on you at all. In America, I suppose, it is run very close to that. It does not tell you anything, does not educate you, does not try to take you over and explain the world at all, but provides an easy cheap form of home entertainment. That's one case. If that is so, the BBC is much too good and aimed at much too high a level of responsibility in terms of media.

Conversely if it *is* really significant and really important and is going to be the dominating means of communication, which I suspect it might well be in the next ten years, it isn't good enough. It should not be allowed to disperse and then dissipate its qualities to the extent that it does. It should be focused on its importance. It should become more aware of the responsibilities to society. In which case, it is not good enough at the moment.

Now I'm between the two schools – I'm not sure which way it should go. I have a horrible feeling that, being in the middle as we are at the minute, we are really building a non-future for the BBC. I think that unless somebody very soon says what our future is going to be, in ten years time the BBC may well be in a very ambivalent situation when, as we all know, there will be a choice of 300 networks. Television in ten years' time must be a question of pushing a button and getting Tokyo, America, pre-recorded stuff, cassettes. So what is this thing called BBC television in ten years' time? Is it going to be a national network, feeding important material, or is it just going to join in the rat race of cassettes, popularity and home movies, entertainment, profit? I don't know. But it is a question which ought to be asked.

# Ian Martin

The clash between the values of show-business and the values of journalism is, of course, particularly acute in ITV as Ian Martin, previously a producer on BBC programmes such as *Panorama*, *Gallery* and *The Human Side* and now Head of Documentary for Thames TV, points out.

If you are a documentary producer you have to fight on two fronts simultaneously. It's no good fighting wholly on the enemy's ground and trying to claim that documentaries can get the ratings, because this is demonstrable nonsense a lot of the time. And so part of your strategy has to be some high-minded stuff about watching the Television Act, about wide showings for programmes of merit. On the other hand there is quite a wide-felt fallacy that documentaries are far more disastrous for ratings than in fact they are, so you have to fight on that level as well and say, 'Look, you will lose a little bit of rating by this programme, but you will not lose so much ratings that it will clobber you for the whole of the rest of the evening and the amount you lose you can well afford to lose and it is your duty to lose.'

*Why do you think that it is their duty to put on documentaries?*

Because I regard television as essentially an aspect of journalism rather than an aspect of show-business and that really does seem to me what the nature of the thing is about. I mean it's perfectly arguable that television is just a long-playing record or the holiday snaps or whatever. But I don't look at it that way. Its prime function is an informatory one. It can't be its function the whole time, but if it doesn't do that, its failing to fulfil its prime function. It takes up so much money and talent, that I just think that amount of money and talent should not be used solely for entertainment – it should have a strong education and information aspect as well.

*You worked for the BBC for nine years before joining Thames Television under Jeremy Isaacs. Did you see ethics of the BBC changing during that time?*

I think the only way to get effective programmes inside a structure like the BBC is to have lots of little kingdoms, even if there's a certain amount of duplicating and mutual antagonism. This is the only way a big organization like that can remain healthy and virile.

Since any sort of power springs from programmes, the closer you have your power to the actual act of production, the more satisfactory your situation is I think. The trouble with the BBC is that there are more and more people, somewhat removed from the business of production, whose main role is to interpose themselves, to demur gently about things, or to be worried.

*How do you think one can get over this problem? Do you think it's necessary in fact to break the BBC down into independent units or what do you think one can do with it?*

I think the problem is that it would be very unfortunate if the power of the BBC were broken to a really substantial extent. I think you have got to have a really powerful instrument whose announced and basic purpose is public-service broadcasting. Not only for what it does itself, but because this is a kind of public proclamation that that is what the community's vision of broadcasting is. But if you have something like that, you have going along with it all the sort of monolithic, authoritarian tendencies that one can criticize so much at the BBC. In order to maintain an internal structure that gives people a fairly considerable opportunity for moving around – if they fall out with someone then they have alternative employment somewhere else – I think you've got to have what to any decent business consultant would be a pretty illogical and wasteful structure. You have got to have overlapping between departments, you have got to have rival barons fighting for the same areas of territory, because one isn't in the business of producing plastic chamber-pots in the most economical way but in the business of putting ideas across and you don't want a situation where people say, 'Ah, that's an idea about science – we have a science department, he must go there,' and the Head of that Department says, 'Oh, that's not my idea of science – that isn't really science. I don't wish to do anything about it.' The danger is that perfectly good stratagems for maximum output at minimum cost are really not applicable to the BBC because the product is different, but because there is a product, and it's visible as a piece of video-tape or celluloid, there may be the danger of saying, 'Well, we could produce that product more cheaply if we slimmed down the departments, if we did this and this.'

# David Webster

1967–9, Editor of *Panorama*; Assistant Head of Current Affairs Group, BBC TV.

*Perhaps the most prestigious of all current affairs programmes is* Panorama. *How do you see its role?*

When you look at a programme like *Panorama* you have to consider not only the programme but also the role that it plays in the whole spectrum of output. If we have nightly programmes, if we have news programmes, if we have song and dance programmes, it is obviously ridiculous for *Panorama* to attempt to be any of these things. What hit *Panorama* some time ago was a crisis in identity – it had had an identity which was built around Richard Dimbleby, and when Richard died what was it? Was it just another programme? *Panorama* having been very well established early on, other people nibbled away at the subject matter. So if you look back ten years – even five years – *Panorama* is totally different. It is different because other programmes were not there. Now, when you get into a situation where you have got programmes like *24 Hours*, the whole mood is changed. News is now effectively transmitting the first sequences of *Panorama* stories; the first two or three minutes is taken off the top. You have then to consider what your role is. Now *Panorama* at one time used to deal with the arts, but obviously after they set up *Monitor* this was silly. One had to find a role – an identity. Now what I did – and I expected to lose viewers – was to say that *Panorama* will never do anything merely because it is interesting and only do it because it matters. In a curious way this did re-identify the role of the programme.

*You expected to lose viewers because you thought it would be much heavier going?*

Yes. But we did not, because people recognized what the purpose of the programme was. So I suppose they said to themselves, 'Well, we'll sit down at eight o'clock on Monday evening and if the world comes to an end they will tell us about it.' That was perhaps their one obeisance to looking at what was going on in the world. The one thing they did know about *Panorama* was that, though it might be quite often a little dreary and insist on dealing with serious subjects, it did carry a sort of massive professional integrity with it. So that, by and large, they were likely to get something pretty close to the truth, and they would see it done in an authoritative way and with people who carried authority. That is what the role of that particular programme is in the BBC.

*But you kept the magazine format?*

No, we did not keep any format – that is the silly thing about it, you see. I've always said that *Panorama* has no format. It's 49½ minutes between the opening titles and the end titles and if you want to stand on your head during that period, OK, it's open for you to do so. If you want to do OBs, if you want to do films or something in the studio you can do that. If you wanted to you could turn the thing into one long interview. What you do is to use all the techniques that are available to you as a television producer in the way which you choose at that particular moment in time. You have all the pressures which come from employing a large number of talented and difficult people, and in a sense the job is to create an environment in which that talent can flourish. Now the glory of not having a great theology about this, but just using it how you want to, is that you can run 49½ solid minutes of celluloid on some subject if you want. Often we go into a situation where some people go off to do a story and they are intending to do a twenty-minute film or half-hour and they strike gold and they send you a cable – say, look, this is wonderful. Well, you take this with a pinch of salt. When you actually put it together you say, 'well, it *is* wonderful' and you say 'to hell with it, let's run', and you run a solid programme on this. All right, maybe you have an argument with somebody else who wants something else, but that's what an editor is for.

# Jeremy Isaacs

Producer, *What the Papers Say* and *Searchlight*. Editor, *This Week*. Presently Head of Current Affairs, Thames.

*Do you think TV journalism has had much effect on its audiences?*

The surveys show that more than half the people in the country are coming to depend upon television as a source of information, rather than upon newspapers. I think that is the principle effect of television journalism. I think it has altered the content and style of written journalism to some extent. I think it has helped to create a more educated public in this country. I was very struck by something that Wedgwood-Benn said on television the other day. He was complaining that an ITN programme about a series of by-elections was treating the thing as a horse-race, that Burnet was treating it as a joke. He thought this was unworthy of the public to which it was addressed and he went on to say: 'If you go around the country as I do, you will find that people are infinitely better informed about the issues, better informed about the economy, better informed about the world outside, better informed about technology than they have ever been before, and yet you people on television treat politics as a joke.' Well, in fact, as someone pointed out to him on the programme, if that was the case, then television is partly responsible for it.

I'm a little bit aware of what television can and cannot do in the way of moulding or altering public opinion. I think it has had some measurable effect. For example, I did several programmes when I was the producer of *This Week*, which I suppose were libertarian sociological programmes. They were programmes about homosexuals, saying: 'Stop thinking about this as a problem, as an argument. Just look at the people.' And I myself would argue that if we have more libertarian legislation in this country in areas of sex and abortion and even capital punishment, then television has played a part in that. I think that there is something more compelling about the presentation of that kind of subject matter in the television medium than in the print medium.

If I can give one absolutely specific example. I do think that programmes hammering away at the thesis that drink was connected with driving accidents altered the climate of public opinion in this country that enabled Ministers to introduce legislation. I think one of the best programmes I ever did, in a tabloid way, was a programme in Christmas 1963 about drinking, which pulled out every possible stop. I mean it cut from dear old Mrs So and So, the victim, to Drunken Driver saying, 'Well, you know, you don't interfere with our pleasures,' and that kind of thing. It also gave the statistics which, of course, were overwhelming. We came out of this to Marples in the studio who was then Minister of Transport and he actually said, 'I'm shattered, but on the other hand, I can't introduce the legislation you are asking me to introduce because public opinion would not stand it.' So we made more programmes until eventually the government saw that public opinion would stand it.

*Are you able to do your job satisfactorily within the present ITV structure?*

The fundamental fact about ITV is it's supposed to make money. The people who have put up the money for it want a return on the money they have invested. Now you can persuade them to give programme-makers a great deal of freedom if they are anyway making a great deal of money. At the moment you have a situation where the thing is so financially tight because of the way in which the government has cut into the profits of Independent Television that programme-makers like myself find it very difficult to persuade our bosses to make more money available for any additional output at all. At the moment, when the financial viability of ITV depends on keeping costs, which are always escalating, down, if possible, below a very restricted revenue and when it also depends upon that margin of revenue which is obtained by exchanging programmes in a network which now comprises five companies instead of four or on weekdays four instead of three, it is very difficult to see where more money for more and better programmes – different programmes – can come from.

*Would you like to have seen the Pilkington recommendation of the revenue side of ITV and the programming side being separated?*

No, I wouldn't. Like everybody else in television, I am engaged in rethinking for my own benefit, and perhaps for the benefit of any Committee of Inquiry, any suggestions that I have to make for improving the system. But that is not and never has been a recommendation which has appealed to me and for this reason I have never understood who would have been choosing which programmes were networked and which were not and which were made and which were not. I do not like the idea of divorcing the revenue-getting side from the programme-making side or, anyway, splitting these two functions. Let me explain this. I actually think there is something in the making of television programmes which is basically publishing and publishing comes from collecting a body of like-minded people together and putting them in a given set of circumstances and letting them get on with it – letting them decide what they will do with the air-time at their disposal. Now on this basis you can blame all the rotten programmes that the network does on the Network and all the rotten programmes – if you think they're rotten programmes – that this company does on Thames. But at least we do them. It's fair to say that Thames is *Today, This Week, Report, This is Your Life, Opportunity Knocks, Max, Callan, Mystery and Imagination, Special Branch.* That's Thames. OK – it's not everybody's taste. But that's Thames. My fear is that if you had a body of people, however high-minded and however excellent, who commissioned programmes from other bodies of people who made programmes, you would turn the people who made programmes into packages, and I think that they would be less individualistic, less idiosyncratic, less varied, on that basis, than they are now. I think that their product would be glossier and smoother and 'nothing-er' than it is now and that is saying something in some cases. In other words, I think Lew Grade and Sidney Bernstein have contributed something to British television.

# Philip Whitehead, M.P.

Worked at the BBC on *Gallery* and *Panorama*. 1966–70, Editor, *This Week*. Since this interview elected Labour Member of Parliament for Derby North.

I see our job here in this particular programme as getting very sophisticated political information on a number of different levels through to an audience of people who habitually read the *Daily Mirror*, and who are not, because of education or interest, capable of going through all the better alternative sources of information. I am not at all concerned whether you watch my programmes or not, because I know that you are reading the *Guardian* and the *Economist* and a bit of the foreign press and you probably listen to BBC radio and you are a selective television watcher. People who watch my programme on the whole (there are usually eight to ten million of them) are people who are sufficiently keen on what we are talking about to stay tuned after a light entertainment programme from 9 to 9.30: people who quite often get no other similarly concentrated view of foreign affairs and the more esoteric domestic issues.

I am very depressed that, even so, talking to people where we live in Derbyshire, about a programme they have seen of yours on the previous Thursday, you find that they abstract images much more clearly than ideas and they remember things they have seen. The second problem is that they abstract facts which fit their prejudices much more easily than facts which are new or novel to them or demand an effort of adjustment in their own attitudes. For instance, we did a programme at the BBC about Robert Kennedy, at a time when Robert Kennedy was first staking out a separate constituency for himself in America, rather different from the John Kennedy vision. This programme ran forty minutes and it was, I thought, a pretty fair assessment of an American political figure in that sort of framework. I found almost everybody up in Derbyshire watched that programme, because it was about a glamorous man and a glamorous family, and they all came up to me in the shops on Saturday morning saying things like, 'Isn't it amazing that he has that number of children.' Every single person I met could have told me to the last one the number of his children. Hardly any of them could have told me anything about the political attitudes he represented.

There is the question of images coming first, not really ideas. I think that in a way they are much more vulnerable to using those images and certain selective facts to boost their prejudice. For instance, we did a programme about eighteen months ago on the exploitation of coloured people in Birmingham. One of the things we showed was multiple occupancy of terraced houses and a lot of people living in them. The overwhelming response of the letters that came in, but also of people one met, who you would expect to have that attitude anyway, was, 'There you are, your programme proved it. They love living in conditions like that. A real rabbit warren.' They had taken out of that programme the one or two simple images and facts that fitted their preconception. So I don't regard any single television programme as being able to change opinions overnight. I think it's a drift effect over a long period of time.

# Desmond Wilcox

Editor, *Man Alive*.

*Do you think TV confirms people's values?*

I think probably the great plethora of mindless rubbish which I see on all three channels in this country – and, by God, there is some – probably does, because in fact it does not attempt to excite any kind of new thinking process in the viewer. And it's only when you try and do this that you might challenge established values. When you subscribe to what makes laughter, or what makes excitement, *without* disturbing or exciting the viewer, then you are of course confirming the viewer as he is.

But, compared with other countries, we have a vastly much greater percentage of challenging television. Where one is frightened is that sometimes the television management fails to recognize what ought to be encouraged, what ought to be slapped down. On the whole the BBC is a thousand per cent better at giving new talent its head than ITV which, instead of a brain, has a kind of rating chart. You see, the whole motive has to be different over there. You are making television for shareholders, for a board room, for a profit.

*So you are not interested in ratings?*

It is certainly one of my ambitions to get as many viewers as possible for my programmes – I don't want to make programmes that are so challenging and so esoteric that only three of us watch them with fascination. I want to make programmes that are challenging and reach those that need to be challenged.

*But why do you want to challenge society? Do you want to shape people's political opinions, do you want to shape their social views?*

It's summed up in a word – illumination, in the literal meaning of the word. I believe that the purpose of the sort of television that I'm concerned with making, is that we will attempt constantly to illuminate corners of our society, which did we not do so, would otherwise remain dark, shadowed, and perhaps unobserved by the rest of society, that is the rest of us. Now that challenges the establishment, in as much that just to make somebody think about the man next door, and produce an understanding of the man next door, might make him do something about the man next door, particularly if that somebody is less well off – or even better off. When I see that I fail to make them aware, I will go on banging, and there are issues like housing, like race, like education, like religious tolerance, where I may never be able to say I've done one programme and my job is complete. What I will say is that until I see the tolerant freedoms that I want in this society, it is my job to go on bashing at that issue.

# Anthony Jay

1962–3, Editor, *Tonight*; 1963–4, Head of Talks Features. Freelance
writer: scripts include *Royal Family* and *Frost Report*.

*People now often talk of that period when you were on* Tonight *from
1957–62 as the golden age of British television. Do you see it that
way?*

Nearly always, in any new art, the great creative period is the
earliest. In painting, in drama, in the novel, poetry, the period
when it first suddenly comes to its full flowering is best. After that,
people are terribly influenced by what's gone before – they're trying to do it differently or trying to take just one area of it. And I
think it's not impossible that the time you're talking about was the
great creative time on television – where really all things that were
technically possible were possible then and I must say that watching television now, in the 1970s, it's very very rare to see anything
that we didn't know about and haven't tried in those years, except
the use of a large participating studio audience for interview
programmes on 'serious' subjects. That's the only really important
addition, I think. Otherwise one just sees the same things being
done that we did – the same mistakes being made, and the same
creative discoveries being made.

One of the things about television expanding so fast is that the
folklore hasn't been passed on. People have had to keep inventing
the wheel, because the chap who invented it before is now a Controller and hasn't got time to show you how to make one. But it's
awfully easy to pick a time as a golden age – I mean there was a
golden age of television comedy play-writing, there was a golden
age of drama series with a documentary flavour. I think that the
*Tonight* era was only one of them. One reason why I think that
that group somehow passed into folklore is that, if you're going to
run a television channel, your real problems are with Parliament.
It's the political context of television that requires the finest and
most delicate handling and the most confidence and courage. And
it is likely that the people who can do that are going to evolve from
current affairs and politics like Huw Wheldon, Paul Fox, Michael
Peacock, Donald Baverstock, Alistair Milne, David Attenborough,

Anthony Jay

Carleton Greene – almost everybody who comes to a position of prominence in broadcasting has come through that route because that is where the fire is hottest. If you can survive that, and fight on equal terms with Prime Ministers and Chief Whips, you're better qualified than someone who's come up through producing Tommy Cooper and Tony Hancock and doesn't know what's going to hit him.

Nevertheless, I think there was something about that time and this is a phrase that Donald and Huw Wheldon both talk about and I think Huw originated it, and that was what he called 'programme dialogue'. That when you have any new skill or new intellectual area to explore, a creative area, a number of people can acquire a sort of private skill of a high order, so that if it's to be passed on it's somehow got to be formulated into a body of accepted knowledge. In other words we know that this works and that doesn't. If you don't accept it, well, accept it for the time being and you will gradually learn and violate it at your peril. Maybe you're a genius, maybe we've got it wrong and we've closed off as a blind alley something that is a great thoroughfare, but you've got to be very good to prove that – there's a lot of people have battled at the end of that blind alley before you. And programme dialogue is the process by which individual intuition and private feeling, seat of the pants instincts, pass into a corpus of knowledge and practice. There was an intensity of learning on *Tonight* forced upon you by the volume of output – because don't forget *Tonight* was five nights a week, at forty minutes a night. There was what you might call traumatic learning. You know, you learnt through errors and disaster and you had to meet in the pub after the programme and say, 'Why was that so awful?' You somehow had to formulate a reason that satisfied everybody that it wasn't going to occur again or it would occur tomorrow night and the night after and the night after that – till the programme was removed, and rightly, by the planners.

Mind you, this was not a group, but a number of warring tribes that met around that Talks Meeting every Thursday morning. *Tonight* was one tribe with deep contempt, because of territorial jealousy, for *Panorama* on the one hand, which seemed to be trespassing and trying to take Cabinet Ministers away from us on Mondays when we wanted to talk to them as well, and *Monitor* on

161

the other hand, which seemed to be taking away all the best painters and sculptors. Our feeling was that *Tonight* was about anything two civilized people could talk about, and they talk about Harold Wilson, or listen to a pretty girl singing or talk about auto-destructive art, anything. Obviously any programme that sectionalized itself was immediately in conflict with us. This is why I felt very strongly in favour of the magazine programme. If you say, well, let's have a programme entirely about art, let's have *Panorama* entirely about politics, let's have a programme entirely devoted to science, then the moment you do that you divide your audience by four. *Tonight* is addressed to anybody interested in what's happening this week. *Monitor* immediately cuts off all the people who aren't interested in the arts, and you have something called *Workshop* which is only for people interested in the arts who like music, or *Canvas* which is only for the ones interested in painting. You could go on subdividing until nobody is viewing at all except the size of audience you could invite to a lecture room.

# Alistair Milne

Former Editor, *Tonight*. Controller, BBC Scotland.

I think one of the key losses is that in the talks field at the moment producers in the old sense are very lacking. There's a vast number of directors around but the man who has a conceptual notion of what a new programme is about – who can sit down with a sheet of paper and say, 'This is the shape of future programmes' – are very rare indeed. There were never very many, truth to tell. It seems to me there are rather fewer at the moment, perhaps because the whole operation has got much wider and more specialist and our trouble in the next five years is going to be finding the lead producers again – the people who say, 'This is the way it's going to operate and we're not inheriting a series of preconceived attitudes and timings and philosophies'. You know, it's very difficult to take *Panorama* over now, after God-knows-how-many years, because it's at eight o'clock on a Monday night and it has fifteen years of history behind it. I think one's own experience as a viewer demonstrates that; there seems to be a running danger of the content being submerged by the technique. And all the technique began to encroach as the equipment became more sophisticated and I suspect now we've got to the point where the techniques are known – the equipment is highly sophisticated and thought should be put back into the picture somewhere. And unquestionably, if the new-generation directors believe that self-expression is all, they're wrong; if you have nothing to communicate in terms of intellectual expression to the audience, if you've got no kind of internal dynamic to a picture, you may as well throw it away. There's a good deal of emptiness on the air.

*But how can the BBC bring about a situation that puts the content back in?*

I think by very rigorous dialectic with the producer, because I wonder sometimes, the television service being as big as it is, whether there's time enough for people to be able to teach through argument – if they've got anything to teach anyway. I think this is a great problem and the service is now so big and there are so many departments and the output's so vast, that the individual producer or director, it seems to me, is almost losing contact with his own immediate fellow-directors. It could be that this process of self-expression just takes over and becomes self-mutilating. In a much smaller outfit it's easier to argue directly about programmes, to criticize in advance rather than afterwards. But with five hundred producers, or something, how do you cope? The departmental head is supposed to be the teacher, but he's attending meetings, writing memos and all that sort of thing. Somewhere along the line it's been lost and somebody'll have to rediscover some way of doing it.

\*

*Although in theory TV current affairs is supposed to be neutral, it is always being accused of bias. This accusation takes various forms. There is the accusation from established society that TV is a nest of libertarian revolutionaries spreading their permissive doctrines, and there is the accusation from the minority groups that TV is too closely linked to an establishment, governmental view of society, and that not enough dissent gets an airing.*

# Malcolm Muggeridge

Journalist and television reporter and presenter. Documentaries include *Twilight of an Empire* and *The American Way of Sex*. Most recent programme: *The Question Why*.

*You've never made an effort to be politically neutral or balanced in any way?*

No, I can't. The whole idea of balance is repugnant to my nature because I don't think any good has ever been achieved from balance, only from violent prejudice and conviction.

*What do you make, then, of the BBC's contortions to keep balance?*

They are just a joke, aren't they? Because there is no balance really. You can only try and apply a corrective. If you have one particular sort of maniac on, you can have a different sort of maniac on. But there is no real balance, and can't be.

*Do you think there are many kinds of maniacs on at the moment?*

You mean among the regular performers?

*Or editors.*

Well, I think they're a fairly prejudiced bunch but that's quite inevitable. And, of course, they're nearly all prejudiced in the same way, which happens to be a way that I don't agree with. I mean, they are nearly all what we call liberal humanists, a position with which I feel a notable lack of sympathy.

Nearly all of them are like that. You can practically always assume that they will think A is a good man and B is a bad man, that this is the right course and this is the wrong course, and this is enlightenment and that is obscurantism. So that if I'm right, that liberalism represents the final death wish of an expiring civilization, this is its ultimate expression in a very powerful position. I mean, these people are all my friends, but their view of life is this liberal humanist view.

*A mass medium like television in the hands of liberal humanists surely would be better than, say, television in the hands of Fascists.*

If that were the choice, yes. I would like it to be in charge of, for instance, Christians. I would find that very agreeable. There aren't any Christians now, but that would appeal to me. I don't think that the alternative to liberal humanism is Fascism.

*No, but as the going is at the moment, liberal humanists are probably not a bad bet.*

Well, they have very irritating ways as far as I'm concerned: for instance, their infinite capacity to fake everything without realizing they're faking it, of suggesting that all is going well when I think it's going very ill. That abortions are good and that sort of thing, which I am very doubtful about. But, anyway, the truth is television is in the hands of those people.

*ITV isn't to the same extent?*

Well, they have the great merits of being more interested in making money than in promoting ideas, and in some ways I think this is a much less dangerous trait.

*Truly, do you think that?*

In some ways I do. Because if people just want to make money it's a very despicable pursuit, but I doubt if it's as socially harmful as promoting what I can see to be wrong ideas. Making money may not be the noblest of careers but it's a perfectly understandable one. When you get into the realm of people wanting to promote a certain way of looking at life, the dangers are terrific.

# Anthony Smith

Editor, *24 Hours.*

Television isn't a neutral instrument in any society in which it operates, even in a system like our own where the whole structure of broadcasting has been founded historically on the idea that it is possible to have a completely neutral institution to do the job. This is normally thought to require a group of neutral human beings to staff it. I think one's plain observation of the facts is that that is not true.

I feel slightly frightened even in saying that. It's telling the emperor he has no clothes. It's a logical and human impossibility that the structure could obtain ideological neutrality but one fears that the existence of everything we have achieved in broadcasting in this country depends upon it. In every country I've ever been in the television community made its centre of gravity left of centre – in America, France, Germany, certainly. You can go to places like Poland and Yugoslavia and you get a very strong sense that there is a kind of awkward television community with common – liberal – attitudes. Television and the press form a large interest group everywhere and inevitably develops a point of view about itself and that point of view has a sort of spill-over on to other things; if you are in the business of communication – public self-expression – you have obviously got to be in favour of it; and if you are in favour of self-expression you are in favour of a whole lot of other similar things. You tend to find that television does accumulate around it left-of-centre people. In the Soviet Union you might say it attracts right-of-centre people. But it certainly attracts the group of people who are concerned about examining the society critically. It may not be right to use the world 'left' or 'right' – but certainly in this country it would be correct to observe that the people who are responsible for television on both sides of the screen, and both halves of the industry are mainly left of centre and the whole direction of television is left of centre. And therefore one has to admit that the television community is un-representative of the public as a whole. You could not people the television medium with a pure cross-section of the population and at the same time get good critical plays, good critical current affairs on the screen.

166

*Anthony Smith*

*How do you see the role of television?*

Well, it is now emerging as a separate estate. And I think its function is to stand over against the political estate, or rather authority in general – and stay there. Its function is to survey permanently everything that is going on in the society and find out that which has not yet been articulated, then to give expression to those interest groups, and those vexations which have not yet been given expression. Television becomes almost a source of authority itself, at any rate becomes a complement of authority – it derives its title deeds – its right to this function – directly from the society and not from the politicians and this is really what the whole controversy currently raging is about, that is the nub of it. We are the primary practitioners of the medium of television – the broadcasters and producers; we have to do – and prove that we are doing – what the society which owns us needs us to do. We have a responsibility directly to our society (to be truthful about it, to the best of our ability) and the politician also has a responsibility directly to the society, however politicians and television practitioners do not have a responsibility to help each other.

*Do you think that ratings competition with ITV is healthy?*

There is competition for ratings that's healthy and there's competition for ratings that's unhealthy. It isn't the pursuit of high audiences itself that's unhealthy. We are a mass medium; the natural state of television – its natural condition – is to try to maximize its audience. I am trying to maximize the audience for *24 Hours*. That is to say I want as many people as possible to watch what we do. But I am not trying to do that which will make the largest number of people watch. Certainly I am in pursuit of ratings. I look at the weekly figures avidly, obsessively, trying to put on half a million here and a million there – put things in the programme and advertise them well on the days when I know that we could get eight to nine million watching. But I wouldn't put on anything that isn't *24 Hours* in order to do that. And I've no idea whether the channel wants me to or not. I've never received any instructions on the matter. Except that one knows that the whole channel is concerned to maximize its audience. I think the ratings can be pursued in positive and nega-

167

tive ways. If ITV knocked us out of the habit of pretending that the number of viewers didn't matter, then that was a good thing.

*What do you see as the negative way of getting viewers?*

The attitude to sport is one of the big things here. Not merely because I find sport boring but because I think we're in danger of creating a new kind of pornography in unlimited coverage of sporting events, and space shots too for that matter. A thing that is put there simply because you know people will watch. You know there's something almost in the physiology of people's viewing habits that can be exploited to raise ratings. Isn't that analogous to pornography? We can't always know the motive of the purveyor – whether the stuff has been put into the schedules because it's the best possible programme available at that time. There's a very important division to be made between that which will capture vast numbers and stimulate vast numbers. It's possible to be bored and watch. The point of American television is that the programmes are more boring than the commercials. You put on programmes that may be boring but certainly will make people watch. The commercials have to be stimulating otherwise they wouldn't work. They attract a disproportionate amount of the available creative energy. I am saying that we should always be concerned to deal professionally with what it is we actually want to put on the screens and then worry about the audience later. The danger is only when the programmes are ordered by the gross, because it's easier to turn television into a series of slots, filled with predictable material – tried and trusted formulas.

# Brian Connell

Formerly reporter and presenter, *This Week*. Programme adviser, Anglia.

I'm considered to take up a very extreme position which makes me extremely unpopular in television, and this is one of the reasons I do so much less than I used to, although I am still very active as adviser to one of the television companies.

You have got a fundamental difference between the world of Fleet Street, which is basically my world, and the world of television. The printing department on a Fleet Street newspaper is a completely neutral production process. The printers and the chaps who set up the form get little pieces of paper on which it says, 'Set up these words in such and such a size of type and put them in a particular place in the page and put them over that headline.' Now if the printers started saying, 'We think this should not go there,' it would be total chaos. You cannot run a newspaper that way. The information in a newspaper is at least entirely under the control of the editorial staff. It is their judgement, good or bad, which determines what appears in a newspaper.

Now in television there is a fundamental difference to which I think few people have drawn attention in these terms: your cameraman, your film editor, your producer, your director, all the people connected with the production process, are in control. But they have not been trained as journalists. The way you point the camera and the way you cut those images together do not necessarily have anything to do with and can indeed run directly counter to what is being said in commentary. There is a tremendous gulf between the two. Now I think it is probably true to say that the vast proportion of producers and directors are of a fairly left-wing persuasion. As far as I am concerned they can have any political views they like. But one is taught in Fleet Street that whatever your political views are, the facts are separate or as far as possible. If you deviate from the facts you have to explain why. But these are all people of limited general knowledge of very strong left-wing persuasions who, when they take the position of controlling the contents of a programme because they have mastered the techniques, do seek out as their collaborators those people who are convenient to them. Which is why you get, to my mind, this gross preponderance of left-wing people who are operating in television.

*Why is a television director or producer's view of the world and news and events and current affairs inferior to that of a journalist?*

I'm not saying it's inferior, I'm saying it monopolizes the box to the extent that it does. I'm politically as inactive as you could be, but I have been in the business of journalism for thirteen years and I am and have been and will continue to be frankly shocked by the one-sided nature of the presentation of information in television. It is perfectly true that unpleasant things have gone on, on the American side in Vietnam. Who is to deny it? But I do not think there has been a single television documentary which has set out to give an account of the atrocities on the other side. And when you think of the evidence of 3,000 or 4,000 corpses in mass graves, where people were simply slaughtered and massacred by the Vietcong, it is not the lack of evidence.

Another alarming element in all this is what I would call the introduction of an artificial parity as a substitute for balance.

A practice has grown up, and in many ways the BBC is more guilty than the ITV companies, if only because they have more current affairs discussions on their two channels, of giving protesters and Marxists the same status and airtime with elected MPs and people of similar public standing. This outrages the balance of political opinion in this country. I remember, within one week, seeing Robin Blackburn, Wilfred Burchett and some other extreme left-winger spouting at great length on *24 Hours*. There was another programme on Granada called *Seven Days* which was a conventionally mounted studio discussion with a permanent panel of four, the 'expert' was a Marxist. They declared their interest absolutely straight away in the first sentence. I've no objection to each of them standing where they do, but what principles does one apply to this? At a general election you get about thirty million voters, take or leave the odd million, in this country. On the latest count, the Communist Party, which is the only form of Marxist expression we've got, I think got 50,000 votes, so that is roughly one in every 600 people. Now if you get three Marxists in a row in a weekly programme or three a week in a daily programme, then you are providing them with a national platform far more frequently than their representation in the country warrants – false parity instead of balance. If you carried this mathematical calculation through to its logical conclusion their entitlement on a weekly programme would be to appear about once every ten years.

*To what extent do you think TV should just accurately mirror society and to what extent do you think it should be in those areas where the discussions are?*

On 11 January 1969 there was a great piece in *The Times* signed by Dennis Foreman, managing director of Granada. Here is an extract: 'So what can television do? It can and must support the democratic machinery so long as this forms the constitutional basis of the country. But at the same time it must give full voice to those critics who wish to change it.' Now I would have thought that was so far contrary to the intentions of the Television Act as to be more like an invitation to sedition than fair comment.

*You don't think the critics should be allowed?*

I would not say they should not be allowed, but to offer television as the platform on which those who wish to overturn society should have their say, seems to me to be going a very long way indeed and a very dangerous way indeed.

\*

*Apart from the structural biases of the institutions and the inevitable human biases of the practitioners, does the medium itself warp the truth it is trying to present?*

# Malcolm Muggeridge

The trouble about it is that it carries a sort of authority because of the camera. The villain of the piece is the camera, the enemy is the camera. We who are accustomed to working with it know that it's capable of infinite deception, probably the greatest of all deception, and yet is accepted as having some sort of objective truth in it. And since the camera dominates the thing more and more, so the possibility of deception grows greater and greater.

*I thought that deception was only in the editing.*

Well, the editing plus the camera. Take, for instance, the Vietnam War; I've known numerous men who've been out there, Americans mostly. Because they go there, they want to get a story. Well, how do you get a story? How are you sure you are going to get on the screen? Everyone's sick of the Vietnam War. So you've got to find something dramatic. You look for something dramatic, which is the first falsification, and then, of course, you may just a little bit set up something dramatic. The result is received by the viewer as the truth. It's not a dispatch, say, from Mary McCarthy or Walter Lippman or someone like that that you've read, but it's the truth that you see.

*But you're bringing into question the whole nature of the communication between one person and another, because every statement that is made excludes all the alternative statements that could be made in its place.*

My point is that the reader makes the adjustment but the viewer doesn't. That's the difference.

*How could we educate the viewer to do that?*

It's impossible. This medium is bound to deceive. Even if you put the truth into it, it comes out as deception.

*And yet the people dedicated to it are enormously honourable people, concerned that they will show the truth.*

Very much so. I had a long talk with Paul Fox last week on it. How do we stop people being deceived by this? How can we really tell them the truth? The answer is, you can't. I mean, he knows quite well that in all the big events of the last ten years – student revolt, Vietnam, and so on – television has been an enormous distorting factor, making some things more important than they are and other things less important.

*Do you think its role in our society is going to get out of hand?*

It's got out of hand, I think. But the salvation is that the parts of it you and I are interested in will diminish, as they have in America. They've virtually disappeared. And it becomes in the end a home cinema with Newzak, which is what it will become everywhere.

*Do you think that's a good thing?*

I don't say it's a good thing, but it's better than dominating, as it does, people's way of looking at life.

# Philip Whitehead

I think the most serious compromise always is the tyranny of the slot and the time scale. I am talking now simply as somebody who produces a twenty-seven-minute political programme every week. It is impossible for me, in the present set-up of ITV and the network, to go to people and say, 'I cannot deploy this argument and these facts and these pictures in twenty-seven minutes, I could do it in thirty-nine.' And they say, 'No dice, old boy. You go away and make two programmes out of it if you want to.' But I then say to them, 'I can't do that, because it's a dense mass of facts, information and reasoning. It has to flow altogether. You can't expect particularly our sort of audience to assimilate half of it one week and then take up that theme again eight days later.' And that gets nowhere at all. So I think the worst compromise sometimes is clipping your material down below the point of maximum comprehensibility.

*The average audiences are simply not aware to what extent things inevitably have to be rigged and so on. Does that worry you?*

Yes it does. Television is the only profession in which the word 'cheat' is an inseparable part of the vocabulary. I think it's alarming that so often, in order to preserve a smooth visual flow and in order to re-create an assumed sequence of events or to prepare a visual montage which approximates to an idea, you do dishonest things. I think one should always guard against that, and the only areas in which I allow myself re-creation are those areas where people are physically endangered by showing the real thing. If I were to be doing a programme about the resistance in Greece, and I wanted to show that a rendezvous took place, after which, somewhere in Athens, we met leaders of the resistance, I wouldn't film it and show it as it happened. I would film it totally dishonestly somewhere else. The real question then is should you say, in those circumstances, that that is what you have done. Well, I don't think you should, because I think there one is, in fact, putting oneself in the position of saying, 'This is how it really happened.'

The camera is never a neutral factor and when the medium is big enough it will more conscientiously acknowledge this fact. There is a very good small essay on this point by David Holden in *One Pair of Eyes*. It is true that, if a camera is in an Egyptian village, the thing that is really going on there is that an enormous crowd of people are gawping at a Western cameraman. The thing that is not going on is that an old peasant on a donkey, uninterrupted, is crossing an otherwise empty landscape from left to right. That's only happening, because you are making it happen.

In all sorts of areas, the presence of television, I think, significantly alters the events. I was very shaken six or seven years ago when I went to one of the first of the Trafalgar Square punch-ups, where Colin Jordan and his mob were holding a meeting, and the massive saturation coverage of that by television turned it into a riot with people actually staging their own battles in front of the television screen.

When I started in television it was axiomatic that you should never ever pretend there was television there. Everything should be like a cinema film. Microphones must never be seen, cameras must never be seen, the reporter was to stride through situations as though he were the star in the movie, and he must be seen in the totally realistic trapping where everything happened as it would have been happening had there been no television. Increasingly, we are coming to see, in studio programmes as well as on film, that this doesn't work. One of the breakthroughs the BBC made was with their late-night programmes, where, for the first time, they showed not merely an audience and performers, but they also showed them in relation to cameras, the technicians, the whole paraphernalia, the very artificial paraphernalia, of the so-called live studio programme.

*You have worked for both the BBC and ITV. Do you think it is possible to produce good public service TV within the present ITV structure?*

I think there is a great deal implicit in the Television Act which was simply not taken seriously by Sir Robert Fraser in the post-1964 situation. Pilkington criticized ITV on three grounds. One was the excess profitability. Bevins thought that a flat levy would solve that one. Second, there was the level of quality and, thirdly, there was the absence of competition. Bevins thought he had a solution by making the ITA responsible for networking and putting the ITA in control and writing into the Television Act specific provisions that the ITA will ensure a wide showing for programmes of merit. This is very explicit and so are the provisions in the Act for the powers of the Director-General, but time after time the ITA says, 'We can only interpret the absolute matter of the Act and where we are in some doubt about the spirit of the Act, we do nothing.' In 1954, 1955 and 1956 Lord Fraser did a great job in holding up the original contractors when their morale was very low and persuading them to work with each other, building up a system of networking by mutual agreement. And to ask the man who had built up that system voluntarily to destroy it was really ridiculous, but there we are and that's why the system hasn't changed. I would like to see the spirit of the 1964 Act interpreted in quite a different fashion by the new Director-General. I would like to see him either exercise or, if he feels that he will be baulked in so attempting, to seek from Parliament, the powers to exercise the right of the controlling figure and to arbitrate in that sense as master to the contracting companies.

*Do you see any danger in fact in putting a lot of power in one man's hands? Surely questions of subjective taste are involved.*

I think there is always a lot of danger in putting power in one man's hands, but then I think most of the major changes in broadcasting came about because individual people of high quality have been able to assert themselves at the right moment or, conversely, because individual people of low quality have been allowed to get away with changes which have harmed television.

The fact is that any Director-General of the ITA taking power now is appointed as a countervailing force to the tremendous commercial impetus of the whole system. In such a system in every ITV company the overwhelming pressure is to try and minimize costs, maximize profits obviously, and what they are really looking at is what the shareholders say at the end of the year, how well the advertising has done compared with six months ago. Given that I think that what the Director-General must have is a degree of expertise in programming costs and a strength of personality and a sheer drive towards merit in all things which is, at the moment, wholly lacking in either the higher councils of the companies or the ITA.

*Do you think that competition with ITV has affected BBC for the worse?*

I think people like Peacock and Fox on BBC 1 have vulgarized television quite deliberately, because they have accepted those values implicit in ITV which most people who work, I think, in ITV deplore and are constantly struggling against, as the norm for the majority BBC channel, and they have used BBC 2 as a convenient fig-leaf. I think it's happened almost deliberately. When Michael Peacock was Head of BBC 1 the only kind of pep talk he used to give was to come along and talk on the subject of the 'inheritance factor' and how you had to plant your maximum-audience-pulling programmes strategically through the evening and how maximizing the audience was the only thing that really counted and this is what we were all told we had to do. We were 'not in a minority business', this was 'a hard fact of life' – lots of clichés about omelettes and eggs. You see that is lethal, wicked, I think, and that's why people go in headlong retreat from the best of the public-service concept.

# David Webster

*Do you think there is too much current affairs on TV?*

Yes.

*How has that arisen?*

It's arisen on the basis that television is a devouring thing. There are a number of reasons why we've got too much. I certainly think that we're spread over too wide an area. We just do too much and there is a limit to the amount of this stuff that people can assimilate. There's a limit to the amount we can do well. One of the basic reasons why this is so is because of the historical division between News and Current Affairs. Now, I don't think that Current

Affairs can solve problems in isolation from News and I don't think News can solve their problem in isolation from Current Affairs. Certainly, in any rational world, if one sits down and looks at the nature of the problem it is obviously necessarily both in administrative management and editorial management that the thing is eventually put together.

I'm very worried about over-communication, and I'm worried about it because I think people have two reactions to being continually prodded by crisis: one is withdrawal and the other is hysteria, and neither is a satisfactory response. This is why I'm in the business I am in instead of the news business. A long time ago I came to the conclusion that regurgitation of fact was not a satisfactory method of explaining what was going on in the world. Now you can wake up every morning, somebody screams at you, 'They're shelling Quemoy and Matsu!' Now you're not quite sure who Quemoy and Matsu are, but they're shelling them. I think eventually this kind of crisis reporting means that people either don't take any notice at all or they get very neurotic. Now that's the television of exploitation, where you exploit subjects in order to make good television. There is also the television of contribution where you try to tell people what the basic position is in the Far East so that when somebody shouts, 'They're shelling Quemoy and Matsu', they have some body and context into which to place this information. I think this is terribly important and I think it's going to get more important for the simple reason that whether we like it or not we're going to have what people cheerfully call the great communications explosion, and this is not a thing which is just broadcasting alone.

One of the basic things which worries me about the development of technology is that its main characteristics, certainly in the industrial urban West, is multiplicity of options. You have a number of choices. Now, in a situation where you have a great deal of choice, you will develop very sophisticated techniques in making that choice. For instance, if your newspaper comes to you as a development of Xerox technology and is transmitted over a cable to your house, you probably do not intend to print the entire newspaper in your living room at breakfast. What you do is select those bits that you are interested in, which means you have to know you're interested in them before you select them. Now, we've all got selection systems and one of the most common is our eyes. We scan books, we scan newspapers. Many a morning you can see a stockbroker going through the newspaper looking for the stock exchange prices, and his eyes are scanning pages as he turns them. Maybe he sees a picture of a pretty girl with very few clothes on, so his eyes stops there and he ends up reading the fashion page. Lo and behold, he has created one of those peripheral interests which is the only thing which holds society together. If his eye is never hit by the lady with a few clothes on and he reads only stock exchange prices he probably loses his capacity to discuss anything with his wife, unless she happens to be a stockbroker too. So one is in great danger, because of the reaction to the multiplicity of options, of creating narrow gauge societies. It's a totally unproven hypothesis but it's something which I think somebody ought to worry about.

# DOCUMENTARIES

Of course, all factual film-making longer than a news item is documentary, a *Panorama* report as much as *Morning on the Streets*. But it is a term that has come to apply in particular to films that contain a larger element of imaginative response than the straight journalistic report. Like all other television film-making, the television documentary developed from a tradition that already existed in the cinema, a tradition associated with the names of Grierson, Rotha, Flaherty, a tradition whose aim, in Grierson's words, was 'the creative treatment of actuality'. This is now a type of film-making that television has made very much its own. Indeed its distinctive development has been one of the great creative contributions of the television industry, until its forms have begun to influence feature film-making itself, in movies like *Poor Cow*, *Midnight Cowboy* and the work of Godard.

The importance and richness of the documentary form is that it has exploited to creative advantage the very disadvantages that the form has as straight journalism. The documentary accepts the film as an artefact rather than a faithful record of so-called 'objective reality'. It accepts the inevitable biases of personal response and glories in them. Many of the best documentary film-makers started with current affairs programmes. Dennis Mitchell with *Special Enquiry*, Jack Gold and Michael Tuchner with *Tonight*, Richard Cawston with the original television *Newsreel*. But with their experience as a base they exploited the conventions of the medium to push deeper into more personal territory.

Although many fine documentary-makers have worked with reporters (Jack Gold, Michael Tuchner, Kevin Billington all worked with Whicker and Muggeridge), in the true documentary the director is king, and anything that undermines his status damages the form. The strength of the documentary is based upon personal response. It is the most responsible of factual forms in the truest meaning of that word. There is a widespread illusion that the more anonymous a film is, the more responsible it is. The opposite is true. But present trends in television particularly threaten documentaries: the needs of scheduling demand predictable and easily digestible product. In the McKinsey world of computer planning and budgeting all films are equal and the director becomes merely a cosmetician who applies a little gloss to make the raw facts of life more acceptable. Increasingly the director is either a despised hack, and if he allows himself to become a mere cosmetician he is rightly despised, or more dangerously he is admired not for his ideas but for the skill with which he can disguise any ideas that might erupt. A BBC executive responsible for documentary programmes stated without a trace of irony, 'We are looking for someone to direct the film who has no ideas.' In such a world the documentary series is king and the helicopter can be seen not as an occasionally useful film-making tool, but as a major contributor to the creation of documentary wallpaper.

In the present climate therefore the documentary film-maker is threatened – his role is not clear. He is not a journalist giving people the facts. Nor is he a playwright creating a clearly fictional experience. In this uncertainty he is drawn towards the disputed territory of the drama-documentary. He is also drawn there because he accepts the artificiality of the realistic film-making conventions. To present something as it happens it is necessary when filming to rig and recreate. But how far should he go? Moreover, how does he balance his desire to show the audience things as he sees them with his need to protect his subjects from exploitation? There is the ever present fear that he may be using people to pander to the voyeur in us all.

If television has a valid social role at all, it would seem to be in showing people to one another. It is in documentaries and plays that television fulfils that role. The documentary and the play are the forms that can bridge the gap between the informational and entertainment functions. It is, I think, no accident that two of British television's most memorable programmes have been *Culloden* and *Cathy Come Home*. These two programmes shook hands across television no-man's land, but it is in no-man's land that advances take place. The promise of documentaries is equal to their vulnerability, threatened on one side by journalism, on the other by escapist drama. The documentary director is vulnerable because, although he is king, he must use his skill to be an invisible being. He must have both the technique and the personal resources of integrity and sensitivity to become transparent, so that in the form of his work people can face one another.

# Richard Cawston

Head of Documentaries, BBC TV. 1950–54, Producer of *Newsreel* (700 edns). Since 1954, documentaries include *Television and the World*, *Royal Family*, *The Schools*, *Born Chinese*, *I'm Going To Ask You To Get Up Out of Your Seat*.

*How long did the cinema go on influencing television films before television really broke free?*

It's wrong to say we were a carbon copy of the cinema; we were a copy but better. It's rather like the Japanese making cameras better than the Germans. They start by copying them and then they simply use the same techniques and go on doing it better. We were undoubtedly influenced by what was going on in the cinema at that time. The documentary world was a mass of what I call documentary sewage running through the cinemas. It was the travel short, that type of thing; it was junk largely and it filled up the gaps between the two feature films.

Now television was in quite a different position because the documentary had to compete for its audience against pure fictional entertainment on the other channel. This did documentaries a lot of good. We had to learn to make our documentaries entertaining in a way the cinema would have never done on its own.

I think the first long film I made was in 1958. It was called *On Call to a Nation* which went seventy-five minutes, and in those days it was a great battle with the Controller to get such a long programme accepted into the schedule. There had been only one or two documentaries of that sort of length before and they had not been particularly successful. I was convinced that there was room for a thing which would run as long as a play. And I think if I have made any sort of contribution at all it would be in establishing the fact that documentaries can run that sort of length, by introducing a sort of story element into them. *On Call to a Nation* was a study of the health service. We did it entirely with doctors making the comments, and it was based on a waiting-room with eight patients sitting in it. As each patient went in to see the doctor, so that patient gave rise to the examination of a different aspect – one went in to have his eyes tested and we did a sequence on the eye services; another went in trying to get into hospital and we did a sequence on the hospital service and waiting lists; one went in wanting a prescription for something so we went into the pharmaceutical services – that sort of structure. That was a very successful film. People wrote in afterwards saying they just did not know how the Health Service worked before that film went out. You could not put such a film on now because they do know.

You see, those of us who were doing documentaries then – there were only a few of us – were playing to an audience who were still largely uninformed. I could make that programme seventy-five minutes long and there might be two or three more in a year by other producers and that would be all. There would only be about four long documentaries a year and they were treated as events, they were given special billing, and the schedules for that evening were different, and so on. They did not form part of any pattern. There was no prescribed length in those days. You used to make your films and say what length it was and then it would be specially placed. It was quite a shock when Stuart Hood became Controller with Donald Baverstock assisting and said there was going to be a long documentary every Tuesday, because I did not think this would be possible.

I think that on the whole it's been a pity that the fifty-minute documentary was established as something that could be shown as often as once a week, because what has happened now is that a great deal of the subject matter has been done – not always terribly well – but it's been done. It's spoilt the market for doing it better.

# Tony Essex

Founder member of the *Tonight* team, in charge of film. Producer, *The Great War* and *The Lost Peace*. Head of Documentaries, Yorkshire TV.

What you see on television is *Tonight*. I had to start a new style of film editing for *Tonight*, a style of film editing which in effect cut out all the linking shots. Most television documentaries in those days used to have an interview, and always had to have an establishing shot – the interviewer arriving at the next interview, and always close it up gently. We wouldn't have had time, we started a style of film editing which nowadays is an accepted thing. What I am trying to do here is to think all right that was OK for *Tonight*, what is right for current documentary?

Most film editing now has been sharpened up to an extent that pictures no longer exist. It's an awful thing, but if you look at the news or if you look at all documentaries now, we are not using shots, we are using scenes. For example – a scene of a ship sinking. People stand all day round a cliff watching a ship sinking, you know, because there is something monumental, something dramatic that you have to watch for hours and hours. But nobody holds the shot now for hours and hours, anything up to six feet that's it. Because they are showing you a scene, they are not showing you an event. On *Tonight* we used to try this: we held a shot for ten minutes, and the reason why we did not hold it for twenty minutes was the magazine ran out, and we couldn't find a way of joining the second reel on to the first reel without the cut showing and the cut broke the spell. Nobody is working in this field on television now. They are doing an automatic six second and then you have to cut. It's terrible.

*You say you are looking for a new editing style. But why if the old one is good?*

Well, that is what they said when they rode horses.

# Dennis Mitchell

Probably the most influential maker of TV documentaries. In BBC films, such as *Morning in the Streets* and *Chicago*, he developed the technique of using non-synchronous voices that has come to be known as 'think-tapes'. He has pioneered the use of electronic cameras for documentaries in films like *The Entertainers*, made for Granada.

When I actually joined the BBC I was familiar with disc recording but also with some sort of rather primitive tape. I found the BBC were not using tape, and they did not use tape for two or three years. They were very slow about it. But I had already, by chance, got experience of making radio programmes out of ordinary people's speech. I used to do quite a bit of this in South Africa. People here had not then thought of that sort of thing, everything was written and done by actors. Not my style. So I had a slight head-start, and encountered all the sort of problems of cutting sentences here and there and that sort of thing. After a few years of that, and particularly a series called *People Talking*, I went on a television course.

*You asked to go on it, did you?*

No, they just said, 'Mitchell, what about it?' And I went. At the end of it, I was attached to Norman Swallow, who was an experienced film-maker, and he said would I like to have a go at making films. I said, 'Yes, I would,' and I told him how I was going to make it, and he said, 'You can't make films like that.'

*Information*

*How did you want to do it?*

Basically by making a radio programme first, and then building a film round part of that radio programme. But having said, 'No, you can't do it like that,' he then proceeded to show me how to do it and he was marvellous.

*Did you find the technique of film-making difficult when you first started?*

No, it never occurred to me that it was in any way difficult, it was just a natural extension from radio.

*Things like large cameras and so on, did you feel these as limitations?*

Yes I did, very much so. I'd always had the pleasure of wandering about myself with the tape recorder, and of course all that was gone. Difficult.

*So from the start you were looking for more mobile equipment?*

Certainly.

*How did you see the function of the documentary, or did you not think of it as documentary?*

Well, you must remember that when I was fortunate enough to get a job in the BBC radio I'd never heard of a feature, but pretended I had. What I was trying to do was to squeeze the sort of smell out of people, situations and that sort of thing. I always hated the word 'documentary' and I always disliked the notion that the documentary was anything to do with fact, like how do you make a sausage.

*What was it to do with?*

Going some place, maybe a back street or maybe another country, and sort of saying, well, this is the essence of it, this is what it smells like.

*Was this process a long one, did it take you a long time to make your films?*

A difficult one to answer really, because the actual film did not take a long time but often the collecting of the material took a

184

long time. In those days, I could wander about as I pleased and only when I pleased. If I felt like it, I'd stay up all night and wander round bomb sites and things like that. I did not start by saying I was going to make a film about drug traffic or whatever it was. I simply went out into that particular area, because I liked the look of it, or because I knew a man there, or there was a good pub or anything like that. Then I would let people talk. If people know you are coming, they think, 'Oh, this is the man from the BBC and he will want to know about such and such.' They have preconceptions about you.

I never went with a preconception of what I was going to do. I let that street talk. Very odd that you always finish up by talking really about the same thing, whatever was bugging them or making them happy. So you would find you would take twenty hours or so and boil it down, throw away most of it. You would finish up with twenty minutes perhaps of the good things.

*Do you look back on your own films with any sort of particular pleasures?*

I never look back. Never. There I think you're getting more to the nub of the thing. I do not know anything about film or the history of film. I distrust the word 'art' because it seems to be part of what I would think was a dead or dying literary culture. It's said that a thing is only valuable if it's written or painted on stout canvas. Georgie Best doing something absolutely marvellous for about five seconds on a Saturday afternoon, isn't art. A painting of Georgie Best, kissing a girl, is or might be.

I've been thinking about this whole question of television. I'm just a practitioner, but I've been wondering why television programmes are not better. When one thinks about these things, I get into a morass, because good, bad or indifferent, television, mass communications are very near the heart of things. So if you put your finger on it you've got your finger on the nerve, on something which is actually hurting. My first explanation would be that the quality of life was declining quickly and sharply, people are shedding the values and beliefs that have kept them going for many many centuries. It seems that a uniquely new world is in the process of being born. The words to explain the new values have not been coined yet. Words themselves may be discarded. So

185

here you have an enormous explosion with communications and nothing to communicate. At the centre of the sound and fury is absolute silence.

It was interesting to me thinking about the BBC and its destruction. Something was obviously lost, something perfectly decent, and one television channel was gained. But the important thing that has happened is that journalists were promoted to key positions. This is an indication to me that television is, like radio, based on the wrong assumptions. I'm pretty certain that television, whatever else it is, is not a newspaper. It seems to me, for the moment anyway, television is more like moving wallpaper than a newspaper. It's part of life in exactly the same way as a man driving home through the crowded streets receives millions of bloody images, colours and people and so on. It's not a whole experience but it's very much an important part of his life. I think that television for most people is like that. In other words, it's a dream machine, it's a stimulator of fantasies. It's not a conveyor of facts, it's not an encyclopedia.

*I think that's true on the whole. Do you think it could be something better?*

What could be better than a stimulator of fantasies? It's dreams that shape the world.

# Tony Essex

*Do you feel documentaries should have a point of view?*

A good documentary needs a cause, always has. All the best documentaries which came out in the 1930s were about housing and unemployment and that sort of stuff; during the war – what a subject – all these great pictures, but propaganda pictures. After that, the great social conscience started churning. You know, everyone started thinking of cripples, unmarried mothers, divorcees. All these are stale old things which we have looked at monthly. You know, 'Look, what a marvellous old dying cancerous woman we have got for you this week; better still, folks, she has got a cataract.'

*Are there any good causes left?*

Christ, yes. There is one which we are working on here. I think the majority have got a far bigger problem than the minority has and it is to do with that lovely old cliché which I used to tell Cawston for years – he thought I was drunk – called quality of life. For Christ's sake, you know, people are happier at work than at home. They don't want to go home. What do they do? Beans and chip supper, or something, and they look at themselves and wish they were someone else. They don't know what to do with themselves, they have got no vision, they have got no hope, they have nothing.

*Well, what can television do to them?*

Well, life is not all that black if you get up and go. We do here documentaries about people who have got up and done something, people who are different, people who are enviable, yet not so far away that you could not be the same, with no problems at all. For instance, we made a documentary here, *Captain RN*. That man has just been appointed a Rear-Admiral. We made the film because he was admirable and enviable.

# Stephen Peet

Has directed three films of Malcolm Muggeridge talking to Lord Reith. Executive producer/director, *Yesterday's Witness*.

The specific response that my film programmes have got has nearly all been on the same theme of, 'How glad we were to hear something direct without anybody or anything getting in the way.' I'm thinking of one specific film, *Sitting Target*, which was about living in a wheelchair. He was a very brisk, somewhat bad-tempered chap. Many of the letters and conversations about that film said, 'Here was a man with a problem, he had overcome his problem, he was a teacher in a technical college, who told us directly exactly what it was like to be a man like him and nobody and nothing got in the way.' And this wasn't a simple film to make. It had an almost continuous track of his conversations while he pottered around the kitchen, as he went about his business in an invalid car and came into contact with students. I felt very much that I was the go-between or the method by which, whatever it was, five or six million people met that chap directly. This is a film made with considerable care, with a long time in the editing, to achieve that effect. That's what I like, being the invisible go-between.

*How does it feel as a documentary-maker, working in a large organization like the BBC?*

Never before in history, except possibly in newspaper offices or magazines, has there been a sort of huge creative factory or factories of hundreds of creative people and hundreds of administrators, who talk two completely opposite languages, trying to learn how to live together. It has never existed before, as far as I know. We are still learning. I know an awful lot of the griping and the fighting, trying to do things *despite* the system, is this clash of trying to talk different languages.

*Do you think this is beginning to produce more and more impersonal documentaries?*

Well, it may well produce, not so much impersonal, but poor ones. I've fallen into the trap myself in organizing the next few months – so many people, so many more films to make, because so many are promised; they've worked out times and now they're discussing subject matter. I can see in this small group the same danger that the huge group is in. The whole purpose of television is providing a service, and what one finds oneself doing is producing a product for the approval of heads of departments or high officials, or for the approval of press critics. One forgets the whole purpose of it – namely the television audience.

*Do you find that because documentaries must compete for attention there is pressure towards a flashier style?*

I'm fighting against it. In fact, I personally feel, in style, the necessity of becoming simpler and, for the same reason, grabbing the audience by being different from the programmes before and after it. You chance things, because you've got no say in what part of the evening or where your programme is going to go. Someone turns the tap on and the evening's programmes run continuously. But I think, or maybe I hope (because this is the way I'm working now), that a large number of the public want to have things milder and simpler and less passionate, and one can, in fact, say what one wants to say, more or less, by doing it in a simple straightforward way. Like a down to earth simple feature article in the middle page of the *Mirror* that really hits home. It's that kind of way that I like to think of these programmes being, amongst all the other fancy stuff around them.

*Do you ever feel that you are exploiting your subject to satisfy the voyeurism of the viewer?*

There is a danger with the film-maker who does this without scruples and makes things difficult for others. The danger there is that someone will come along later to the same place or the same town with, one hopes, a bit more scruple and they are told, 'No, I'm not going to. Look what happened to so and so down the road who was made a fool of or made use of.' So we are cutting our own throats by being too sensational. We have met this several times, particularly when filming in a town after the hit-and-run kind of people in *24 Hours* or *Man Alive*, whose method of working is, from time to time, fairly unscrupulous, to put it mildly. People are becoming more and more careful about appearing on television and yet I find it also very worrying that the magic words 'Television' or 'BBC' have never been queried when one asks to go into somebody's house. I just say, 'I'm from the BBC', 'I'm from the television.' Never any query, never asked to show our identity or anything. It is very worrying. And the things that people are willing to do, act, say, in front of the camera. I've cut out things deliberately rather than use them, because the person isn't aware of what damage or ridicule they are putting themselves to by appearing on the screen doing that, or saying that. . . .

*Why do you think people do that?*

*Information*

I don't know. There's a great glamour and all this old business of a public confessional. It's a mystery to me, I don't know why they do it.

*What do you feel your responsibility is to the people who appear in documentaries?*

Very considerable. It's a question of attitude of mind and I think it shows on people's films whether you *respect* people or *use* them, if that's the right comparison. Films in which people are obviously used as objects to prove a point of the film-maker is, I think, a disrespectful way of using people, but films in which the people appearing in them are given, by the film-makers, the best possible platform for showing themselves in their most truthful light is using them respectfully.

# Peter Bartlett

Cameraman on countless BBC documentaries, including *The War Game* and *Royal Family*.

As a cameraman, you've got to be very much of a film-maker if you're doing an actuality-type documentary. Say you go into a room where a party is happening. Now, there are two ways of doing that sort of sequence. You can either direct it and use the people at the party as actors, and usually pretty bad amateur actors, or say, 'Fine, just get on with your party. We know we're going to destroy the atmosphere totally because we're going to hang these lights up and there are going to be a couple of chaps wandering around with a camera, a tape machine and a microphone. But just enjoy your party.' Then it is very much a matter of interpreting the situation as it exists. You're not imposing anything on it. You're inhibiting it slightly because you're there with a camera, but if you're careful you can get people to accept the presence of lights and the camera after a while. The first half-hour to an hour of that sort of thing, nothing happens. You shoot film but it's terrible. And then suddenly everybody gets fed up with the

190

camera and they have a few drinks and then it happens – it comes across.

*You have made your reputation as a* cinema-verité *cameraman. What excites you about that style?*

We had acquired cameras that you could handle easily, so you had broken through the sort of barrier of the machinery. You were able to inhibit people less by having smaller equipment and being able to work quicker with it rather than filling somebody's house up with a film studio. You were able just to walk in – in those days, of course, we were in black and white and if you could see, you could shoot. If you were able to put lights in – you got a much better technical result. But it's a matter of trying to compromise between whether you were going to inhibit the situation by putting lights in and thereby losing what you're there for, or whether you're going to slightly degrade the technical result but get greater content. Now, to my mind, content has always been uppermost in actuality filming. Not to the total detriment of technical quality – but content is all important. You can get a beautifully lit, perfectly shot, lovely looking picture that is dead, because you have so inhibited the situation you are trying to film.

*You are implying if someone says, 'Oh, my goodness, that was beautifully shot,' there's something wrong with the story?*

Not at all. It can be both. I can remember in the early days when the *verité* thing started, there was what I thought was a marvellous film done about the Beatles' tour in the USA – not shot by anyone in the BBC I hasten to add. I saw this film, and thought 'God, this is what it's all about. Marvellous.' I went down to see my parents and I said, 'Did you see this fantastic film last night? Just what we're trying to do.' And they said, 'Oh, we turned it off.' I said, 'Why?' They said, 'Well, we couldn't really see; the pictures were all a bit fuzzy and we could not hear what they were saying and we did not know what it was all about.' To us it was an interesting picture and to them – they couldn't see it, they couldn't hear it. So I think what we try to do and certainly what I have always tried to do is not to destroy the atmosphere but at the same time never to degrade the thing so badly technically that people couldn't understand or see what was going on. It's a compromise.

191

## Information

*Those involved in documentary film-making are sometimes accused of invasion of privacy, of exploiting other people in order to make film.*

There have been times when one has been very conscious of this. One of the early occasions was when we went down to Aberfan. We arrived there three days after and we were filming away and there were children still being dug out of this mess and mud and everybody was scrabbling around – digging away. I felt useless. All right, I was only there because I had a camera in my hand, but I felt that I could have done more use with a shovel. But really that wasn't my job. My job was to take pictures.

On the day of the mass funeral we were invited into a house of a family that had lost a child in this, and the whole family were there. We put a couple of lights in and myself and a sound recordist went in, and we were given cups of tea and sandwiches. There was this terrible atmosphere, obviously, and one felt very much an outsider and an intruder. But we were there – we had a job to do and when the moment came where they had a family prayer and the mother and father suddenly burst into tears – what do you do? – you zoom in. You go in for the close-up because that is what you are there for. And when it was all over, we, myself and the sound man, came out and we sat down on the kerb and we just sat and looked at each other for fifteen minutes and just felt absolutely rotten. But that is your responsibility. I could not bring that child back to life. Neither of us could. We had not pushed our way in, we had been invited in. I don't know whether that's invasion of privacy. I tend to think it isn't. It is an invasion sure. What's important surely is why you were there. If you're there for sensationalism, that's very, very, wrong. On the other hand, all these children had been killed. It needed to be recorded. If in some way that film could have helped to prevent it happening again all right. One's not making oneself out as a great sort of social worker with a camera, but it was a job to be done. One had to do it.

192

# Ian Martin

Producer, *Six Sides of a Square*. Editor, *Cause for Concern*. Now Executive Producer, Documentaries, Thames.

I think over the last few years, drama has made quite a lot of raids into documentary techniques and documentaries haven't really made very many compensating raids into dramatic techniques – that's one of the reasons for the slight stodginess of a lot of documentary output. First of all people get pretty neurotic about the whole business of re-creation and faking and so on, and periodically you have some great uproar. Often thoroughly justified – at other times a bit trivial really. Everyone who's made a film knows perfectly well that it's impossible to make a film in a way that controllers of programmes afterwards sometimes claim that they should have been made. So people are a bit wary of anything that smacks of setting up, and also lots of documentary directors have no dramatic training and are a bit nervous and frightened of using actors.

I'm sure that there's a great amount of territory that will never really be properly tackled, and that needs to be tackled, using standard documentary techniques. All this business about not distorting the situation that you find by setting things up – in fact, the mere act of filming most situations distorts them almost beyond repair. A great deal more imagination has got to be given to the problem of tackling social problems in new ways. Because so many of our standard techniques for a lot of subjects are beginning to reach the end of their useful lives. But such things still need programmes done about them – particularly critical programmes.

# Hugh Burnett

Producer, *Face to Face*. Producer/director, four films on South Africa, including *The Colour Line* and *Afrikaner*.

If I had to choose, I'd say you can't mix drama and documentary. I say you can't although you can, but it's very dangerous to mix them. If actors are acting out a true situation, something like *Cathy Come Home*, and then wild tracks of real people are added, from life, and they're mixed together, and the viewer isn't clear about what's going on, you're involved in a very elaborate process of fact and fiction which is very dangerous. On the other hand, to flip into the opposite camp and say you can't possibly put on eight women actresses acting the parts of real people under the banner of a *Wednesday Play*, that's nonsense, because it should be possible to put on a play with actresses and credit your audience with enough intelligence to know that this is a *Wednesday Play* – announced as a play, labelled as a play. You can announce it again at the end if necessary. Whether it's *necessary* to do that is another question again. It's probably far better to go to the original people and interview them. If the people aren't good enough, can't express themselves, find other people who are good enough or wise enough for the role. I think there are lots of dangers in making scripted, artificial, documentary-style drama productions where for some reason the process has gone round the wrong way. A young producer in drama comes in believing that there's a technique in documentary programmes – a particular style. Sometimes there's a technique in a documentary, sometimes there isn't. Sometimes there are film cuts which aren't as good as they ought to be, not because it's intentional but because it's the best way one can get it. That becomes, for the drama director, a method, a style. So he goes away and makes a deliberately badly cut series of acted scenes, juddering camera shots, and calls it television documentary journalism or drama journalism or the documentary style. And it's a sort of dream in his own head. But once he has dreamed his dream, other people think the bad cutting is a technique in itself and another piece of nonsense emerges, a mystique about documentary film.

# Jo Durden-Smith

Producer/director, *Stones in the Park*.

I don't see that television is a profession, exactly, it should be like talking on the telephone or passing information to people in other ways. I don't know how many television-film-makers there are. Let's say a hundred. There aren't many more. It's like – there are only a hundred telephones in the country. Everybody else has got loudspeakers. There are only a hundred people who can transmit through the telephone. Well that's the wrong way to use the telephone, it's the wrong way to use television. It should be available to everybody. This superiority the television people feel is absolutely spurious and certainly only temporary, I hope.

You'll find there is a point at which people in television either suffer from great nervous stress and break down completely and this has happened a lot with people whom I know, or they drink a very great deal, so do journalists. Now, I don't think that's an occupational hazard so much as a kind of feeling that that mystique is probably spurious and then they don't really know what it is that they are doing that's so very special. And people drink because they're under stress, really, of a peculiar kind, not because there's time to spend in a pub and it's a good place to meet. It's not a good place to meet. They're crowded and they're too noisy. You can't really talk. I mean in Granada, Manchester, for example, there's a pub called 'The New Theatre' to which everybody went, to see the same people that they see every day. They didn't talk to them, they were just there together. It was a preservation of a mystique.

*Do you think that competition between ITV and BBC is healthy?*

It seems to me a kind of an impoverished argument to claim that television must appeal to a broad audience otherwise it's not worth doing. That's even straightforwardly false, and yet it is the basic assumption on which all television is now based. The problem with the BBC I think is the problem with financing. The BBC have to go cap in hand to the government every so often and say, 'Please could we have more money from licenses', and the government says 'yes' or 'no'. Now the BBC work on the assumption that they're likely to say 'no' if the BBC are not pulling in huge audiences. I know a number of people believe that the setting up of the ITA destroyed the BBC. Well, I don't think it did. I think it was the setting up of the ghost market that we must compete otherwise people will say that we're not doing our job properly. Therefore, we will produce the same homogeneous product.

*But that would not have happened without the setting up of ITV.*

I think that competition is on the whole very healthy. It is a pity it's competition on this false level. Of course it's wrong that the television companies themselves should pick up advertising revenue. Of course it's wrong that the decision to make programmes should be geared absolutely to financial interests. Of course it's wrong that if a television company renegs on its promises that television company should continue to operate, and of course it's wrong that the financial structure of a company should change radically, as has just happened with this ABPC–EMI–ATV hook-up. Of course it's wrong that Grade should have interests in two television companies; however, it's put through. Of course, it's wrong that huckstering and horse-trading on the network in programme committees should go on. Of course it's wrong that local programming has been killed off because of that hustling. But the system can be made to work. It can only be made to work if the Independent Television Authority puts gloves on instead of simply holding the ring for the big boys. This is absolutely fundamental – it is very wrong that programmes are not made because it's cheaper not to make programmes. It is much cheaper to buy American films, or alternatively, to make films which cost nothing at all – you know, discussion programmes. I think the standard of Independent Television is insulting, it's based on a spurious logical structure which seems to make sense. I mean, to put it in a very crude way, if the three channels put on 'A Log-fire Burning' at eight o'clock in the evening, the channel which had *Coronation Street* before it would get a larger audience than the other channels, so that their 'log-fire' would be better than the BBC's 'log-fire'. Therefore, 'log-fire' programmes are intensely popular and I'm afraid that we must have many more of them.

196

# Peter Batty

Producer/Director, *The Fall and Rise of the House of Krupp, The Battle for Cassino*.

*The network thing is rather bad at the moment, isn't it, because all the ITV documentaries are going out rather late?*

It is, yes. And this is where the weakness of the ITA is evident because it's not prepared to say 'boo' to the Lew Grades of this world. Lew is bound not to want something which he thinks doesn't get the ratings to go out – I mean, he wants to fill the night with Tom Jones, because it gets the ratings and satisfies the advertisers, and this is part of the fault of the system in commercial television, because it doesn't allow any room for what you might call a fastidious sponsor. Whereas in the States they do. *National Geographic* magazine can suddenly put out an hour of *Whither Siberia?*, you see, in prime time because it's got *National Geographic* magazine, which makes everybody perk up and think, 'God! This is prestige', and it panders to all the snobbisms, and also, in a way, it gets the prestigious advertisers – you know, your Ford Motor Company or your Mogul Oil. Unfortunately, because we hate the sponsorship notion so much we're not prepared to tolerate this thing. Somehow one's got to allow a loophole. This is the one way in which you can satisfy the Lew Grades, bearing in mind that the future is going to accommodate Lew Grade types, i.e. one-hundred-per-cent commercial beings who are not interested in the standards as we think of standards. He's interested in certain standards which are more moral standards. It's far more difficult to get a four-letter word past Lew Grade than past the ITA.

*But not for moral reasons.*

He thinks that the advertisers will start swtiching off on the strength of a four-letter word. This is where your problem lies. The commercial system is, by definition, far more rigid than the BBC. In the BBC, when you get down to it, it's a question of personality. You've got to satisfy your head of department, he's got to satisfy the head of his group, the group has got to satisfy the controller, the controller has got to make certain of the DG, and the DG is worried about his governors. Only as a last resort does anyone think about the viewer. I mean, that's life. It's crude. But in commercial television you're worried right from the word 'go'. An individual producer like me was digging direct at the managing director and you knew the pressures that he was under. It so happened that the minute before I went in to get him to spend £15,000 on a programme his advertising director had gone in and said advertising revenue was 2·8 per cent down this quarter, you see, and obviously my timing was awful. Those sort of pressures are going to be there.

# 9 · BBC Executives

The foundation of ITV faced the BBC with a dilemma. As an institution they had stressed with passion over a long period the essential connexion between a monopoly and good broadcasting. If their original theory was correct the logic of competition was apparently the inevitable destruction of the BBC's standards. No institution could possibly face that kind of logic. So the first response was simply to ignore the existence of a rival. Until about 1959 they were able to maintain this stance, firstly because of the period of serious financial difficulty through which ITV passed in the first two years and then because it was some time before ITV approached equal national coverage with the BBC. But in 1959 the BBC found themselves with only 32 per cent of the audience. What were they to do? They began a serious competition for audiences while at the same time disguising the fact with a vigorous PR campaign against the iniquity of a system based upon sordid commercial considerations. This PR campaign was articulated by the formidable figure of Hugh Carleton Greene: 'I am not being critical or aggressive, I am just stating a fact when I say that commercial broadcasting in whatever form exists to sell goods and public service broadcasting to serve the public. Commercial broadcasting is part of a country's business apparatus.' I am personally sympathetic to the anti-advertising position. Advertising has, I believe, general social disadvantages and specific disadvantages as a means of financing a television network not because of its source, but because of its fluctuation. Good television requires long-term planning and confidence and a steady income at whatever level is most likely to provide that. But to attack advertising on moral grounds was to disguise but not solve the central dilemma of competition for audiences. Whatever their motives, the programme companies wanted the same thing as the BBC, large numbers of people watching their programmes. A fatal split was beginning to take place between need for ratings and the philosophy of the BBC enunciated by Carleton Greene:

> Then we come on another of these loaded phrases 'giving the public what it wants'. This phrase is linked with democracy and with trusting people – the simple faith preached by many men who are not at all simple, that what most people want, all people should have.
>
> To use the word 'freedom' in this connection is an abuse of language. What we are in fact concerned with at this point is tyranny – the tyranny of the ratings or of the mind machines. There is, to my mind, mortal danger for the broadcasters in erecting the ratings chart into a kind of token, contradicted only at great risk. I have already said that we broadcasters are public servants. Yes, but what is the public? How little in fact the ratings tell us. They tell us simply how many people watch a particular programme. They tell us nothing about the people themselves. . .
>
> The ratings tell us hardly anything about the things which, as responsible broadcasters, we ought to know.
>
> If you substitute for 'giving the public what it wants' the phrase 'giving everyone what they want' you expose its essential falsity. You cannot give everyone what they want all the time. But you can, under what I should call a free broadcasting system, do your best to think sometimes in terms of the few, sometimes in terms of the many; and even if, as must inevitably be the case, there are many interests which you cannot satisfy, you can at least not kid yourself into thinking that the studied neglect of minorities is justified on democratic grounds.

This is a telling critique of the direction in which BBC policy has been inexorably pushed by competitive scheduling. The BBC decided to submit to the tyranny of the ratings for two reasons. On political grounds they felt that the constant need to increase the licence fee, which they saw coming, could be resisted by Parliament unless the BBC could be seen to be delivering approximately 50 per cent of the audience and unfortunately the only way this could be demonstrated was in the crude terms of ratings. On broadcasting grounds they needed the audiences in terms of self-esteem. A generation of professional television makers was coming to creative manhood with a need for that brand of virility that large audiences gave them. Of course, all communicators want to talk to large numbers of people, not to an empty room. What is at issue is a sense of proportion and a sense of the realities of delivering an audience.

We must always bear in mind when examining the imperatives of competitive scheduling that the connexion between size of audience delivered and the quality of the programmes transmitted is minimal. The imperatives of scheduling are as follows. The audience tends to watch one or other channel all evening. The object, therefore, is to induce them to watch yours all evening. This is known as channel loyalty. Channel loyalty depends upon an audience who will not make active choices. The horror facing programme controllers is the switch-over or the switch-off. The switch-over is worse than the switch-off, for that at least means your competitor hasn't won either. It is the need to avoid any encouragement to switching over that has placed the BBC in an insoluble scheduling dilemma with channel 2. I will deal with that separately. What, therefore, a scheduler must encourage is a passive but hooked audience. He must avoid the danger of a powerful reaction against any programme on the part of anyone because he is losing that viewer not only for that programme but for the rest of the evening. This is the meaning of consensus television and this is why it encourages pap. The only safe place for a controversial programme is late in the evening because if there is nothing to follow it doesn't matter if you lose all your audience.

Accepting the concept of channel loyalty the crucial moment is when people switch on for the evening. There has therefore been steady pressure to start the peak-viewing pattern of programming earlier. Peak-viewing is usually taken to mean 7 P.M.–10 P.M. From 1958 to 1965 *Tonight* occupied the first half-hour of that time with a diet of moderately serious journalism. Its replacements have been pushed to both sides of the evening, *24 Hours* in general to after 10 P.M. and *Nationwide* from 6–6.45. At 6.45 the evening starts with a serial (*Z Cars* and *The Doctors*), to hook them, followed by comedy. As is clear in the interview with Paul Fox the pressures to start the pattern earlier are building up, because the channel that hooks them earliest lasts longest. But having persuaded your audience to switch on your channel, the inheritance factor comes into play. This is the expression of a demonstrable truth that following a very popular show a high proportion of the audience will stay to watch the next show, not out of choice, but out of inertia. Related to this is the phenomenon of pre-echo, that is to say following the same inertia principle, the audience will tend to settle down in front of the channel on which the main programme they want to watch that evening is situated. They are prepared to suffer a certain amount before it, to make sure that they don't miss it. This characteristic is helped by the fact that BBC and ITV do not have common programme junctions.

Pre-echo is dependent on having a clear and assured popular hit. But programme planners have little faith in either the taste of their audience or the quality of their producers' programmes. So they introduce a more reliable form of pre-echo which is to attempt to schedule their big audience pullers a few minutes earlier than the opposition. Thus if both channels are showing a feature film and one starts theirs ten minutes before the other, the earlier starter will, regardless of quality, tend to gain a bigger audience. The BBC has recently introduced a more sophisticated version of this technique, a suitable demonstration both of Paul Fox's scheduling mastery and of the almost total unreality of the whole system. Live sporting events start at times which are not set by the programme controller; moreover, as in the case of the World Cup, both channels are transmitting the same pictures from Mexican television. So what is the poor programme controller to do? He constructs a non-programme around the actual event so that he can start before the opposition.

The combination of all these factors makes the ideal schedule for the delivery of audiences one that starts at a reasonably high level as early in the evening as possible, builds rapidly to a high plateau and holds there as late as possible.

Of course, these tactics are often justified by the claim that they also enable much larger audiences to be delivered for worthy minority programmes than would otherwise be the case. It is, of course, true that when *Panorama* follows *Steptoe* it gets a much larger audience than if it follows a less successful comedy show. But *Panorama* still loses audiences. Indeed, it would lose audiences more drastically were it not in fact scheduled against *World in Action*. The logic of competitive scheduling is never to lose audiences if you can avoid it. If one accepts that logic minority programmes in peak hours will always be under pressure.

But there are of course countervailing pressures so that to the extent that standards have been lowered and will continue to be lowered by scheduling pressures, this decline is not dramatic. Any programme controller works within a tradition which he can do little to alter except in emphasis. An examination of the schedules destroys the myth of a recently departed golden age of British television. While there have been variations of quality both up and down, they have been around a norm of great consistency. But if one compares the schedules in 1955, before ITV came on the air, with the BBC schedules now one sees how rigid and un-changing British TV really is.

Within this rigid structure, the big change has been the decline of serious programming, not only in peak hours, but right across the schedules.

1st Week in November (BBC 1 only)

| *1960* | *1961* | *1962* | *1963* | *1964* |
|---|---|---|---|---|
| 2 Plays | 2 Plays | 2 Plays | 2 Plays | 2 Plays |
| 2 Docs. | 2 Docs. | 1 Doc. | 2 Docs. | 2 Docs. |
| 1 Arts | 1 Arts | 2 Arts | 2 Arts | 2 Arts |
| 1 Music | 1 Music | 2 Music | 2 Music | |
| 1 Science | Royal Ballet | | | |

| *1965* | *1967* | *1968* | *1969* |
|---|---|---|---|
| 1 Play | 1 Play | 1 Play | 1 Play |
| 1 Doc. | 2 Docs. | 1 Doc. | 1 Doc. |
| 1 Arts | 2 Arts | 1 Arts | 1 Arts |
| 1 Music | | | 1 Science |

The golden age, such as it is, coincides, as might be expected, with Pilkington. Then a slow decline set in, which became precipi-tate when Michael Peacock became Controller Channel 1 in 1965, when the policy of three feature films per week started, when the *Tonight* current affairs spot was moved out of peak time, and when the Saturday play was replaced by an American film series and later by a feature film.

The irony is that all this activity has not, in fact, very much changed the competitive position with ITV. According to the BBC Annual Report the audience split 50 : 50 in 1962–3. In 1964 the BBC's share was 45 per cent, in 1969 it was 56 per cent but the BBC now has two channels competing against one. The audiences in fact split BBC 2 – 12 per cent, BBC 1 – 44 per cent, ITV – 44 per cent. Moreover, as all this competition is in terms largely of one or the other, it is only concerned with minute, virtually immeasurable, margins, i.e. to obtain a 5 per cent turn-round in audiences you have to persuade 2½ per cent of the audience to prefer your programmes a fraction more than the opposition's or at any rate dislike them less.

Because there is such a tenuous connexion between audience size and programme quality and because programme controllers do not make programmes, but are responsible for delivering audiences, it is very easy for scheduling requirements to take precedence over programme values. The formula reigns supreme. Programmes become pre-packaged slot-fillers, as predictable and uniform as possible. There are documentary series, *Horizon, One Pair of Eyes, Bird's Eye View*, rather than one-off documentaries, drama series, *The Expert, Codename, Softly-Softly*, rather than one-off plays. There is an increased obsession with star names not only in drama, but in documentary (*Cameron Country, Philpot File*) and in arts programmes (*The World of Georgie Best, The World of Gracie Fields*). The formula approach to programming is not only imposed from above with increasing force and inevitability; formulas are actually sold as concepts of artistic value. The logic of competitive scheduling, the tyranny of the ratings, leads to a view of your audience as masses. Raymond Williams has accurately diagnosed the state of mind that increasingly reigns in BBC TV: 'The conception of persons as masses springs, not from an inability to know them, but from an interpretation of them according to a formula. . . . The formula, in fact, will proceed from our intention. If our purpose is art, education, the giving of information and opinion, our interpretation will be in terms of the rational and interested being. If, on the other hand, our purpose is manipulation – the persuasion of a large number of people to act, feel, think, know, in certain ways – the convenient formula will be that of the masses.'

The BBC were forced into this position by competition and they saw their escape route in a second channel. They mounted a massive effort to persuade the Pilkington Committee to recommend a second channel for the BBC.

The BBC got what they asked for from Pilkington but as Greene said, 'Perhaps when one looks back one is tempted to think that we did almost too well.' The founding of BBC 2 brought two sets of problems to the BBC without relieving them from the strait-jacket of competitive scheduling as was hoped. The first problems were scheduling problems. If you decide that BBC 2 is to be a complementary network its schedule is tied to the schedule of BBC 1 as a positive to a negative. BBC 1 has the job of wooing the mass audience and must continue in that role at least until BBC 2 achieves full national coverage. If, therefore, BBC 1 is successful and if the logic of scheduling holds good, then the BBC 2 schedule must be a disaster in audience terms. Indeed, if a true complementary service is to be provided, the more successful BBC 1 the more disastrous BBC 2. The BBC has always denied that they wish to turn BBC 2 into a specialized minority channel. But how are they going to avoid this? One way would be to make BBC 1 more of a balanced channel than it is at the moment and allow BBC 2 to capture substantial audiences from it without at the same time expecting BBC 1 to replace that loss by capturing audiences from ITV. What seems to have happened so far is that BBC 2 has creamed off that portion of the audience who in spite of the efforts of channel controllers remain obstinately selective. With the sophistication of scheduling technique now available, ITV and BBC 1, so long as they directly compete, will split the remaining audience approximately 50–50. Now the BBC considers it undesirable to gain consistently much over 50 per cent of the total audience for fear of driving ITV into ever more competitive programming in order to survive. Therefore, they must limit the growth of BBC 2 at a certain point, because if, for instance, BBC 2 captures 20 per cent of the audience and the rest is split 50–50 the BBC will then have 60 per cent of the audience. Unless of course they do an about-face and allow BBC 1 not to compete. Then you would have a danger of the pattern of radio repeating itself. When the BBC set up their three-channel radio service they aimed for an audience split of Light 50 per cent, Home 40 per cent, Third 10 per cent, but what happened was an uncontrollable drift towards the Light so that the actual audience split ended up Light 70 per cent, Home 29 per cent, Third 1 per cent.

More serious than this unresolved scheduling dilemma were the administrative problems brought to the BBC by the foundation of a second channel. In spite of its apparent advantages it can be seen as the straw which broke the camel's back. 'Some straw, some back,' you might retort. In brief, with channel 2 the BBC grew too big and too poor at the same time and this resulted in pressures on programming which reinforced those of competitive scheduling. The BBC was not given the funds with which to finance a second channel and, ever since, the overriding concern of management has been economy. These economies have had to be made in a service which thorough independent outside inquiries, one by West German Television and one by the American management consultants McKinsey, at the invitation of the BBC, deemed already to be outstandingly efficient. McKinsey said 'BBC television programmes are produced more economically, considering both cost and quality, than anywhere else in the world.' This would lead one to suppose that if the BBC were to reduce costs more than marginally they would have to reduce quality. This is exactly what is happening. This process takes several years severely to affect the programmes on the screen because a television service can live off the fat of its past. For instance, the creative atmosphere of a particular period produces programmes such as *Tonight* which splits into *24 Hours* and *Nationwide*. It uses, watered down, some of the talent developed by *Tonight*. But where is the thrust for new current affairs programmes going to come from? But economies bite in more hidden and insidious ways. They attack the development of writers and directors. There is less money to nurture promising dramatists to replace the Mercers, Pinters, Alun Owens and John Hopkins produced in palmier days and the writers who do appear are forced by economic pressures to over-write. You cannot live as a TV playwright on less than three plays a year, so you either do hack work for series or you leave the medium or you burn yourself out. The same applies to directors. There was a time when the BBC nurtured such talents as Ken Russell, John Schlesinger, Jack Gold, Ken Loach. It is now rightly proud of the contribution these men have made to the British film industry, and wears the occasional programmes they still contribute like jewels in its crown. But the atmosphere that produced these talents no longer exists. A standard of production is accepted on *Review* that would never have been tolerated on *Monitor*. No one is given time to train and learn any longer. Documentary series

like *Horizon* and *One Pair of Eyes* depend upon directors churning
out one film every three months year after year.

Why don't production staff make a fight for standards? Because
power has been taken out of their hands. It is claimed that the
implementation of McKinsey's proposals puts power into the
producers' hands. Charles Curran stated on 14 November 1969,

The McKinsey philosophy is one of devolution to the point of accountability. . . . In the minds of senior management devolution is the art of
being able to pin the responsibility on somebody else. There are many
in the BBC who will welcome the process, including myself.

The essential wrongheadedness of the McKinsey doctrine as
applied to BBC television is that it pins the financial responsibility
on the producer at the very moment when creative responsibility is
removed. The use of the word 'pin' is indicative of the way in
which BBC management regards its creative staff. It is the police-
man's view of the criminal. His liberty must be curtailed at all
costs.

McKinsey were baffled by the BBC. It did not conform to the
industrial cost-effective norms. Normally, they said, they identified the fifteen decision-makers in an organization and most of the
managerial problems were solved. But at the BBC there were between 1,500 and 2,000 decision-makers. The solution to this daunt-
ing administrative problem seems to have been the creation of
fifteen decision-makers. Creative decisions of importance are increasingly taken by programme-controllers and departmental
heads. As they are not going to be making the eventual programmes they create programming formulas, strands of output
which conform to pre-set time, budget and content limits. This
trend is strengthened by another strategy for relieving financial
pressure, the co-production. Programme packages, such as *The
History of the British Empire*, are negotiated with organizations
like *Time–Life*. When the business deal has been made, the producer is called in to execute the project. Here creative control is
handed over in part not only to a middle-management editor, but
to an outside organization with no real interest in the British
television audience. The BBC claim that they do not give up
editorial control, that they never make as a co-production a programme they would not wish to make anyway. This editorial

control may not be imposed from outside, but the realities of international marketing dictate some tailoring of the product for that market. The BBC seems to be tiptoeing in the wake of Lew Grade.

What is happening in television is a normal process of industrial growth. As Huw Wheldon has pointed out to his staff, BBC television is no longer a cottage industry. It is now entering the mass-production phase and producers are becoming mere wage-slaves. The position of management *vis-à-vis* their wage-slaves is being strengthened in certain key creative areas by a process of casualization. The BBC has an agreement with the Union it recognizes as representing its production staff, the ABS, that short-term contract employees must never exceed 30 per cent of the staff. One must accept the assurance that this agreement is being observed, but even within the terms of the agreement there are causes for disquiet. Short-term contracts used to be of from 2 to 5 years. There is an increasing tendency to use temporary contracts of one year or under. The shorter the contracts the larger the pool of labour that can be contained within the 30 per cent. The unchanged percentage figures undoubtedly disguise growing job insecurity and hidden underemployment in just those areas, drama and documentary, where the greatest push against management pressures is needed. This situation is of course exacerbated by factors outside the BBC's control, such as the temporary end of expansion in television and the recession in the film industry. But it is related to the BBC's huge size and therefore power as an employer. It is an important factor in the changing power structure at the BBC.

No one disagrees that television is becoming more and more like the motor industry. The area of disagreement is about the desirability and inevitability of the process. The present management seem to accept the trend as not only inevitable, but desirable. An increasing number of their creative staff disagree and deplore the direction in which the BBC, as the dominant institution in British television, is heading. Huw Wheldon states that the BBC's only aim is excellence, the only enemy mediocrity. No one would disagree. But who is to decide the nature of that excellence and that mediocrity? This is what the growing demands for producer power are really about. Do the people who make the programmes set standards or those who organize the budgets and schedules? To paraphrase Dean Acheson, it seems to many both inside and outside the BBC that, after Pilkington, the BBC gained an Empire, but has yet to find a role.

# Lord Hill

Chairman, the Board of Governors, BBC.

*What should be the relationship between a broadcasting organization and its public? Although the ITA is supposed to maintain standards and although the BBC was set up as a public service, neither organization can ignore the pressure of public demand expressed in crude ratings figures.*

Take Independent Television first of all, for it is there that the pressure of numbers is much clearer. Its income depends on numbers. Now one of the roles of the Authority in its application of standards, taste and balance is to apply a counter-pressure, a check, to the uncontrolled pressure of numbers. It does this in various ways. For example, I recall in my Authority days an art programme was required of every programme company. The Authority didn't say what kind of art programme: it said that it would not approve their schedules unless there was an art programme. In general the Authority's job is to see that there is a public service attitude in a commercial service. Bearing in mind the inevitable and compulsive pressure of numbers, particularly in these days of falling income, the ITA has succeeded in this remarkably well.

This leads on to the BBC. Parliament decided on competition between a commercial service and a public service and this has worked well. The qualities, or opposite of qualities, of one tend to rub off on the other. In Independent Television there is a basic respect, an admiration for the BBC with which it is competing.

On the other side of the coin, it is sometimes said that whatever may have been the good results of that competition, one result has been that the BBC has gone all out for ratings. Incidentally, some people ignore the existence of BBC 2 when they do their arithmetic on that subject. But at first sight there is something in this criticism. But don't let's think of numbers as invariably sinful. It is not a bad thing even for a public service to attract large audiences. The real test, taking BBC 1 and BBC 2 together, is the extent to which the Corporation succeeds in meeting the needs of the minorities as well as the majority. It surely satisfies this test. But say on Saturday night, when the great British public seeks relaxation, there's nothing to be ashamed of in seeking to please the largest number on BBC 1. Above all, it is excellence that matters in both programmes for the majority and those for minorities. Indeed, even in programmes that begin on a minority basis, it is often their excellence which leads them to be at least less minority in appeal.

The majority of the great British public look to television for relaxation. Criticize them for it if you will, but the fact is undeniable. A large number of people come home from a day's work and their first two questions are, 'What's for supper, dear?' and 'What's on the telly?' The programmes should be examined as a whole. An acid test is the willingness to put on a minority programme in peak hours. The BBC does this, sometimes with a startling courage. On the other hand, there are kinds of programmes that will only meet the wishes of the minority. Where figures matter in such a series is whether the audience declines or grows in relation to its target of a relatively small audience.

*In the past, because TV was constantly expanding, the BBC was able to constantly renew its creative personnel. Now expansion has stopped, how do you solve the problem of 'dead wood'?*

Until the last year or two, because the number of licence holders was steadily rising every year, the BBC's income went steadily up. Expenditure was not unrestrained, but expansion year by year was relatively easy. That phase ended as saturation point was reached in the number of licence holders. Now there has to be more careful budgeting. It also puts on to Governors a heavy responsibility to get the licence fee up to the level of the BBC's need, bearing in mind that politicians seem to think they will lose votes if they put the licence fee up. This is a nonsense and they know it's a nonsense. We are losing rather more than £7 million a year by default. It's a vast sum. It is a fact of life now that, apart from reducing the number of defaulters, increasing the licence fee and the number of colour-viewers, we have a limited sum of money within which to live. It is of the order of £100 million a year. Don't think that poverty of resources is the consequence of this development. It isn't. But we have lost the old lush days in which we could almost do anything that our human resources permitted. But, compared with so many industries, broadcasting is an expanding industry.

*The BBC had its first strike at the end of 1969. Are you aware of the possibility of growing industrial unrest within the industry?*

I'm aware that this industry cannot escape what is happening in industry generally. Obviously it cannot. We cannot expect not to experience the surges that one sees elsewhere and the increased demand on the part of those who make the product to participate more in management. That's a widespread phenomenon outside as well as inside.

I will take one aspect of recent unrest following the publication of *Broadcasting in the Seventies*. It seemed to suggest a fundamental disrespect on the part of the creative man for management generally. Yet there must be management, there must be a financial organization, there must be a personnel organization. And when I think of the gusts of freedom that blow through the Television Centre, I hardly get the impression that there is a heavy or a repressive management. But management there must be and creative people are often well equipped to become managers. Some are managing now and doing it superbly well. Some will never succeed at it and are glad of it.

*You said that there is obviously a mood throughout the country of people who make the product wanting to get involved in management. If this continues in the future, how do you see the BBC being able to restructure itself to do that?*

There's a basic problem here. A way has got to be found of providing a forum for consultation, for the expression of views of creative artists of all kinds. I accept that unhesitatingly. For their part, creative people have got to accept that there has to be give and take within themselves in the expression of those views, that the formulation of policies involves the compromise of consensus. It's no good having a vast and lively body in which everybody disagrees with everybody else and enjoys doing it. If you want to deal with the hierarchy in your organization you have to co-ordinate, canalize and express in precise terms. How best can it be done? It might, I suppose, be much easier if the creative people had their own organization or their own group within a larger organization. Now to make this work is going to require a kind of self-discipline on their part to yield up some of their individuality. Given this desire to co-ordinate, to canalize and to yield something up in individual terms, then the BBC will and should adapt itself to such a development. Now we come across a very real problem. I suspect that a bread-and-butter body finds difficulty in meeting all the needs of creative people. It may be that the Union of the future has to have within it, or in relation with it, a different kind of body, essentially for the gathering of the views of the creative groups.

*Suppose that such a body grew up, would it have representatives on the Board of Governors?*

I wouldn't have thought so. The Board of Governors is the buffer between the broadcasters and the outside world. If we don't sustain that role, there will be a new body set up, an external consumer council. Nothing should be done to make that more likely, for it would go right to the heart of the independence of the BBC and the freedom of the producer. I think the Governors should remain what they are, amateurs, who assume a responsibility for what is broadcast, who gain an understanding of how the BBC works, who reserve the right to say so when it has gone wrong, but whose task is to defend the independence of the Corporation, resist the pressures on it and to defend those who work in it. Board of Management, that's another matter. If you are aiming at a place for the voice of the creative people that's the place. But that voice is there already in the person of creative men transferred to management.

*Do you feel the outside pressures on the BBC growing?*

I do. Spiro Agnew just can't be swept under the carpet. He said one or two things that are rather disconcerting amongst all the other nonsense. So why are we going into this phase of vulnerability? It may be because of the stunning impact of this medium.

212

Those in authority may envy the strength, the pervasiveness of television as part of a kind of love/hate relationship. You can't expect television to grow in strength and in influence without having movements afoot to check it. One thing that disturbed me in recent months was the way some people criticizing, say, *Broadcasting in the Seventies*, as they were fully entitled to do, sought to bring the government in more and more and so to give the government an excuse for invading our autonomy. Fortunately, government resisted the temptation.

*Do you think there is any strength in the argument which I think a lot of people are making even within broadcasting, that television and radio should be split up into two separate public corporations?*

Obviously bigness has always had its dangers and always will have. We employ 23,000 people. It is a vast organization and that of itself creates its problems. In the absence of positive arguments for a break up, I think I'm sceptical of it for this reason: I want a strong single body to be able to resist pressures in the future. You may think I'm obsessed with this question of external pressures. The strength of the External Services is the greater because they are part of the BBC. The independence of a unified BBC is safer than it would be with the organization broken into parts. There are great advantages in the sharing of services. Career prospects are greater in a single service. Those who advocate a breaking up should produce their arguments for such a change, and show why their proposals would be better for broadcasting.

*Have you ever considered a system in which the BBC might not survive?*

No. The BBC is strong in the affections of the people of this country. It is part of our national life. Its record is outstanding. Its independence has been maintained. Don't let's dig away at the foundations just for the love of change.

# Charles Curran

1947, Radio Talks Producer; 1951, Monitoring Service; 1953, one of the first two BBC administrative trainees; 1959, Head of External Broadcasting Administration; 1963, Secretary of the BBC; 1967, Director of External Broadcasting; 1969, Director-General.

*One of the main criticisms of the BBC made by those who work in television is that the BBC has grown too big for its own good. Do you think there is anything in this?*

On this front the real question about television, as about broadcasting in general, is 'How can you manage it?' A given amount of television takes a certain logistic base no matter what way you approach it. At any one moment it will either be slightly too big or slightly too small, but the general bigness will be there because we have to fill that much air-time. If it's split up into little bits and you add up the little bits it will probably add up to the same – and if it doesn't add up to much the same it won't be able to do the same things. If we had, say, a specialized television network showing things like specialized documentaries – science, for example – it would be very hard to find the funds which would sustain that kind of network with all the equipment which is at the disposal of *Horizon* today. *Horizon* depends for its assets on the existence of *Up Pompeii*. If you go in for small-audience programmes you can't really guarantee the logistic support which they need to be at their best unless you also have the big audience stuff. The question is not: 'How big is television?' – because it will be big if it's good. The question is how the bigness organizes itself. So what I am concerned with as a management problem – and this applies to the BBC as well as to the Television Service – is: 'What are the right bits which have a natural life by themselves? How do you put those bits together so as to take advantage of the mass of financial support which is available to us as a single organization and which would not be available to smaller organizations and certainly could not be as economically managed?'

Now, whatever way you organize broadcasting – whether as a system of little groups or one large group – broadcasting has to accept that it is living in a society which calls for financial accountability. I think myself that broadcasting is particularly vulnerable

214

to public pressures. It needs size if it is to have the kind of independence which I think is necessary to the production of the best kind of programmes. Just suppose we had fifty little organizations all doing their own bit. Let us say that *24 Hours* was one little organization, and let us suppose *Man Alive* was another one, and so on. Let us suppose that somebody decided that they did not like one particular little group and all the pressures kept going after it. I believe that its natural vulnerability would be the greater if you did not have a relatively large body to protect the little groups each of which will be liable to provoke public criticism from time to time. I think broadcasting is naturally vulnerable, because if you are going to do anything worthwhile, you are going to express new ideas – and, frankly, nobody likes new ideas. People like accustomed facts. So once you go into the field of ideas you are going to upset people. If you are little, once you upset them, they turn round and ask why should you be there at all. There are good things which come out of this possibility of provoking people and it is much easier for a large organization to do the provocation than a small one.

*Well, one of the comments we received from ITV is that BBC 1 is now virtually the same as ITV and the BBC salves its cultural conscience by having BBC 2.*

It is very good propaganda but it is simply not true. But should it not be put the other way round – that ITV is now really like BBC 1? ITV is rather different from what it was in 1955. I agree that BBC 1 is not very different now from ITV and I do not think this is a bad thing. After all, the BBC was 'ivory tower', and I believe that the facts of the market place do tend to drive people out of the 'ivory tower'. I think you can go too far in either direction. What people may be thinking about BBC 1 is that it has gone too far towards the market place. I do not believe that, but that would be a legitimate line of criticism. I do not think it is a legitimate line of criticism to say that it is like ITV.

*But don't you think that this is a criticism of the state of television in this country that the two main channels should be so similar?*

I think it is a fact about competition. In 1954–5 this country decided to have competition in television. If you have competition the competitors get more and more like each other. It is absolutely inevitable. If you make that decision then you must accept the consequences. Let's move on to the second part of your statement – that BBC 2 is the cultural conscience of the BBC. If this is simply a reflection of the fact that the people who make this criticism see on BBC 2 the kind of programmes they would like to see, then I do not mind it, but in that case BBC 2 is not a reflection of the BBC conscience. It is a reflection of their tastes. The fact about BBC 2 is that it is planned to complement what is on BBC 1. Now, the more BBC 1 becomes like a revised ITV that has responded to the BBC, then the more it is likely that BBC 2 will be extending the area of possible choice of programmes in television, because it will be going away from that area into which BBC 1 has been brought – which I have described as being out of the 'ivory tower' and half into the market place. BBC 2 won't be retreating into the ivory tower but it will be looking at other places in the market place.

*If we can turn to the question of economies in BBC television, I read that you had said in a letter to the Writers' Guild that the drama budget would be slashed . . .*

What I actually said, after a general explanation of the impossibility of giving a pledge that any particular part of the budget could be made sacrosanct, because that would make it impossible to change anything, was this: 'I can say that any cut-back next year will be slight, that we have no intention at the moment of altering the balance between original drama and what you call derivative drama, and that nothing which our Drama Group feels is really worthwhile will be less likely in 1970 to find its way to the screen than it did in 1969.' Now, if that is an axeing of drama budgets I am a Dutchman.

*I have talked, of course, to the drama people, and there is a feeling that drama is so expensive that it is one of the areas where economies are bound to be made.*

This is what happens when people take one part of the picture. There is a cut-back in general programme expenditure because we have to work within a budget, but that cut-back is made after providing for the maintenance of the present standard of output.

In other words, we have a given programme rate for BBC 1 and for BBC 2 and we add a large percentage to it to make it possible to maintain the same standard as the previous year. Not to put anything on to meet rising costs would automatically be a depression of standards. After adding what is needed for that, we say we are going to take a little bit back because we are in a financial difficulty, and that little bit is less than what we have added on. In real terms the cut-back, so far as it goes, is slight in relation to the history of expansion.

*Now, has the expansion of cash budgets throughout television also been subject to this minor cut-back because of the overall financial depression?*

What I say to Huw Wheldon is: 'This is our financial state. What are your proposals to deal with the television part of it?' He then says, 'On programme funds I shall add so much, as usual, in order to maintain the standard, and then I shall require my people right across the Service to make a general saving.' But it is for him to discuss with the heads of departments and with the network controllers and with everybody else, including the engineers, how this applies. I don't say: 'Cut it off drama.' I don't say: 'Cut it off all departments.' I don't say: 'Cut it off OBS', or 'Cut it off Light Entertainment.' That is a Television Service matter and it is the only way this place will run – by making the people responsible for the Service actually responsible for its financial well-being.

*Is there any probability of putting greater pressure on either this government or the next for further increases in the licence?*

What puts pressure on the government is public opinion, not the BBC. If the BBC got up on its hind legs and said, 'We are pressing you, the government, to do this for us', the government would be perfectly entitled to turn round and say to the BBC: 'And who do you think you are? Are you elected?' And there is only one answer to that – 'No'. Pressure is generated by public opinion. If our programme service is rated worthwhile by the public then pressure on the government is automatically there from the right quarter. If we have not enough money, we really have only two courses open to us. One is to ask for more on the grounds that we are doing what the public expects us to be doing and what the government has asked us to do on behalf of the public, and the other is to say: 'Because you are not giving us any more money we shall have to reduce the service that the public have demonstrated that it wants.' Now you can reduce the service in two ways. You can reduce it by impoverishing the quality and you can reduce it by cutting the extent of the service – either in the number of hours, or in terms of coverage to the country. Cutting coverage of the country is pretty unacceptable because it means that you take money from some people and don't give them the service. I think that is unfair, so there is really only one answer – to reduce what you are doing on the air. I think the impoverishment of the programmes is the one certain way to damnation.

*Would you say that the BBC's financial position at the moment was a critical one?*

It has been critical ever since television really began to grow in the early 1950s, because the costs of providing good television were bound to rise at a rate which would outstrip the steady expansion of the number of licences, for which saturation point would be reached very quickly. We did not have a financial crisis between 1922 and 1939 because there was always an expansion of the market. We did not have one between 1939 and 1947 because of the war, when we were on Grant-in-Aid. We did not have one between 1947 and 1950 because television was growing pretty slowly. From 1950 onwards we have been in fairly continuous financial difficulty for one reason or another, but the main reason has been that the speed at which political decisions were made was lagging behind broadcasting necessity.

*Why should the licence system survive?*

Because it is the only one which anybody has been able to devise which leaves the BBC reasonable independence. There are two kinds of independence. There is constitutional independence and there is financial independence, and one is no good without the other.

*In terms of BBC expenditure didn't the BBC suggest to the government recently that educational broadcasting might be paid for in some other way?*

218

The case which we put to the government was twofold. First we believed that there was a proper national case for the development of educational broadcasting as a part of the educational system. We believed that educational broadcasting, including schools broadcasting, was becoming more directly part of the curriculum than it had been in the early days, when it was a kind of enrichment for use by the teacher. But it was becoming more and more an essential part of the educational apparatus of the country, and it could be argued that, to the extent that it was an intrinsic part of the educational system, a part at least of the cost should be borne by the educational authorities rather than by the general licence fee. We thought that there was room and need for development. I do not think we carried total conviction on that with the Department of Education, and there is a real difference of opinion between us on that issue. But we believed very firmly that, if we were doing educational broadcasting, it was in the interest of education and it was in the interest of the BBC that educational broadcasting should retain a visible recognizable independence. We therefore proposed that we should continue to find from the licence fee a substantial part of the cost of educational broadcasting. We were not saying: 'Pay for the lot.' We were saying: 'Pay towards a good deal of it.' Further, we were saying that we believed that there was a suitable set of instruments for preserving the independence of educational broadcasting, in the shape of the School Broadcasting Council and the Further Education Advisory Council, and we did not believe that taking government money meant submission to government dictation any more than taking the grant for the External Services meant a loss of independence for them.

*Many people in the BBC feel, I think, that management consultation with staff, over* Broadcasting in the Seventies, *for instance, is a farce. That meetings are held, objections are raised from the floor and then management goes away and does exactly what they planned in the first place.*

That may be because the objections were not very sound.

*But do you recognize a feeling of uneasiness?*

This is always going to be the case when a coherent plan – and it surely ought to be coherent if it is thought fit to be presented by management – is heard by people who, because their association with each other is not cemented by the pressures of responsibility, will not have coherent opinions to express about it. It is always likely that those opinions will be diverse, and therefore their effect on a coherent plan is bound to be fairly marginal. There is a kind of assumption that those people in management who are preparing the plans don't know very much about broadcasting, or know less than the people to whom the plans are to be presented. The fact is that the people in management all come out of broadcasting in exactly the same way as the staff who are being consulted, and they have come out of broadcasting in many cases at the 'sharp end'. They are not from outside the world of broadcasting. They are still in it, and they know a great deal about it, so they ought to have got the answers right. If they present plans and their answers are all wrong, then they ought to be fired. They don't, on the whole, present plans in which the answers are all wrong. Therefore the impact of criticism ought to be marginal. If the impact of criticism is major, then the plan must have been wrong inthe first place.

*But do you think that if the criticism was more co-ordinated it would make more sense to management?*

It is certainly easier for management to consider criticism if it is co-ordinated. It does not necessarily mean that it is more effective, because very often criticism which comes up from the floor will reflect precisely the criticisms which have already been ventilated at management level, and to which the answers have already been found at the management level and after a particular course has been chosen rather than another because those criticisms were not thought to be strong enough to stand in the way. One thing that one has to remember when presenting any management plan is that there are very rarely perfect answers to any problem. What you are almost always presenting is the imperfect answer. You know that it is imperfect before you present it, and you have taken into account its imperfections, so when you get criticism of the imperfections what you are getting is a confirmation of your own doubts about the plan – doubts which you have already rejected. Now there are points where criticism is valid in itself. There are other points where criticism reflects a state of opinion which is important to the carrying out of the plan. If you do not have people's feeling with you at certain points, then the plan becomes much more difficult to carry out. You have to take account of the fact represented by opinion, and you may alter your plans accordingly.

*But do you think there is a gap between management thinking and creative thinking and an inevitable tension between the two?*

I think it was *The Times* recently which said that the people in the senior management of both Independent Television and the BBC are bound to be concerned with political questions much more than are the people in directly creative activity. There may be a gap between the two kinds of thought, but it is perfectly clear that the one can't exist without the other. You cannot have the creative activity without the political, technical and financial structure which makes it possible for the creative to operate. I do not engage in political discussion simply for the fun of it. I engage in it because it is a necessary pre-condition for the programme-producing activity. Unless I can get the right constitutional conditions, the right financial conditions, and the right technical conditions, nobody can really produce programmes in ideal conditions. I suppose you might say that there never are ideal conditions, but they should be as good as they can be. My pre-occupation is with programmes in the last resort. I see a lot of programmes and I listen to a lot of programmes. When people say: 'Do I have any spare time and what do I do with it?' I say: 'I listen and I look.' Now, I am not looking here for sympathy, because I like looking and listening. Unless I am really preoccupied with what comes out at the other end, from the people who are doing the same sort of job as I once did myself, then nothing else that I do really matters. I may be arguing about political freedom; I may be arguing about violence on television; I may be arguing about whether the BBC ought to pay Selective Employment Tax or not. All these things in the end come back to the one point – producing programmes.

*When the BBC was set up, its purpose was defined as being to inform, educate and entertain. What do you think its purpose is today?*

It is exactly the same. We still have to entertain, but entertainment is not simply relaxation. It can be very demanding and

221

should be, as often as not, demanding. If you look at broadcasting, whether it is radio or television, a great deal of it is bound to be entertaining, whether it is relaxing or the demanding kind. It is that kind of a medium and that is why most people are willing to hand over their money to a public service organization by way of a licence fee – because they expect to be entertained. So entertainment has to be given in quantity. Then you come to information. Of course, it is part of the duty of a public service organization, which is using a public franchise in the shape of a frequency, to contribute to the enlightenment of society. That means its political, social, cultural enlightenment. We have the limitation, because we are using a strictly limited medium, of making sure that all significant points of view have their appropriate opportunity for expression. That is what I mean when I talk about balance. Some people have said that I seem to be preoccupied with balance. Balance, to my mind, is only a gauge. It is only an instrument to make sure that the enlightenment job which we have to do is being done with reasonable fairness. There is a need, then, for enlightenment in the schedules. You cannot measure success by whether enlightenment brings you large audiences or small audiences. You can only measure it by asking yourself all the time whether you are doing what you know perfectly well you ought to be doing as your contribution to society. That is the final criterion. Now, if you come to education, we are living in an age when technological change is so fast that most people are going to have to change their jobs once at least during their lifetime. That means, in true human terms, that they will be out of a job, unless you can retrain them. I reckon that it is part of our job in broadcasting to provide some part of the education which enables people to retrain themselves. In other words, there is a vocational element in our education which we did not think of twenty or thirty years ago, when broadcasting was a pioneer adventure, and this, I think, is an extremely important role for the broadcaster.

# Huw Wheldon

1952, entered TV. Producer, *Press Conference, Facts and Figures, Portraits of Power*. 1958–62, introduced *Junior Wranglers, All Your Own*. Edited and introduced *Monitor*. 1968, Controller of Programmes; 1969, Managing Director, BBC TV.

*How do you see the BBC in relationship with its audience? How do you resolve the dilemma between giving the public what it wants and giving them what you think is good for them?*

My view is that the question can no more be put to a television programme-maker or to a television programme executive than it can to a novelist or a publisher. The question is actually irrelevant. *Twelfth Night* wasn't either what they wanted or what Shakespeare thought they ought to have. If you allow the question even to reside in your mind, then you are bound to move in one of those two directions and go for either pot-boilers or sermonizing. What you have to do in order to establish a proper relationship with the audience is respond to your own needs, to the needs of the subject and to the needs of the audience in a very complex amalgam of pressures. And if in the end you find that you can't do that then either society is wrong, as it was with Cézanne, or you are wrong.

*In the competitive situation in which the BBC finds itself, isn't it being inexorably driven to produce the same programmes as ITV because it is competing for the same audience?*

I think that even had there been no ITV there certainly would have been a BBC 2. The BBC situation is that if you're going to do a public service broadcasting job you have got to have two networks in order that you can provide choice, and in order that you can take in the great minorities as well as the great majorities. One of the limitations is that you are unquestionably dealing with the large audience. You are not in the audience-of-hundreds league because television is too expensive for that. You are inescapably in the seven-figure audience league on both networks. Given, however, that you've got two networks, then the requirements which are put on you, or which you accept, or which you invent – to carry out journalism, to carry out art, to carry out a vision of the contemporary and a vision of the past and so on –

these various responsibilities can, I think, be accepted. But two networks are essential. While you're doing that, I agree you have also got to do two other things. You have got to maintain a competitive situation, otherwise you're thrown out of business; and secondly, you have got to do it in such a way that there is some evidence to suggest that you are providing either delight or insight or pleasure to the nation at large, whether persons in the nation find themselves at a moment in time within a minority, or within a majority. I'm glad there is competition actually. I think it puts an edge on things. But the first basis of policy is to use two networks to broadcast what you think ought to be broadcast.

*What happens with the relationship between BBC 1 and BBC 2 when BBC 2 is a full national network? Because, at the moment, BBC 2 inevitably plays second fiddle to BBC 1 schedules, rather than the other way round.*

There are twenty-three million people now who have BBC 2 sets together with the necessary antennae and so on. And there is evidence to suggest that, gradually, the notion of being able to choose between three, and not two, networks is taking hold. By today there is some reason for believing that those who've got BBC 2 look at five or six BBC 2 programmes a week. By the time we come to 1974, the twenty-three million will be much increased and it will be virtually national. Secondly, I believe that the number of BBC 2 programmes watched as against BBC 1 or ITV will also be increased among those who have BBC 2. Now, if those are facts, they also tie in with the actual policy which is that under no circumstances should we drive for a situation in which BBC 1 is the Home Service or Light Programme and BBC 2 is a Third Programme. That is to say, that in terms of eventual policy the two networks should be of equal weight. Of course, they should have their separate flavours. I like the idea of BBC 2 being a channel for enthusiasts, a channel where the odd-ball programme pops up, a channel which cheerfully takes big risks. Given a different flavour, however, and no more than that, the important thing is that the channels should be of broadly equal weight so that you could call them BBC Lime and BBC Grove if you wanted. Above all, they should provide programme by programme choice so that between the two we get a full two-channel operation.

*But if you're successful in that, it will radically change the present preconceptions about scheduling, won't it?*

The scheduling operation now is that BBC 1 maintains a first position and you arrange BBC 2 in such a way that it responds to BBC 1. It will inevitably get a little more veiled – a little more shadowy, so that if BBC 2 particularly want to do something, then BBC 1 will have to respond to BBC 2 scheduling. But I think it will prove possible step by step and week by week to bring this about smoothly without making any sensational or radical alterations in the way the schedules are built.

*I know that you feel that things are much easier for the BBC during a time of national unity such as during the Second World War whereas now society is more pluralist.*

That's right. There are lots of voices now that wish to be heard. I don't think that makes programme-making or scheduling difficult. What it makes difficult is the standing of the BBC *vis-à-vis* the country. As you just said, broadcasting was easy during the War. You spoke for and to the nation. But when you have discordant voices, all of whom feel that they're either right or on the way towards a proper vision of the future and they are different from each other, then you have a new problem. There is no great difficulty, I believe, in actually making programmes some of which are humanist and some of which are anti-humanist, some of which are entertaining and some of which are less entertaining, some of which are more serious in this way and others that are less serious in that. The real difficulty is always how to do them well. Mediocrity is the enemy all the time. But good or bad, you do them at a cost. The cost is that at a divided and anxious time, one man's programme meat is another man's programme poison. You cannot but run into a lot of criticism. The question is – what do you do? What you do I think is two things – firstly you recognize the facts and bear in mind that this is going to be the context in which you live and work. Secondly, you've got to accept that since there are going to be difficulties of public stance, it becomes more important than ever to fight against mediocrity and aim for excellence.

*Do you think everyone agrees about what a good programme is?*

Not entirely, of course, any more than anybody agrees with what

a good picture is. Like you, I have seen lots of very good programmes which were very largely dismissed, and poor programmes
which were praised. Also, as I said, there are deep and genuine
differences among people. But on the whole, I think excellence is
recognizable. We've been brought up to think because of the history of art over the last hundred years that these things are arbitrary, but in point of fact, they are not as arbitrary as all that.
That George Eliot programme the other day – with Sheila Allen
playing the part of George Eliot – was very widely regarded as a
good programme. The *Six Wives of Henry VIII* was very widely
regarded as a good play series. *Take Three Girls* was widely regarded in the same way; Dudley Moore and Peter Cook are
widely regarded as making what is genuinely a good programme.
And so on. Equally there are certainly programmes which are
widely regarded as second rate and once you've tasted them, you
also say – 'Damn it, this is really not very good!'

*Now TV has become such a huge industry, many programme-
makers feel that there are growing pressures from above that
militate against excellence – that they are increasingly being asked
to fit into scheduling formulas. Do you think there is any truth in
this?*

I don't think so, no. Mind you, it's always difficult to tell. At one
time I was below and I felt that the pressure from above was
appalling. Now I'm above and I feel that there is no over-pressure
from above but a certain lack of pressure from below. Pressure is
a funny thing, because what you want nowadays is not simply
more programmes. At one time, when BBC 1 hours were gradually increasing and BBC 2 was starting, what you needed was
simply additional programmes. Good ones, if possible, of course;
but above all more programmes. If there was pressure from somebody you were only too pleased. 'Thank God, we can now fill up
Tuesday evenings on BBC in March.' But today, it's tougher,
because BBC 1 and BBC 2 are full of established programmes,
and if something new is going to come on, it must come at the cost
of something else. This needs real pressure, and not simply a
shouting match. If you want to replace *The Money Programme* or
*Softly, Softly* or *Europa* or *Sportsnight With Coleman* you need to
have a very strong programme idea indeed. These programmes

are not so easily pushed aside. It needs the pressure of actual brilliance, and brilliance does not grow on trees.

On the whole, I think that the way in which programmes claw themselves on to the air is reasonably satisfactory. When I was a producer I did not think so, although things were much easier in those days. In that sense the situation remains very much what it was. Any theory that ten years ago producers were always terribly pleased with the schedules is nonsense. They kicked against them then, as they kick against them now. Quite right too. It's like publishers and writers or editors and reporters. Each think evil thoughts of the other! Having been both, this seems to me not only unavoidable but actively desirable. In other words, you need pressure from below.

*As a result of the McKinsey recommendations the BBC has intro-duced a system of total costing so that individual programmes are charged a true porportion of the overheads. This should allow a more flexible use of resources. Many people fear that it will also lead to a more flexible use of staff, through casualization. Does the BBC plan to use more freelance staff?*

Not in the immediate future. Who can tell what'll happen in three or four years' time? At the moment, I think we've got a reasonable balance. There are established staff producers and there are short-term contracts. And then there are temporary contracts. Now from all sorts of points of view, you need, as it seems to me, all three. And the question of making the correct equation between the one and the other is always a tricky one. Round about 30 per cent of our people across the board on the programme side are either temporary or short-term contracts, and round about 70 per cent staff contracts. There is no policy which involves changing that. If, however, you are anxious about any short-term or tem-porary contracts question at all, let me say this: you always need a certain amount of temporary work. I certainly couldn't have done *Monitor* if I hadn't been able to bring in this chap for three months to try and that chap for six weeks to try and in that way all sorts of people were brought into the operation, some of whom became staff and some didn't. I personally have always thought it a good thing to have a greater number of temporary contracts among the very junior – among research assistants and young production assistants. My experience suggests to me that when you meet somebody and work with him for three or four months perhaps, even in that period, it is not easy to know whether he is likely to be a good producer or good editor or a good film editor or a good programme executive or whatever. What is more, it is very difficult for the people themselves to know. From that point of view, the notion that you no sooner walk into this place than you become established staff is a very dangerous one. Of course, the situation has changed over the years. When I was Head of Documentaries, it was quite difficult to find really good documentary makers outside the Department itself. Now the situation is different – I don't want to deny the possibility of Jack Gold or Kevin Billington or Ken Russell or Jonathan Miller or Patrick Garland or whoever making programmes. That is to say, there are now an awful lot of very good directors and producers outside the BBC (most of them BBC-trained as a matter of interest). It is a new phenomenon. And they are pressing at the gates. They want to make occasional programmes. We want them to make occasional programmes. I think that's reasonable. What we must not do, however, is move from the broad 70/30 basis unless we do it with the greatest consideration, and that would take a long time. We have not started on any such examination, at the moment.

*What does the public service role of the BBC mean to you?*

It is difficult to talk about it without the justifiable accusation of insufferable complacency – and I can only grope my way towards it by references to the two-channel operation, to the foundation of the licence fee, and so on. Because in so far as the BBC is any good, it is not I think because Mr A. is so marvellous or Mr B. is so wonderful. On the contrary, they're quite frequently not all that hot. It's the organizational foundation that makes it possible to work well and achieve excellence. The older I get and the more I knock about the world, and see television and broadcasting, the more I get the feeling that overwhelmingly it is committed to the second rate. It is very largely either propaganda, with a bit of entertainment pushed into it, or pap, with a bit of news and current affairs pushed into it. The power of money and the power of government play upon broadcasting organizations all over the world. And this is what emerges all the time – that it is either pap or propaganda. Now, coming to the insufferable complacency stakes, I do not actually believe that the BBC has ever been a very propagandist organization, nor one devoted to pap. I do believe that we put on a certain amount of pap. And yet it's awfully difficult to say what the pap is. I wouldn't say that a series by definition was pap. *Softly, Softly* is not, in my opinion, pap. On the other hand, I actually feel quite frequently that documentaries and so-called serious programmes are more frequently pap in the sense of being clichés, or statements in a fashionable mould, than are many so-called light programmes. So of course, there is pap. Which is again an aspect of mediocrity. Given that there is pap, however, the thing that impresses me all the time is the capacity for excellence. Whether it's *Harry Worth* or whether it's *Billy Budd* or whether it's *The World About Us* or whether it's *Chronicle* or whether it's *Dud and Pete*, the capacity for excellence is constantly reaffirmed. The singularity of the Corporation does lie in this – that its foundation, the licence situation plus the two-channel television operation and the multi-channel operation both on sound and here, allow excellence to be courted. We often fail but sometimes we don't fail and that itself is so singular that I believe it is unbelievably important to keep governments and commercial power at bay.

*Of course, one wants to keep commercialism at bay and government at bay, but the problem is how you do it.*

When the chips are down – if it is true that in most parts of the world you can feel the existence of the committed second rate and that here you can feel the possibility of the first rate – then what you have here is not to be lightly or tritely dismissed. On the contrary, it is what has to be defended.

*You said that television is taken, rightly or wrongly, as being powerful. Do you think television really matters?*

It undoubtedly matters. If people – the very old and the very young, widows and children and professors of statistics and dustmen – if they spend eight or nine hours a week watching television, which is a very minimal number, it cannot not be important. To what degree it changes the attitude of the nation towards the world or of people towards the world, who can tell? People have tended to think that it is much more powerful than it is. It doesn't change a Conservative into a Socialist. Probably, in human terms, it comes down to the everlasting situation that what you get out of things depends very largely on the type of person you are. If what you want is vulgarity, then you will find vulgarity. If what you want is sensitivity, then you will find sensitivity. We make sufficient programmes that are good in their own right to be factors of experience which are agreeable. Wise men learn more from fools than fools do from wise men. And wise men will certainly learn from BBC television when it is good, and when it is bad or indifferent; and if it's good they learn a bit more.

*The sheer size of the BBC is clearly beginning to cause problems. Do you think the BBC should be split up?*

BBC Television Service is in itself fairly big with 6,000 people. But if I had to choose between having a smaller Television Service running one network and a Television Service as big as it is running two, I would certainly go for the latter. The cost of a two-channel operation is size and although being big is difficult, I think the cost is worth it, because a two-channel operation is absolutely essential.

*It could presumably be organized with two channels joined only at the scheduling level?*

I don't think it could. Quite apart from being very much more costly (which is a huge factor incidentally) there is great gain to be got from the fact that everybody here is serving the BBC Television Service. A two-channel operation, unless it is complementary absolutely right across the board, in terms of servicing and construction as well as in terms of scheduling, is not really a two-channel operation. It may be easier to go back to radio and see it at a distance. I think if the old Home Service had been run from Broadcasting House and the old Light Programme had been run from Daventry and the old Third Programme had been run from Cambridge, I don't think that sound radio would have been as good and as brilliantly inventive as it was. I also believe, in the final analysis, that you are forced into an absolutely definite policy choice between being competitive or complementary. You can't be partly one and partly the other. They are attempting that in Sweden. And we'll see whether it'll work. I can't believe that it will. If you're going to be complementary so that you can handle contemporary plays, classics, series, classical series, serials and classical plays and so on in such a way as to cover the waterfront, then I believe you need two channels on which to operate, both in terms of choice and in terms of the spectrum. If you had a second BBC drama outfit operating from Edinburgh, then in the end it would have to be competitive.

*Yes, creatively competitive.*

It doesn't matter what word you put in front of it. Once you move into competition, it is competition. The huge example is NBC, CBS, ABC, competition in the States where competition means literally competition right across the board: Western against Western, news against news, contemporary play against contemporary play, film against film and so on and so forth. Above all, it means limitation of spectrum. You don't cover so wide a waterfront.

*But you wouldn't be competing in that sense if you were planning two channels as complementary. You would only be competing in the sense that a playwright would have a choice of two Heads of Drama.*

That exists already with the ITA set-up. But once you allow competition to come into the BBC in your sense and muck up the complementary foundation, you in fact muck up the operational spectrum. You can't avoid it. You'd have a Head of Drama on BBC 2 who could not abide not to be contemporary because how can you be a Head of Drama and not do contemporary plays? You'd equally have a Head of Drama on BBC 1 who also could not abide not doing contemporary plays. You have not got room for contemporary plays competing against each other. It is unthinkable to me that a good television service should not have contemporary plays written by contemporary authors on contemporary issues. But you have also got to have classics. You have also got to have series, which in my opinion has brought out some of the best writing on television so far. In order to be able to handle this whole spectrum and make sure that you do everything, you need two channels so that the scheduling operation then becomes a process of choice as between programme and programme across a wide front, not between spectrum and spectrum, both limited. Equally, directors and producers and designers and the rest need to be able to move from one to another. It is important that a director on, say, *The Expert* should be able to do a *Thirty-Minute Theatre* or part of a classical serial. It is part of the nourishment of the Service. For really good complementary programming you need conjoint activity running right through. Given that, you have some chance of meeting the immense demands which the public, quite rightly, puts on BBC television; and of meeting the immense demands which BBC television, equally rightly, makes upon its producers and engineers and designers and film editors, indeed, on its staff in general.

# Paul Fox

Controller of Programmes, BBC 1.

*You are responsible for one of the main national television channels. What considerations govern what goes out, when and so on?*

There are certain landmarks around which the schedule is built and you start from there. The landmarks include things like the News, *Panorama*, *Omnibus*, the *Tuesday Documentary*, the weekly play, variety on Saturday and a number of feature films.

*These are inherited landmarks?*

Traditional landmarks. One of the facts about schedule building is that there is never a clean piece of paper, that the *status quo* really is the key thing. You've got, as I say, traditional things, that are there because certain programmes work on certain days and don't work on other days. *Panorama* has been traditionally on a Monday for fifteen years – because it happens to work on Monday. I think if one moved it to another day it would not necessarily work. The same thing applies to other programmes.

*Would you like a clean sheet of paper?*

The only time there was a clean sheet of paper was when BBC 2 started, and I would not have thought that the first schedule of BBC 2 was a very effective sample. I think it's very difficult to start totally from scratch. There are certain things that have got to be there. The News is obviously one. One would like to get the News to another time. One of the problems the BBC faces is that we work in twenty-five- and fifty-minute modules and, therefore, you can never get to the hour or the half-hour. Therefore you get all these odd timings like the News at ten to nine and something else at 9.10, and I do not think that that is very satisfactory.

*Why does the BBC work in twenty-five- and fifty-minute modules?*

Because of the imported programmes and, of course, no commercials. This is the international length. If we want to sell anything at all we must sell it in twenty-five- and fifty-minute time segments – modules. Those are, unhappily, the internationally recognized time periods.

*At what stage do you look at ITV schedules?*

I think the process is our landmarks first, new programmes that come in, the quality of our programmes, then the competition. Obviously one will change occasionally to meet the competition. I keep one eye on the competitor's schedule and if they change or do something to oppose us, OK, one will try and move against them. Take an example. The *Tuesday Documentary* could easily be moved from Tuesday at 9.10. It's in a very exposed position really, up against things like Tom Jones and now *Family at War*, and if one were bothered by what the competition put against one I suppose one would move it to Thursday where it's in a slightly more protected position. I try and protect new programmes by putting them between two fairly strong established programmes. I prefer this to worrying about what the competition does.

*Are there any circumstances under which you go out to try and slam one of theirs?*

More on events really. I think on sport and public events one will make a major effort to compete hard, possibly by having better build-up, by starting earlier, things like that. Better inheritance. The inheritance factor is a key thing. Take things like the Cup Final or Elections or Budget programmes. I think one will make

233

an effort to provide a good lead in to that programme and, therefore, hope that the audience will come with one to the main event.

*Do you think, because of the rules of scheduling and the pressures of peak time viewing, that competition makes ITV and BBC more and more alike?*

A lot of nonsense is being aired now about similarity in look and feel between BBC 1 and ITV. There isn't any channel, any network that can do a regular Play of the Month such as *The Three Sisters*, such as *Howards End*, and then follow it with an *Omnibus* programme every Sunday night. How anybody can say that that is like ITV Sundays is talking nonsense. Come back to the *Tuesday Documentary*, a documentary not at 10.30 at night where ITV place it occasionally, but at 9.10. A regular spot for the *Wednesday Play*; it is the only spot where there is new and contemporary writing done every week. I think one's just got to look at the schedule, look at individual nights to see that there's a considerable difference between BBC 1 and ITV.

*There seems to be a clash between journalism and show-biz. Do you find that?*

I would have thought there were about four or five or half a dozen attitudes, all fighting to get programmes on to the screen. The arts people will fight, they'll want to get their things on. *Omnibus*, ideally, feels that it ought to be at 9.30 on Sunday night and there should not be any opposition on BBC 2. Why have *Rowan and Martin* against it, or why have *The World About Us* against it. There should be nothing against it by and large. And the same thing is true of the *Tuesday Documentary*. They worry now, they say *Family at War* is against us. They don't want anything there; they certainly don't want Morecambe and Wise there. Obviously all sides are fighting to get the best possible placings for their programmes, and why shouldn't they? I'd be very unhappy if they didn't scream blue murder and said, 'Oh, you're putting us on too late.' I mean, *24 Hours* will complain every day that they're on at 10.30 at night.

*You think that's healthy?*

I think it's a reasonable attitude that everybody wants to be on

234

earlier and in a better place, wants to have more time, wants to have more money. Why shouldn't they?

*But you have to balance out these pressures. How do you decide between giving the audience what it wants and what is good for them?*

It comes back to the fact that there are certain parts of the BBC 1 schedule which I won't give up lightly. There are certain things one says, 'OK, these things are going to be here and we're going to do the best possible job with these programmes, we're going to do them well, we're going to promote them well and they're going to have a run at that particular time.'

*Regardless of ratings?*

Not entirely regardless of ratings. I think it would be absurd to say regardless of ratings, because there are certain programmes maybe in a wrong time period or on the wrong day, and one may say, well, it doesn't work because it doesn't work on this particular day. Try and shift it to another day and it'll do better, or try and give it a better lead-in programme or a better programme following it so that it may work better then. I think it would be absurd to put a documentary out at eight o'clock. I think a documentary programme is suitable for ten past nine after the News. To a considerable extent one goes by one's own tastes, after all, when oneself is ready for that type of programme. It would be out of the question to put the *Wednesday Play* on at eight o'clock; quite apart from the watershed situation of wanting to put certain adult types of programmes after the News, I think it is the wrong time for it. The evenings do start much earlier now. Just because we in London feel that we're never home before 7.30 or eight o'clock in this job, or in London anyway, we feel that programmes early in the evening are sort of pap stuff. I'm surprised – delighted really – how well *Nationwide* has done early in the evening, even though I can't really see it at home.

*Sitting at your desk with big decisions to make about what sort of programmes go out, do you feel that you have to bring any social or even moral considerations into what you're doing?*

Yes, absolutely. Certainly there are restrictions, one has inhibitions. Some of them are reflected in the time period one ought to

235

put a programme out, others are reflected in saying, 'Well, I don't think this programme is suitable for going out at all at any time.' I have inhibitions about mixing fact and fiction, really because one has been brought up, trained, as a journalist. To my mind this is a far more worrying thing in television than sex or violence.

*Why?*

Because I think mixing fact and fiction knocks and denigrates the whole integrity and authority of the BBC. One of the great things we've got going for us is the authority and the truthfulness of the News and Current Affairs services, and if we start mixing fact and fiction I think we lose that credibility. It then endangers the whole News output, and people then really cannot distinguish between fact and fiction any more. I'm all in favour of dramatic experiments but I think there's got to be a limit to them.

*Have there been rulings laid down on this subject?*

No. It's just a feeling I have, my own view really.

*Given that personal feeling, to what extent can you impose your taste on your output departments?*

Obviously one doesn't like everything that goes out on the screen. One's got one's personal taste.

*But, widening the issue, the Heads of Departments are very powerful barons. Do you say, 'I want so many plays, so many light entertainment, so many documentaries', and trust them to get on with them, or can you influence what each single documentary is about?*

No, of course not. It's a process that evolves over the year. There are two or three big sessions in the year known as the Offers Meetings when Head of Output Groups and Output Departments will come and offer X, Y and Z in their particular fields. They will know in advance how many productions I can take, how many plays I can take, how many documentaries I can take, how many comedy programmes I can take. It's up to them then to get on with it. As you say, they're powerful people, that's their job. We discuss the question of money and lengths and facilities and so on, but the content of what goes into the *Wednesday Play*, what goes into the *Tuesday Documentary* is up to those chaps who are running the Departments. I would not dream of interfering with them.


# Robin Scott

Controller of Programmes, BBC 2.

*To what extent can you actually influence and control what goes out on your channel?*

Well, obviously one can and does. It is of course a fact that when you get translated to a position of considerable responsibility of this kind, when you get lifted as it were off the studio floor, to some people you become more remote because anybody who takes decisions in terms of other people's work is bound to have some remoteness; you also become invested with a kind of papal authority in some respects which clearly no single person is entitled to have in all sincerity. The important thing in exercising control is to retain the confidence of the professionals you are working with and on whom the network depends. A controller does not run a network by the negative process of using his 'power of refusal' – but by positive acceptance of the best offers and suggestions or by encouraging the teams of producers and directors through their departmental chiefs to tackle new ideas and formats. All that, in fact, one is trying to do is to encourage the best talent and the best ideas and to develop them within the realistic framework that you have to work within, the realisms being money and general policy, available talent, what people can do and are capable of doing, the number of hours which you can broadcast and so on.

*Do you feel yourself considerably limited or do you regard the problem as one of freedom and what to do with it?*

Well, there are a number of restrictions but not in terms of 'freedom'. The first restriction is the number of hours; the second restriction is the amount of money available: these are banal restrictions which everybody knows about. The third restriction, but I think it's a justified and proper restriction, is the one which requires one, partly because of Pilkington, partly because it's developed in that way, to provide alternative programming and complementary programming to BBC 1 which happens most of the time to be complementary programming to ITV, although the programme junctions, of course, don't relate to ITV's programming.

*What you put out on your channel is very much governed by what goes out on BBC 1 because it was there first and it's got national coverage.*

Yes. And the main problem is to achieve a good 'vertical' pattern of programming whilst observing the 'horizontal' alternative requirements.

*Do you, therefore, get the schedules from Paul Fox before you do your schedules?*

Yes. And if he makes an advance change, then I will know about it. I know his exact pattern at least six months ahead. Though we both decide on our 'programme mix' up to a year ahead. But that doesn't mean to say that we're not going to make a lot of changes, both of us, and that maybe the unexpected will happen and there'll be a sudden complete revision of BBC 1's pattern for very good reasons, some big event or maybe it's a public holiday and Paul feels the need to juggle the schedules completely. Then it's a question of whether I react immediately, or whether I say, 'Well, no. Actually that programme always goes out at that time on BBC 2. Why should I change it for the people who watch it simply because what is now the alternative on BBC 1 is different from normal?' Sometimes I 'chase' and sometimes I don't and I have to justify myself each time if I don't.

*What has experience led the BBC to consider legitimate alternatives? Are there rules such as heavy Current Affairs opposite light entertainment, sport opposite drama?*

No, there aren't and I moved drama actually. It used to be on a Tuesday night opposite *Tuesday Documentary*, I felt it would be better as an alternative to sport and so I moved what used to be *Theatre 625* and now is the regular BBC 2 drama play, to Thursday night opposite the Coleman sports programme, and the figures went up. I may be quite wrong, but I have a feeling that we did better with *Henry VIII* opposite the sports programme than we would have done on a Tuesday night opposite the documentary.

*Now what made you feel that it was a better alternative?*

It was based on the notion that you should not put drama opposite drama, story-telling opposite story-telling – as some documentary is. However, it doesn't always work out to my complete satisfaction. The placing of the BBC 2 series *The Borderers* – and more recently *Codename* – is a case in point. I planned for a Tuesday run and it was tied in with a whole lot of complicated scheduling; when the BBC 1 film moved to Tuesday evening from Wednesday I found that I was in an impasse and I couldn't respond, because I couldn't move *Borderers* to anywhere better, where I didn't find myself also against 'story-telling'. It meant a radical change in the schedule which after using up a whole lot of paper I decided wasn't possible.

*How far ahead do you have the ITV schedules?*

I don't see them until *TV Times* is printed and I wouldn't (and couldn't) work on them anyway. There are far too many regional variations for a start. I only exceptionally avoid certain programme times because ITV is doing something similar. For instance I knew when the Thames *Dickens* programme was scheduled so I avoided a clash. And it would be absurd to place *Review* opposite *Aquarius*. My schedule is planned in function of BBC 1. I can't do a double thing with ITV.

*The normal philosophy of scheduling, as I understand it, is to build a nice audience curve which reaches a peak and goes away. Now if Channel 1 is doing that, you're committed almost to breaking all the normal rules of scheduling.*

Yes.

*Is this very frustrating or is there any way of getting over this?*

We have a particular weekend problem because Saturday evenings are generally considered to be entertainment evenings. This is the British way of life, Sunday morning is for reflection with coffee and the newspapers and Saturday evening is for sheer forget-it-all and if sheer forget-it-all type programming is going on on BBC 1, and justifiably so, then what do I do? Put equally forget-it-all escapist type material on 2? The answer is no, because even though the audience may be relatively small it is one of the purposes and advantages – the privileges of the network – to be able to offer a different pattern of programmes to a selective audience which finds entertainment and pleasure in other ways. But when BBC 2 goes for a 90- or 120-minute special programme – like a full opera or ballet or major documentaries such as *The Violent Universe* or *The Mind of Man* (which Philip Daly is producing – with large co-production involvement – for autumn 1970) then I will devote almost a full evening on the network to it – running right through programme junctions. BBC 2 is after all a network in *its own right* – and increasingly so. David Attenborough set this precedent – just as he inspired much of the programming which brought BBC 2 to maturity – and I welcome bold strokes of this kind.

*We all feel that 2 is a minority academic channel – for things that won't get as many viewers. If it's likely to get a lot of viewers, put it on 1.*

Yes, I think academic is the wrong word, because, in fact, theatre is minority, good cinema is minority. A lot of good talk is minority. Programmes about history are minority in a way unless you dress them up and call them *The Six Wives of Henry VIII* – or present them like *Chronicle* does. And one shouldn't expect that one will have large audiences for everything. When I hear it said that BBC 2 has been a flop because it doesn't attract big audiences, you can't in fact have it both ways. You can't on the one hand demand that there should be a network which exists partly for 'serious' programming, for what people claim to be the good things that are worth talking about, excluding most of what is described as trivial, and yet expect big audiences. I think, in fact, that you have to steer a middle course saying, for instance, we will go for an audience here and we'll love to have it and if at the same time the programme that follows gets twice as many customers as it would otherwise that's splendid. Actually, it's not difficult to get big audiences – with feature films, for instance. But I'm sure that if *Civilization* had just been part of a universally 'grey' output, however worthy, that the audience for *Civilization* and the attention paid to the programme would not have been as great. Instead of that, there's the *Morecambe and Wise Show* one week and there's *Pete and Dud* the next and they switch on by the million. All right, some of them don't like the *Wednesday Play*, they switch to *Morecambe and Wise* and they're surprised to find *The Six Wives of Henry VIII* is marvellous and it gets over 20 per cent of the BBC 2 audience which on other networks would be ten million plus. If you can give the impression that the door is open then maybe people will watch other things. To that extent it's a kind of Reithian principle, if you like, which derives from the programming policy of BBC 2 which is to provide alternatives, but which enables the network to provide a wider range of programmes than any other I know.

# David Attenborough

Director of Programmes, BBC TV.

*How do you perceive the function of public service broadcasting?*

The first thing to say is that it should be crucially different from any other form of broadcasting. It is not the same as government broadcasting; it is not the same as commercial broadcasting. My working model is that, like a publishing house, it should find from the community in which it is rooted the voices that are most interesting, most amusing, most prophetic, most gifted, most informed, most significant – the list is immense – and that it should provide the wherewithal, the technical facility, for those voices to be heard by the rest of the community. That, of course, is a very different thing from simply reflecting the community. These voices are selected – and that, of course, is the editorial problem which a public service broadcasting system, like a publishing house, must face. But I would add that one of the measures of the success of the system is the range and variety of the voices it relays. Within the limits of the laws of the land about libel, and so on, and paying proper regard to the sensitivities of the audience, that you have no right to gratuitously offend, those voices should be allowed to speak in as untrammelled a way as possible.

*But there isn't, for example, any direct way minority groups in our community can be on television without going through this highly facile broadcasting process. Is there a case, supposing there were several million Jehovah's Witnesses, to say to the Jehovah's Witnesses there is a programme – you represent so many people – have that programme? Like they do in Holland.*

Yes. I think there is. We do it to a certain extent in *One Pair of Eyes*. The trouble about giving a programme to three million Jehovah's Witnesses is deciding who actually produces the programme. Certainly not a committee of those taking part. No good programme would ever be made by a committee. So one person in the end produces. And he has to be technically competent. *One Pair of Eyes* reflects individual points of view. We also represent group interests in other programmes – indeed Jehovah's Witnesses did put their case in a programme with Muggeridge. They had thirty-five minutes – which is not bad – to talk seriously about what they believed.

*Because television producers tend to be drawn from a liberal humanist élite, do you think there is a danger of unconscious censorship?*

If the BBC were what a lot of people think it is – an organization which produces nothing but messages from within its own vitals, which broadcasts in a patronizing way to a populace which simply lies inert and has programmes sprayed over it – then I would agree with you. But in fact there are many television producers in this building whose job is not to project *their* views but to get the views of doctors, bankers, teachers, coal miners and whoever and make sure they do get on to the air in as untrammelled a way as possible. There *is* certainly a danger that we might produce nothing but programmes in our own image – but one is doing one's best to try and prevent such a thing from happening.

*In large areas of broadcasting, surely, you are not going out and finding voices, you are creating entertainment to popular demand. How do you relate the two?*

242

Galton and Simpson's voices *are* voices from the community. They are also marvellously entertaining. It is our responsibility to find more Galtons and Simpsons – and Martys. They say a great deal of things which have quite profound importance and reflect attitudes which are not BBC attitudes. Now, of course, there is a certain amount of undemanding television of no particular significance. Nor do I disapprove of it. I am quite sure that the pace at which a great number of people live means that when they get home, they don't actually want another deep, profound, soul-searching, stimulating examination of the decimal system. Why shouldn't they have Sing-along with somebody or other, or indeed why shouldn't they have over-the-fence gossip in a daily serial? I see no reason why they should not. It seems to me a perfectly proper palliative to the frenetic pressures of the day. It would only be wrong if all programmes were that.

Voices like Galton and Simpson's are first heard because there are producers in a comedy department who are interested in comedy writing and who either should or do know where all the best talent in this particular sphere is. It is their job to be out and around and try and find it, and encourage it. Monty Python came, not from me, not from a network controller, not from the Head of Light Entertainment group, but from a perceptive energetic producer who saw talent around. That's what it's about. No one man, no matter how polymathic and inspired, can possibly handle by himself the job of discovering all kinds of new talent.

*But the editorial problem remains. How do you balance what your producers think is good and valuable and what the audience thinks is good and valuable, because they are so often different?*

The audience doesn't think anything good or valuable. That's far too big a generalization. The only meaningful way of examining such questions is to consider what proportion of the audience thinks what. But accepting the generalization for the moment, there is certainly a pull on the one hand to get vast audiences, and, on the other, to do something which you are interested in because you are a broadcaster. The BBC calculates the total audience split over a week. At the moment, according to our figures, the share is 52 per cent to ITV, 48 per cent to us. I don't mind whether it's the other way. As a matter of fact, I don't really mind whether it's

40 per cent to us and 60 per cent to them; or indeed 60 per cent to us and 40 per cent to them. What I mind very much is if it is only 30 per cent to us and 70 per cent to them, because then I know that vast numbers of people in this country who by law are compelled to pay money to the BBC are not getting their money's worth. They are not getting enough programmes that they wish to enjoy. On the other hand, if it were 70 per cent to us and 30 per cent to them, I would equally believe that we weren't being daring enough, that we were relying on well-tried propositions and we ought to be trying new things and chancing our arm a bit more. I agree it's purely a arbitrary way of looking at the thing, but it is a useful yardstick. Nor is it something I've just dreamed up; it is a proposition that is well known to heads of departments.

*Supposing it drops down to 40 and you'd like to get it up to 50, how do you set about getting it up again?*

The art of scheduling is not as mysterious as all that. You can improve those figures, at least in the short term, by artful changes in the schedules. For example, if you have two feature films on both networks the one that starts first will, by and large, win unless you have an enormous puller just beforehand. I can think of a particular night now where that happens. The BBC film starts three-quarters of an hour later than the ITV one. If we wished, we could bring it forward, by putting the three-quarters-of-an-hour serial that now precedes it at the end of the evening. We would increase the audience of the film by doing so, without question. So why do we not? Well, in the first place because a lot of people like to have a fixed starting time to their forty-five-minute serial. It is convenient for them. If you put it at the end of the film – because we don't cut films to fit time slots – the serial would start sometimes at 9.45 and sometimes at 9.30 and sometimes at 9.55 and people would be fed up about it. I don't say the majority would, but quite a substantial number. Secondly, there are quite a number of people who like to have their meal and then watch something after dinner. Now, if you start your film at 7.25 they are denied a choice of joining until later in the evening – that is to say if they have only got BBC 1 and ITV. If they don't start viewing at 7.25 they have had it for ninety minutes. So we didn't make the change, even though we know that it costs viewers. There are plenty of other things that you can do, but by and large the competition between us and ITV is not as cut-throat as many people would have us believe. It is intense in a professional sense in that, for example, we are keen that we should do sport better than they should. But ITV equally know that they could increase their audience by doing certain things, by, for example, not scheduling such documentaries as they do schedule or by taking *This Week* out of peak hours and putting it on late at night.

There are three ways of getting a bigger audience. One is the scheduling jiggery-pokery I've just described. This certainly can bring a temporary change but not a fundamental shift because the other side is then forced to adopt similar tactics and you end up largely where you were. A second way is to change the content of the mix – the kinds of programme in the schedule. The third way is to make the same programmes better or more popular. I say 'or' because I don't actually believe that there is any correlation of any sort whatever between audience size and quality.

*Many people working in television feel that the BBC has grown too big, that lines of communication are too long. What problems does the size of the BBC present you with?*

When we were small, a producer went along to the head of his department, or even to the Head of the Television Service, and asked for what he wanted in terms of cash or scenery or studios or whatever. The Head of Television then doled out what he was asked for, if he could, from his central pool of technical facilities and money. But then, as we grew, the facilities became so enormous and so varied that the whole planning operation became vastly complex. As a result, producers began to feel it was getting very impersonal. Furthermore, below-the-line facilities were, as you might say, up for grabs, and nobody really calculated what they cost in pounds, shillings and pence. One of the things we have done recently is to make everything required for programme production – not just those bits requiring the expenditure of cash – measurable in financial terms. Producers are then given budgets, and within certain rules have the freedom to spend their money within those budgets in whatever way they want.

Size also affects what you might call ethos. In the old days, all producers had a pretty clear idea of the general policies of the BBC on all sorts of matters, because everybody knew everybody else. Now there are 6,000 people here. There are about 350 producers alone. Furthermore, a new kind of producer has appeared who is not interested in the ethos of any broadcasting organization. He is only interested in his own programme. Nor does he mind who buys it – as long as it is bought. And who am I to say that such a man shouldn't exist? At any rate, there is now a shifting body of producers. Years ago there was, without any question, a very acute sensitivity amongst all producers as to what the BBC's view was about bullfighting, or programmes on Eire, where you stood about advertising, where you stood about obscenity and so on. People imbibed it as they joined and after a year they were BBC people who knew what the BBC form was. But that is no longer the case. The need is greater than ever; the obstacles are also greater than ever. So people, such as myself, who are responsible for nurturing the ethos must be around and must be available, must go to departmental meetings, must arrange seminars, and so on.

*Do you think the growth of a body of freelance producers is a healthy development?*

I think that it would be a nice thing if it were possible for a man to earn a living as a free voice, speaking in the language of video-tape or film, and finding places where his voice could be heard whether it was on the BBC, on ITV, or whether it was in the commercial cinema, or the underground cinema. It seems to me that one of the dangers of the BBC when it had a monopoly – and I was a member of it in the monopoly days – was that once you got into the BBC you never left. It wasn't because you were so cowardly or timorous. It was simply that there wasn't any other job. If you were a director of electronic cameras in 1953 and you actually enjoyed it, and you fell out with the BBC, whether on personal grounds or policy grounds, you had had it. I don't think that's a healthy situation.

*Many would say that the BBC is such a dominant employer that the situation is still unhealthy. Do you think one should pursue the logic of freelancing and split the BBC into competing creative groups?*

No, I don't think so. There is a great illusion about the mono-lithic nature of the BBC. If ever it was monolithic once, it is cer-tainly not so now. There are plenty of examples of people who didn't get on in one department and who have wanted to move to another department and did. It wasn't the network controller, the great man in the middle, who put the black spot on him and decreed that he will not be a member of this organization. The BBC is a collection of small empires. Nor am I in favour of competing creative groups for the sake of competition. One of the fundamental truths of broadcasting, it seems to me, is that com-petition leads to similarity. I imagine that there were naïve people who thought that by introducing independent television, you were providing a choice. Competition produces similarity. The United States provides the most extreme example. The only way to get variety in broadcasting is to have one body which provides a shelter as it were for a great deal of different activities – some more popular, some less – and that's what in fact the BBC is supposed to be doing. I believe it would be useful for certain people to have an opportunity to freelance. But I am absolutely clear on my own part that the majority of the people who work for the BBC wish to see the BBC as their career, and should be able to do so if they want to.

*What effect do you think imminent technological developments like cable systems, satellites and cassettes will have on the future of BBC television?*

As far as cassettes are concerned, I don't think they will have any more impact on the BBC than long-playing records have had on radio. The second proposition is that there is the multi-channel cable. Now if this means that the audiences for the great television networks are to be eroded away to a stage where those networks could not continue in their present form, then I would be very worried. There is what you might call a baboon theory of com-munications. A troop of baboons remains one troop as long as a baboon on one side can communicate very quickly with a baboon on the other. If a lookout warns of an enemy, the whole troop can immediately respond. Now if the troop gets so big that the chap on the one side can't be heard by the other side – then very soon you get two troops. I think it is true to say that one reason this

247

country has remained one country in spite of the vast increase in population and also increasing economic and political freedoms is that the media of mass communication have grown commensurately. Now Edinburgh hears what Exeter hears; middle-aged conservatives are aware of what radical students are protesting about – and, equally important, students hear the views of the middle-aged. And that includes drama as well as current affairs. If you break down broadcasting so that you don't have one, two or indeed three national services, but fifty small independent voices, then the nation no longer is aware of its component parts and of what is happening to it.

In all this talk about having fifty or a hundred channels by cable there is one enormous element that's often ignored – the economic factor. What is economic to show on these networks? However much one would like to pretend otherwise, quality programming depends a great deal on the amount of cash that is available. If you have fifty stations all broadcasting, each one of them must reckon to get a fairly substantial audience if it is to survive financially. That would be difficult enough if the system was immediately available to the entire population, but it will take a long time to build up. If they decide you can send it all through the gas main or something, so that immediately fifty-four million people in this country can see fifty channels, then it might be viable.

*Television seems to be under pressure from the politicians. Is this because they have started to tumble to the political force of television?*

I think the political force of television is greatly overrated. Television, by and large, reinforces existing views and existing tendencies. This exposes one of the fallacies in one argument going on about violence on television. Some politician in the United States said, 'The broadcasters expect us to believe that you can show soap powder on commercials and so persuade people to buy it; and yet when they show so much violence, they expect us to believe that people are unaffected.' The point about commercials is that they operate by reinforcing known likes. When there isn't a likeable characteristic of your product, then you link it to something that *is* a known like. So that lavatory paper becomes identified with flower petals and motherhood becomes the same

248

thing as margarine. I don't know of a single example anywhere where people have been shown to be made to like something if they started off by actively disliking it. That is why I remain unconvinced when they say that showing violence encourages people to be violent who otherwise would not be so.

*Certainly a lot of people would allege that you report a students' revolt on television and six more universities say, 'Look what they're doing up the road – why don't we do it?'*

I think that proposition is arguable. Within large and complex societies, it is very important that a minority group has a platform from which its voice can be heard by the majority. If you deny a platform to that minority then it will, in fact, grab a platform in the most violent way. I suspect that one of the reasons why the Sorbonne students actually had to burn down part of their building before they were heard was because there was no voice from any Sorbonne student heard on television, or in the newspapers, before it happened. Similarly in America. You didn't see groups of long-haired protesters on American television before the Berkeley riots. The fact that television here did provide a platform on which students could speak their prejudices, their moans, their objections, their worries, their aspirations, may well be one of the reasons why, in fact, student protests in this country are relatively peaceful.

*What then is the role of television in either facilitating or checking the rate of social change?*

I think it facilitates social change, whether we like it or not. To take an extreme example, if you go back 300 years to Jacobean times somebody could have a riot up in the north of Scotland and it didn't have any effect whatever on London, until some chap on a horse with a letter belted down there, which may have taken a week. Well, now we actually see it happen. So of course it speeds change. In other areas, however, it may reinforce existing attitudes. These enormous generalizations are very dangerous. What television should do is make society aware of itself and the changes that are going on within it.

JOAN BAKEWELL

# 10 · ITV Executives

The state of mind of ITV executives at the moment stems from the tension between commercialism and principle. That is not to say that the private enterprise programme companies represent only commercialism and the public guardians of standards, the ITA, represents principle. Far from it. The interplay of responsibilities is far more complex than that. But it is inherent in the structure of ITV since its beginning.

The Television Act of 1954 set up the ITA as the public body controlling the new commercial channel, to build, own and operate the transmitters, appoint the programme companies and control the standards of both advertising and programmes. This was and is a non-profit-making body appointed from among men and women in public life by the Minister of Posts and Telecommunications. It was a compromise solution to safeguard our commercial channel from the evils of sponsorship and runaway commercialism.

Indeed, had the companies been created without the watch-dog supervision of the ITA and been able to declare an intention of making as much profit as possible by going only for ratings, then the situation would have been much clearer. The fact that it isn't results from four factors: the powers written into the Act for the ITA, the federal structure of the companies, the limited duration of the licence which makes the companies answerable for their policies, and the fact that a number of ITV executives were formerly programme-makers with professional instincts for programme content and scheduling. The conflict in ITV continues to be between profit and broadcasting standards as the fundamental justification of its existence. The critical problems of ITV today can be traced to an interplay of these forces. First financial: the

250

fact that a number of companies in ITV are not making a profit, are not returning a dividend and are worrying about survival is a known state of affairs. The reasons given to the press are also familiar but we should perhaps examine their plausibility.

First, company incomes are down because advertisers are spending less on commercials. Advertising money has to earn its way more thoroughly in a time of economic stringency and slow economic growth. Media buyers in advertising agencies have turned to point-of-sale promotion – plastic flowers, competitions, give-away premiums – and have invested their money here. Investment in television commercials has fallen. Faced with this trend the companies cannot at the moment put up the rates they charge for an advertising spot, even though colour is thought to give commercials far greater impact. Colour-set viewing is not yet widespread because of the nine-month down payment on rental agreements. Until this goes, the advertising rates for colour must stay down. Nor can ITV companies claim increasing viewers for existing black-and-white sets because saturation point has been reached: even the two-set family won't remedy this. Two sets in one household don't increase the number of the family though they may increase frequency of viewing.

The Exchequer Levy is the second great check on ITV income. Prior to 1 July 1969 the Levy was expected to yield £26 million annually, dependent on revenue remaining stable. It was then increased to bring in a further £3 million – that is £29 million in one year – more than a quarter of ITV's income and quite apart from income tax and corporation tax. On 15 April 1970 the scale of the Levy was adjusted, reducing its annual total to £23 million – but primarily bringing relief to the smaller companies. None the less, the fact that it is on income rather than profits puts the pressure more directly on programme budgets and creative plans. These have certainly suffered.

The purely commercial instinct under such evidently pressing circumstances would be to streamline the companies. As it is at the moment the resources of ITV are not distributed to maximize profit. The federal structure is wasteful. But it is at this point that principle stands firm: that principle is regionalism. The federal structure of ITV, with five major networking companies and ten regional companies, was set up as a deliberate counter-structure

251

to the BBC. Regionalism is not economic but it is vigorously defended as a culturally healthy and socially desirable system. First of all it produces a harmonious working unit: Anglia, mostly housed in a converted market hall in Norwich, employs a staff of 425. The atmosphere is of a single enterprise at work, more cohesive than the BBC's staff of thousands. Again Southern, with a new colour studio complex that cost £2½ million, has a staff of only 400. Both Anglia and Southern interpret their role as regions in terms of winning their way on to the network by supplying programmes where the network companies are weak; Anglia with drama or Southern with children's and women's programmes which are networked in off-peak time.

Secondly the regional structure supports local identity. All the regions run daily local news magazines after the evening news – and each takes pride in the high ratings and local interest they arouse. But the regions stating the most vigorous and insistent case for their licences are the ones that contain national groups: Border, Grampian, Scottish and Harlech.

To streamline the industry by scrapping the regional system might be commercially plausible. It has happened in other industries and regrettably in the press. But in a medium whose very existence is built on an ability to communicate with people, the loss would be grave. There is another principle, too, that checks ITV's wholesale surrender to the ratings and financial pressures. It lies in the character and professionalism of the broadcasters working within the companies.

Many of the people who hold or have held executive positions in ITV were once with the BBC. They took with them to the commercial channel a passion for making programmes, an eagerness for success and a knowledge of scheduling policy based on other things than ratings alone. They had to readjust violently. Some of them made bad businessmen; some of them wanted a quiet life in a prestige position; and some wanted opportunity, new challenges, the chance of making their kind of programmes. But the belief is widespread and instinctive that a good programme is good for its own sake.

ITV's greatest value in theory at least should be the great diversity of choice available from different companies. One of its major problems is that there is too much programme-making capacity overall. With the arrival of Yorkshire as the fifth net-work company, the time available for each of the others was re-duced. The recurring theme of our talks with Big Five executives was the familiar cycle of pressure: financial difficulties, low in-come, programme budget priorities, networking time, scheduling, ratings, income. ITV's greatest weakness at the moment is at network level. The network planning committee and its sub-committee has failed to sort out and co-ordinate what the different companies have to offer. There is no such thing as an ideal ITV schedule of programmes: simply a lot of separately made pro-grammes strung together on the network. Again this is something the executives themselves feel uneasy about, a recurring subject in their examination of the ITV structure.

# Aled Vaughan

Formerly Head of Documentary and Features, BBC Wales. Pro-gramme Controller Wales, Harlech.

*Why did you leave the BBC for Harlech?*

I left for a variety of reasons. I felt that I had run the course of my experience in the BBC and one likes to move on to experience new things. I like taking gambles. The idea of a company that's autonomous, without any strings at all, appealed. Eventually, too, there was the possibility of doing more for Wales.

*What is your policy for programmes in Welsh?*

One's policy for Welsh language programmes for Wales is per-haps a little broader than the policy for English language pro-grammes for Wales. I take the attitude that the only television in the Welsh language done in the whole world is done here in Wales, and, therefore, the world is your oyster. We, in fact, do pro-grammes of an international flavour in the Welsh language. We do current affairs programmes that deal with international affairs. We have dubbed more documentaries from overseas into Welsh than into English, because the subjects are catered for in English by television companies in England.

*How do Harlech's programmes reflect the region?*

Well, I'm a great believer that one should exploit one's strengths, and one's strengths in these terms are the things other companies can't do, by virtue of the fact that they are elsewhere and we're here. This means programming about and from the area. I would say that our main strengths are music, especially opera and choral music, and the documentary. Also, we have good talkers. I think we have a marvellous area for documentaries because we have voluble people, people who express themselves well, who are keen to express themselves, who have very firm views on many things, who are philosophically inclined. We also have such a contrast between the old and the new. You get a place like Port Talbot, a massive complex of steelworks, and about three miles up the road you get a small Welsh village where they speak Welsh and where life must be very much the same as it was fifty years ago. This inclination towards the documentary doesn't mean that the Welsh don't like laughter; they like the documentary to be serious, but on the whole I think they like their drama to be slanted towards comedy.

*One of the criticisms you had as a BBC man was that the money came from London. What about the budgeting situation in Harlech?*

The money is ours – we can control it. We can do whatever we like with it, really. And that in itself gives you a feeling of freedom. That isn't to say there's necessarily any more of it. It isn't a matter of amount. It's a matter of where the power is. One feels freer as a person, and I feel, well I can do anything I like providing it is responsible. For instance, one feels more free than the BBC to attack the Establishment in Wales.

*Do you give more coverage to the whole Welsh Nationalist movement than other programmes?*

Well, I'll answer that one in a roundabout way. One of the things we on the Welsh side in Harlech decided on when we came in was that we would concentrate more on the youth of Wales than was done, in my time certainly, in the BBC in Wales, because the young Welsh form a particularly interesting group of people. I think they are more aware of their heritage than the older generation and, therefore, by giving them increased programme time one inevitably reflects this national feeling more. This isn't being political – one of the duties of a television service is to reflect the main trends in the society it serves.

*Would you like to see any changes in the network system?*

I would say that in an area like Wales, which is a nation, and Scotland and Northern Ireland, there should be another look at the networking system in terms of these particular areas. I'm saying really that there should be more programmes from these areas on the network, for they are national rather than provincial. They reflect a way of life that is quite distinctive. They have, therefore, more to offer television in terms of something that is different.

# Wynford Vaughan-Thomas

Director of Programmes, Harlech.

*When did you give up the BBC to create Harlech?*

Well, when the franchise came up for renewal, John Morgan rather fired me with the idea. I thought here's a challenge I must accept – at this stage of my career it would be a very exciting thing, firstly to come back to this country where I was born, and secondly, to come back taking part in a fairly top-level enterprise such as this, in which we could get a fair return for the money. We would, as we planned it, have a circuit into which we could direct interests in the arts, in creative work, in stimulating the whole artistic life of the region. And this was a very exciting prospect. I'd done all I could, particularly in television, as a performer. The next stage had become to stimulate the performers and try to build up a creative organization.

What we were hoping eventually is that we would be able to pay back our money and our loan stock and make a fair profit in the last two years of franchise. That was it, and no further. But that first year, in fact, we paid 8 per cent. We had hoped to pay about 16 per cent.

*How hard did the Levy hit you?*

It wasn't so much the actual scale of the Levy, although it's pretty galling suddenly to have to find £350,000 you hadn't projected for, but it was the fact that we were a new company. We hadn't any sort of reserves. We hadn't taken part in the bonanza period. We'd never had a licence to print money, or indeed wanted one. Therefore, we had to try and weather the storm as best we might by back-pedalling on our promises and hopes in one respects.

*From the moment the Levy hit you, did you cut back right away on your programme budget?*

We've cut back our programmes as hard as we possibly can. We sacrificed our dreams first. The things that we were really keen to do, something different from the ordinary commercial company. Alas! These things had to go. Then the next thing was to try and economize not only in programming but in other areas of the company's operations. We tried to run the thing more economically. With the crushing imposition of the Levy you're eventually down to counting the pennies in every field. Even to stop painting the walls!

We have now got to the stage where we are going to lose some of our most cherished schemes completely, and we are getting down to basic services which we are determined to maintain. We've got to maintain our news bulletins, we've got to try and at least do something that inspires the staff now and again with a special type of programme.

# Anthony Firth

Controller of Programmes, Scottish.

In Scotland we are expected to reflect Scottish culture. Well, it must be said that the vast majority of the population of Scotland remain, except for a handful, indifferent to this. This isn't to say they should be indifferent nor to say that we should do nothing about it. But it will take a very long time and a great deal of money before it is an enormous success with the working-class, urban Scot, who is in fact the vast majority of our audience. So get the money straight. This isn't a question of making money, or of keeping money, so much as a question of deciding on what level you want to fund programmes and then what you want to do with the rest of it.

The present structure reflects what is surely one of the most honourable ideas that anybody ever had about broadcasting: this whole new and exciting medium should have strong regional roots. I think it is now apparent that, in a general sense, this is not an economically viable pattern, so if you want to keep broadly to the same pattern you'd have to subsidize it directly or indirectly. But the problem is that both Scotland and Wales are areas which, on the whole, are unable to support the level of broadcasting which culturally and socially they might be expected to want to enjoy. Everyone says Scottish Television and Grampian should merge. But something could be lost along the way. The same with any other kind of merger proposed – the degree of real regional service is going to be diminished. If it's going to be less regional, you're not really talking about regions any more. You are talking about economically viable units of television production. I would have guessed that there would be five or six of those at the most.

*Pilkington proposed that you should have a central authority who would collect advertising revenue and arrange the schedules, and that you in fact would just make programmes. Do you think that is viable?*

I would be very reluctant to give that much authority to any central body. My experience of people who tend to cluster in such organizations is that they are not the kind of people I would, on the whole, describe by the adjective first-class. Also, I don't see how they could do it if they weren't involved in the programming themselves. What one wants is more of the people who are involved in or actually have at some time been involved in programmes, running the industry. The communications industry in this country is on the whole run by people who aren't really communicators in any sense of the word. We surely need more and more people who are, or have been, writers or producers.

*Do you see your schedule in competitive terms with the BBC?*

We are first of all in competitive terms with BBC Scotland: this is different because we do have one of the most autonomous and vigorous of the BBC regions, so we have to keep more of an eye on the BBC perhaps than almost anybody else in the United Kingdom.

Our audience is very much a large number of manually working, urban Scots. They require of us – and if we do not supply it they go elsewhere – a great deal of sport, for example. They require of us as many Westerns as we can possibly lay our hands on. They require of us a good deal of escapist programming.

Of course, one is trying at other times to offer them different things, and seeing the response is sometimes very encouraging. It's rather a serious-minded audience in some ways, so it will watch serious political discussions of a local kind. And it likes to see its own imagery, its own colour.

# James Bredin

Managing Director and Controller of Programmes, Border TV.

I believe there's a good case to be made for the continued existence of regional television – even when we consider a future which will include a second channel for ITV and pictures by satellite which will disregard not only regional but national boundaries. It is even arguable that there ought to be more and smaller regional stations rather than a merging of existing regions to form larger ones.

Take Border as an example: it's the smallest but one of the ITV regional companies; it's geographically large but has a population of only 600,000 and they are a mixture of 45 per cent Scottish, 55 per cent English and 10 per cent Manx. When it started, the then existing companies assumed that you couldn't successfully run an independent television station in this country for a population of less than a million. At the end of three years we were viable – we declared a profit for the first time, we paid a dividend of 10 per cent and directors took fees for the first time. Beyond the purely financial aspect of viability, Border has justified its existence with its local programmes which gain a very large proportion of the television audience in its very mixed area. We do it by taking seriously a part of the country which wasn't taken seriously before and which wouldn't now be taken seriously enough if we were to be part of a larger region.

*How much original programme output can you do economically?*

Four hours a week, which is a very realistic appraisal by the ITA of what we're capable of financially and in terms of resources.

*So inevitably a company of your size is forced to be a sort of satellite of one of the big companies under the present structure?*

Yes, it's endemic in the present setting. You would be fooling yourself in a company the size of Border, or of most if not all of the present Regions, if you thought you were there to get splendid programmes about Cumberland or about Galloway on the network regularly. Border could go bankrupt in six months by trying to make two or three forty-five-minute documentaries about the Lake District or the Lakeland Poets. What is important for a company of our size is the regular five half-hour programmes a week we do by way of a local news magazine programme – and we get 80 per cent of the audience every night with that programme. You could argue that Granada or Scottish Television or Tyne Tees (our immediate and larger neighbours) would do this programme just as well for the Border Area and possibly better because they have larger resources but I don't believe that would happen and I certainly don't believe that it would look as if it was happening to viewers in the Border Area.

*But the original idea of ITV was that programmes could originate in the regions. Would it be healthy had it happened more?*

Of course, it would but it can only happen if the Regions do in fact produce more programmes of network standard and that isn't going to happen if you decree that Grampian is to do three documentaries for the network every year, Westward five, Anglia seven, and so on. This would be programming by Committee and that has never made sense. The way it works now is just about the way it should work. Someone in, for example, Grampian makes a programme which he is absolutely convinced is the best he can do, the programme is submitted to the Viewing Sub-Committee of the Network Programme Committee and, if it is judged to be of network quality, then it goes on the network.

*How is this Sub-Committee made up?*

It's made up of representatives of each of the five major companies and two representatives from the Regionals.

*Would the Regions fare better if the ITA took a hand in schedules?*

The ITA does take a hand in the schedules. It can and does have its say on what kind of programmes are scheduled where and when. I don't think the ITA should do much more than that. Good programmes don't happen because someone outside says they must happen. They happen because someone inside is burningly convinced that they should happen and that he is the man to make them happen.

# Berkeley Smith

Controller of Programmes, Southern. Formerly with Outside Broadcasting, BBC TV.

I think I prefer Independent Television because its method of operation is simpler. It is an enormous believer in the use of the telephone and trusting things that are said on the telephone. A great deal of the business between the fifteen companies is done this way – the day-to-day changes on the network are given out, discussed and agreed on the telephone and that's it. There is nothing like the amount of paper confirmation that goes on in the BBC. And because I prefer talking to writing I suppose that is one reason why I like the independent way of operating.

*Did you pick out from the beginning where you would like your strength to be, what you could do and make your own?*

Well, there was no doubt where we had got to be strong if we were to remain in business and that, of course, is our regional broadcasting – our *raison d'être* – the justification for our existence. But I also wanted – we wanted – something more than that – we wanted to make more impact on the network and it seemed sensible rather than just making programmes we thought we might do well or which interested us, to see where the area of weakness on the network lay. Children's programmes was an obvious area which should lie within the competence of a large regional company like Southern. So we set about it and now we are, I suppose, one of the largest providers of children's programmes on Independent Television – something in the order of about eighty programmes a year. Not peak time because it's madness to think that that could be a runner. No major company is going to give up large slabs of peak time, nor in my view should they because even a large region like ours would not normally be geared to deliver to peak time with any regularity. So it was not so much a question of what programmes I wanted to do but where the outlets would be. And I am delighted now that we chose children.

*What are the main concerns in your position about television now?*

The main concerns must be the uncertain state of the industry. Working on short-term licence contracts as we do is hardly reassuring and don't forget we, including in a sense the BBC, have been through some pretty traumatic times during the last two years. In the long term one must be worried by the growing tendency of politicians to try to control television, often understandably for their own reasons. The strong bastion against this over the years has necessarily been the BBC and I would be very worried if the BBC's basic independence as well, of course, as our own was damaged. Because this is what is happening to television in other parts of the world. I would have thought there is no doubt that the American administration is going to take a damn great swipe any time now at their networks. These are certainly the indications at present.

*What about redundancy?*

There are really two sides to this redundancy problem. The patches of redundancy now in the industry are largely a result of uncertainty about the future, and there is also the problem of senior production staff who are starting to run out of creative steam but who still have virtues, perhaps administrative, and certainly virtues of experience and wisdom. The BBC is much better off here – they have got those marvellous parking lots like the training school and overseas appointments where this kind of man can go. There are really no parking lots on this side of the fence and it is going to be a problem. My impression is that there are probably just enough senior people dying to make this problem bearable at the present time, but it will increase.

*What changes would you like to see in the structure?*

Well, I would certainly not like to see regionalism – one of the great success stories of Independent Television – impaired, but I believe it could be discharged as effectively and certainly more efficiently by a smaller number of companies over all. I think there should be a fourth channel which should be given to Independent Television and in each area it should be run by the existing company as a complementary service – I would be worried for the programme standards if you had two companies competing directly in the same area. BBC 2 is strong in our area and we see the enormous advantage the dual service gives to that organization. Some people say that a second channel is not on financially – we think it is and we have certainly got the capability to run it in the new complex we have just built in Southampton.

# Peter Cadbury

Chairman, Westward.

*James Callaghan recently alleged that certain programmes with violence were having an effect on the criminal behaviour of the British.*

I think this is nonsense. Violence is part of national and international life. I think this is exaggerated quite frankly, and of course we know that there were a number of people in that Government who disapproved of the whole principle of independent television. They don't like seeing anyone making money bascially. They deliberately caused the present crisis. They engineered it and quite irresponsibly have reduced our regional companies to a state where they will either have to close down or become insolvent.

*Have you cut back on programme budgets at all yet?*

We've cancelled our whole colour programme for the time being, insofar as we have not ordered any colour equipment. We don't propose to go into colour at all, unless we can afford it, and we won't be able to afford it unless the Levy comes off completely. The extent to which we can go will depend on how we can adjust the other overhead charges, such as the rental to the ITA.

*Where do you think the strength of what your company provides really lies?*

In its local flavour. I think that this is what will be destroyed if instead of Independent Television you have another enormous elephant of a business on a central basis like the BBC. The BBC can't be regional, except to a very limited extent, because it can't identify itself with a region. If you go down to the West Country, everyone regards Westward as their television station. It belongs to them. It's run for them, The people in it live there and all our programmes are produced with local people and are about local things. No national corporation can compete in that sense.

But it is very difficult for a regional company to get a fair share of the network time. I suppose I can understand it in a way, because every half hour put on by a regional company means that the network company has got to keep its production units idle for that amount of time, so it's obviously not in its own interest to put regional television on the network.

There is an argument for having regional companies independent, but I think they should have their boundaries extended, so that gradually the whole country has the choice of two regional contractors. We'd be delighted, for example, to have our programmes generally received in Bristol, and I know the Bristol people would welcome Westward because they don't like being a satellite of Wales. We'd like to extend our area westwards, and we would be perfectly happy for Harlech or Southern to extend their regions into our area.

# Brian Tesler

Director of Programmes, Thames.

*How do ratings influence a commercial channel?*

I have, just as Paul Fox has, a personal pride in success at the level at which I intend success or hope for success with programmes. So that if *This Week* gets a rating of five, which it never does, then I would put up with that and so would the advertisers, whatever dissatisfaction they might feel, because they are interested in the prestige as well as the popularity of ITV. I do not think there would be a complaint. I do not expect our *Tuesday Documentary* to get into the Top Twenty. It is not made that way. They are made to do a job. *Today* is not made to be consciously popular – *Today* is made as a service to the viewers. It so happens that because it fulfils that function very well indeed it is popular. It is a successful programme. But my concern is if something is *meant* to be a successful programme with big ratings then it has *got* to be a successful programme with big ratings.

My job is to schedule all these so that the inevitably less popular programmes are hammocked in such a way that they catch as many viewers as possible, so that those viewers will give them a chance also. This is one of the basic ploys of scheduling and it is important to me that the schedule works as a *whole*.

*What was your reaction to the scheduling of similar programmes opposite each other as part of the competitive game?* Panorama/ World in Action *is a classic example.*

Well, that was enforced by the ITA. *World in Action* was never opposite *Panorama*. The ITA said 'It will go at eight o'clock on Monday nights.' This was before the new contracts, long before the new contracts. As a scheduler I would not have done that. I have not put *This Week* against *24 Hours*.

*Who takes the initiative to take the avoiding action? ITV or BBC?*

Well, either side can take the avoiding action. There is no negotiation with the BBC. We do not know what the BBC schedules are. But they can know ours very much more in advance than we know theirs, because our schedules go out to advertising agencies months in advance and theirs do not. They can play it very close to their chest. Both Donald Baverstock and Michael Peacock have said that when they were at the BBC – because the *Radio Times* has a later press date than *TV Times* – they used to wait until the *TV Times* came out and then change their schedules competitively. I suppose the BBC does have this slight advantage in that it can operate far more flexibly with rather more advance notice than we. But what happens is that someone puts out a schedule and the other side puts out a schedule, and after a week or two of the airing of both schedules we make adjustments, we both make adjustments.

*That is all part of the game, really, isn't it? Couldn't it be easier than that, don't you think?*

Well, it could be very much easier than that if ITV had two channels. Then our 'schedule game', if you like, would be played by us, for us, between us and the BBC's schedule game equally. The very fact that you would have four schedules would mean that you would not have to schedule competitively one channel against the other. If two channels are complementary to themselves and the other two are complementary to themselves, then it is a marvellous opportunity for the viewer who has all kinds of programmes to see at any given point in time. It would remove the obvious counter-scheduling. That would be my ideal.

*Are you ready for it?*

Well, the existing companies are ready for it. You cannot run two channels in Ulster or two channels in Westward and the other smaller areas, but as far as the main areas are concerned we are ready for a second channel if we are responsible for it. If the Postmaster sets up an entirely new system with duplication of studios, duplication of resources, then no one is ready for it. The country is not ready for it. One of the troubles with ITV is that there are far too many resources. Every one of the major companies could do far more than it is doing at the moment with what it has got in terms of studio facilities and staff.

# Howard Thomas

Managing Director, Thames Television.

What I learned coming out of a monopoly* into a commercial system was the importance of allowing the producer to be a power in the company, so that he wouldn't be too much over-ridden by executives. The more he was an executive, the more responsible he became and the more freedom he obtained. So, therefore, in this company all the executives are ex-producers, every programme boss here has come up the producer way. They are not civil servants. That's the principle I learned, and I resolved never to handicap producers with too many administrators.

*What are the restrictions on what producers put out on the air?*

First of all, there are no advertising restrictions at all. When we first started commercial television many of us saw nothing wrong with the American system of sponsored television. When eventually the British brand came in, when the advertising was separated from the programmes, at first I wasn't attracted to it. But of course time proved that it was the ideal system. There is no pressure at all from advertisers. We can move any programme to any day we like, any time we like, and drop it, improve it, produce it. There is no pressure at all. Where pressures do come, of course, they are Establishment pressures as with the violence problem, the moves by the Home Secretary, who is intervening between two authorities set up by the state, and proposing yet another body to come on the scene. That sort of government intervention

* Howard Thomas produced *The Brains Trust* for BBC.

266

in any aspect of programming is, of course, of much concern to people like me.

You certainly have the Mary Whitehouses ringing you up or writing about you. You've got press pressure on you, and of course one meets criticism from government people and the Church. We have to deal with everyone here. You are surrounded by pressures, as in all communications jobs. In fact running a company like Thames is very much like running a newspaper.

You certainly get the protests, but we assign responsibility to a great many people, and trust those people. Sometimes you are let down, but on the whole it works. Admittedly, there must be a pyramid of organization, but all the companies are totally different in composition. There are all different men at the top. There are five programme controllers: they are all, I think, between thirty-five and forty-five. Fifteen years ago, they were twenty-five, so the people who were once in direct control of programmes, like Lew Grade, Bernstein, myself, are no longer in that job. We've either moved up or moved out. There is a new generation of people and there will be a new generation to succeed these, so really it's not in the hands of a few, it is in the hands of the professionals. Our job all the time is to look around for creative people and discern who has the ability to move up next.

*To what extent is it frustrating that you don't have total control? You have to accept a certain amount of programmes from other people.*

No one company can afford to make programmes for the whole network. There are benefits in the system, that you've got five drama units each working under a different drama producer. The BBC has got one big drama unit, and that reflects again the mind of the man who runs it. ITV drama, I think, gains in this respect that there are five different minds putting out different kinds of programmes. So although you sometimes have to take programmes that you don't think much of, nevertheless you must accept that for the sake of different viewpoints. The difficulty is that London audiences are different from the provinces, and I think we would probably put on more sophisticated programmes ourselves than we sometimes take from regional companies.

Originally, let's face it, all the controllers in new companies wanted to demonstrate their skills. They all wanted to put their programmes into every slot. But they've now come to the point where they do decide on merit and they say: 'For this time, in the early evening, it's better to have a slap-stick comedy programme than a more sophisticated one'; or 'Perhaps this one is too adult for early evening, do you think it would be better to put it on at 10.30?' The five programme controllers have reached an accord and that's why we are doing better again now in ITV. We have got the audience back now, because our people have now got together to plan.

When it comes to the money side of it, we have token prices, the description we use is 'a tariff price', so that a one-hour play we say is valued at X thousand pounds. Many of us will spend much more than this on a programme, but we have this price as a unit between us, and then we share that price according to the respective sizes of our audience. London has the largest audience so, therefore, London pays the biggest chunk. In other words, you've got a play costing, shall we say, £20,000, to be divided among four companies. Yorkshire pays the least, London pays the most, Granada pays another price. Fixed tariff prices mean that you haven't got to argue about 'your play is worth more than mine'. If any company chooses to put on a highly expensive play, then it is their own concern.

*How do you arrive at the sort of money available for programmes?*

Costs have gone up and the income has actually gone down. There is quite enough money flowing into Independent Television for everything, so long as the government doesn't take too much away. The present income from advertising is £95 million. We were paying a Levy of £26 million, and when the Treasury increased it to £29 million we reached breaking point. Now the Levy has gone down to £23 million, but we are still paying about 25 per cent Levy. Now we are coming under PIB I daresay our finances will become state-controlled. The government of the day will be saying how much we should spend on programmes and how much we can retain in profits. I think that will be the outcome of it.

*A lot of the critics of the ITV system felt that a lot of money was taken out of the system and not put into programmes?*

That was so in the past, when profits were too high, but time has regulated that. Take a company like Thames, which has a capital of £7½ million, and has just spent £2 million on colour equipment alone. Thames actually receives nearly £18 million in advertisement revenue, but by the time we have paid Levy we are down to £10 million. The profit for last year was £1 million, less Corporation Tax. A million pounds profit on £7½ million capital on a six-year contract is not enough. After all, if you are earning £10 million in any business you should be able to retain more than £1 million out of it. Apart from the sheer finances of it all, when you are in this job you need to have money for bold ventures. We couldn't make another *Mountbatten* now, because *Mountbatten* remade today would cost us £500,000. We cannot afford to invest £1½ million to make another twenty-six one-hour *Avengers*.

*But you recently put money into covering the GLC election results?*

I think the audience for that programme after midnight probably will be very small but this is a public service we should perform. We will earn no ratings, it will earn no revenue but it is a part of Thames' area and in our opinion we must do justice to an important GLC election. I could be criticized for this at a time when we are trying to economize, but I believe it is the right decision.

# Stella Richman

Controller of Programmes, London Weekend.

I think the existence of the separate companies with their different business interests is non-constructive to good programming. This is why we are all in trouble because everybody, particularly programme controllers, are currently unable to exist without being constantly aware of the money problems, the shortage of revenue, the cost of making programmes, the normal escalations from one year to another which is abnormal really: they are higher than the rises in any other industry. Unless the programme controllers of the Big Five can have many of the day-to-day money worries taken away then I think there is no hope at all for any of us for the future. Luckily, since I have become controller, which is just three and a half months now, the need has been seen by people within ITV. Whether the separate business interests of the Big Five will prevent a change in the system, we shall all see, in the future.

*Are you saying in a sense that the idea of competitive companies running television doesn't work?*

I think it may have worked five years ago, ten years ago, when there was a lot of money to spend in the country. I think the way the companies operated ten years ago is not relevant to life today. It is a question of the survival of the fittest and we need to make ourselves strong by working as an entity, much more than is being practised at the moment. We're all involved in sharing a too small cake.

Always there are groups of creative people who think they should run television companies and, as a creative person basically, I would hate to see that day come. I would hate to work with a committee composed of only creative people. My experience is that if you get ten creative people together they're lacking a businessman and an objective sense of direction. You need a man who is able to be the devil's advocate. A tough businessman but not the accountant type. If creative people take over entirely then we're in terrible danger of them doing the programmes they think the public want. Now that is not very closely knit, often, to what the public actually want. I don't mean by that that the public should be regarded as morons. I think that is absolutely ridiculous. But I do see a danger if you get a group of creative people, forming a board of a company, the dangers are you would argue for many a day about content of programmes. We could find that we'd be getting on to the network some lovely programmes, really smashing programmes, but for ourselves. And the cost! I think the thing is, whether we're in a bad economical position or not at the moment, programmes have to be made for a price in any company.

# Tom Margerison

Chief Executive, London Weekend.

*What did television look like seen from publishing and Fleet Street?*

Very similar. I think there are tremendous similarities between them. Both of them involve the management of creative people. In both fields, in all cases it's very hard indeed to apply the classical rules of economics. You can't say this programme or that article is cost effective. The return you get from investment in a programme is unpredictable and usually indeterminate. All you can say is that if you put the right amount of money into the right thing you will get good results from it. But if you have a bad idea, however much money you put into it, you don't get good results.

When the London Television Consortium was set up, it was a group of programme-makers. They wanted financial backing and the question was where should it come from? They wanted it to be highly respectable, and spread over a sufficiently wide spectrum of financial interests for no one body to have a major financial control. In consequence, nobody within the company, no one financial backer, has more than 12½ per cent interest, which is very much spread, much more so than in most other companies.

The Board, therefore, is one in which no one financial interest is predominant and one of the virtues of this is that the programme-making interests are in a stronger position than they are, perhaps, in any other operation.

*After the management crisis in London Weekend, when a large group of programme-makers departed, did you sense a great loss?*

You are always sorry when somebody who is good goes and you always feel at the time that a terrible blow has been struck. What always happens again is that the person who seemed absolutely indispensable doesn't turn out to be quite so indispensable at all. We haven't tried to replace the people who left in exactly the same way, because one of the things you learn about handling creative people is that some people are strong in one area and some are strong in another area. So you tailor your management to take account of the strengths and weaknesses. If you change the people you almost inevitably change the responsibilities that they carry.

*It has been suggested that you hadn't fulfilled the promise of those programmes. In fact the most conspicuous one was the folding of the Current Affairs Department. Why was that folded?*

It was part of a general re-organization in which the Current Affairs Department became part of a more generalized Features Department. We had high hopes originally that we would be able to introduce a major current affairs stream at the weekend and, in particular, we saw ourselves doing something of the job that the present *News at Ten* does. The whole of the application was written before *News at Ten* started and we thought that there was a requirement in ITV to have a programme (tentatively called *Seven Days*) which brought together all the news stories of the week and presented them perhaps in rather the same sort of way that *The World This Weekend* does on the radio. In fact, by the time we got there ITN had done, I think very courageously and in fact as it turned out very successfully, a daily half-hour programme during the week which covered precisely the ground that it was intended that our programme would do at the weekend. But I do want to go on and say that we've by no means lost out on the current affairs stream. We have continued with the Frost programmes. Both *Frost on Friday* and *Frost on Saturday*, in a rather lighter vein, have been concerned very much with the area of current affairs and have brought people into the studio for discussion. We have also been running *Man in the News* on Sunday afternoons and a number of other less regular programmes, such as *For the Record*, some of which were extremely successful. Looking at the whole picture I think we have fulfilled much of what we originally hoped to do.

*What have you learnt about the difficulties of scheduling for the weekend?*

One of the problems is that the BBC choose to put their strongest programmes into the weekend and have made and continue to make a very, very strong attack on the weekend. We have only three evenings plus two afternoons in which to programme and those three evenings happen to be the ones which are traditionally strong BBC-wise. While that situation holds good we find that the BBC place very strong entertainment programmes against us right the way through the period. We are left with nowhere to put a programme which doesn't come off, which isn't a hundred per cent success, or one which is serious and cannot command a large audience. We're hamstrung by not having sufficient hours. We are limited by the BBC's insistence that the number of hours shouldn't increase. You see, if the hours of broadcasting were increased the BBC would need a larger licence fee to cover the increased costs, which is politically unacceptable. The BBC recognizes this and fights tooth and nail to prevent ITV having any more hours, believing that, if ITV had more hours than it did, the BBC would be at a disadvantage.

*What special problems do you think you had in coming into ITV?*

We didn't realize all the problems that arise from the federal system of ITV. ITV has some strengths in being federal. The BBC has some strengths in being national. Our problem, which we didn't foresee, is that the BBC really competes only with London. If I were sitting in Yorkshire or Lancashire or the Midlands and I changed my schedule the BBC wouldn't bother to change their schedule to meet mine. They would be quite happy to lose out in Lancashire, or wherever it may be, provided they did well in London.

If we change in London, the BBC will change to meet us – as they did only a few weeks ago with the Sunday afternoon pattern.

*Do you find that you are basically concerned with ratings and competitive scheduling in your position?*

Obviously we have to be. It is the nature of the way in which ITV works. We are automatically the popular service. We have to get the audience in order to attract the advertisers. If we don't, we have no money to make programmes. There is no other source of revenue. Therefore, people like me have always to look at ratings. What we hope to be able to do, because I think particularly in this company we're idealistic in our approach, is to improve the standard of programmes that achieve high ratings. This is what we strive for all the time.

On the other hand, the BBC's revenue comes from licences and it arrives irrespective of whether a programme gets good ratings or not. So that the BBC has this enomous opportunity to lead people, to cater for minorities to a much greater extent than we can ever do. We can't afford to provide more than a proportion of our programmes to cater for minority audiences. We could do more if it wasn't for the fact that the government has snaffled a large proportion of our revenue in Levy.

*Would you like to see a percentage of ITV profit put straight back into programme reinvestment?*

This company, and I think this is true for all the new companies in ITV, haven't paid out any money at all to their shareholders, so you could say all the profit has gone into programme reinvestment. Our shareholders have lent the money they've put into the company absolutely free so far. All they've done is to lose money.

But to be practical, since we are asking outside people, whoever they may be, to invest in the company, these people do require some return and the question is what that return should be.

*What would you like to see changed in the structural situation of ITV?*

I think it's very uneconomic in the sense that there is too much equipment and too many people employed. ITV has studios dotted around the country so that the number of cameras, telecine machines and VTR machines employed in providing one ITV service is higher than the total number used by the BBC. Then each company has its own sales department selling advertisements, all going around the same group of advertising agents trying to sell the advantages of advertising in Grampian or Southern or Harlech or wherever it may be. Now does it make sense to have fourteen sets of people all busily employed on calling on the same group of advertising agents all hopefully wooing the same detergent manufacturer to get advertisements? I would have thought that a simpler structure, perhaps similar to the BBC's regional structure, would make a great deal more sense.

*Do you think the BBC and ITV are good for each other?*

I think they are. I like the two systems running in parallel. I used to be very much against ITV as a matter of fact. I didn't really believe that you could set up a network which worked effectively on the basis of finance from advertisements. I always feared – I'm talking about 1955 – I always feared that programme standards must inevitably become subservient to the wish of the advertiser. That has been proved not to be the case. I now feel that the double system of a tightly coupled commercial ITV operation and the more loosely politically coupled system with BBC is perhaps the ideal arrangement, and one which has a great deal to offer to the world at large.

# Sir Lew Grade

My whole effort, as far as I'm concerned, is in television, production of television programmes and sales of programmes overseas, because what I found when I really went into the selling business was nobody knew that British television existed. And everybody looked upon America as *the* country in television production. I said 'This is going to stop. We're going to sell all there is.' Everybody seems to say that I tried to Americanize the programmes. For example with my variety shows. What is my alternative? Keep on putting on Dusty Springfield, Lulu, week after week? At least I give them new faces. In my film series that I produce they say 'You Americanize them.' I don't care if it's a Japanese actor – if he fits the part and can play the lead, I'll take him. I wish I could find twenty Patrick McGoohans and twenty Roger Moores here. And, of course, we are selling a considerable number of dramas; people overlook the amount of documentaries that we sell all over the world. They just look upon us as films and variety shows. But that's only a small part of it. Just examine what we're doing. Granada do nine documentaries on a Tuesday, Thames do ten, I think, Yorkshire do nine. We do nineteen. Our documentaries are consistently seen by more people than those produced by any other company. *The Tribe That Hides From Man* was seen by nearly ten million – so far as I know that's a record! People forget

275

the trends that we started. We were the first people to do religious programmes on a regular basis. We were the first people to do a programme such as *Probation Officer* which was socially informative, educative and entertaining. We were the people to do *The Power Game* and *The Planemakers*. We were the people who did *Emergency Ward 10*.

*What do you think of British television all round?*

In comparison with television anywhere else in the world, all other television is farcical. Look at the three American networks. From 7.30 to eleven o'clock it's entertainment, except with an occasional documentary. You don't see any dramas. But look at Independent Television. There are dramas every Monday, dramas every Saturday. In Britain, both BBC and Independent Television have dramas which are balanced programming. They don't appeal to everyone, but we should encourage it because it brings forth new writers. People think that we ignore the fact that the creative element is the most important thing.

Of course the restriction of hours is the most crazy thing possible. Ridiculous! There are many ideas regardless of the financial implications that we would like to do. People recently have been asking are they going to spend more money on programmes when they get relief from the Levy. We have never looked at the cost of a programme. There is no fixed budget. There's a rough guide – I've never known our producers to stick to it.

I try to have a schedule that I think is a good schedule, a balanced schedule. Of course, we have a different formula from the BBC. We can't schedule exactly the way we'd like to because we network other companies' programmes and they have different ways of scheduling. We try as much as possible to schedule the way we think would be a good evening and afternoon's programming for the people. You see, people ignore the fact that our responsibility is to the majority, not ignoring the minority. We must never ignore the minority and we don't do so, but in the main our responsibility is to the majority.

I think I am the average person in this country. My tastes are the average person's tastes. That doesn't mean to say that I don't like to see a documentary. Yes I do, because I'm an average person. But I wouldn't like to see a documentary every night. If

I'm going to watch for two hours, I don't want to see an hour documentary every night. I want to see current affairs programmes once or twice a week. I like news, same as the ordinary public, I like a documentary at least once a week. And then I want to be entertained by good dramas, by the variety shows, by good escapist adventure series. Because it's all escapism. That's my opinion.

*How would you say, then, that your scheduling philosophy differs from that of the BBC?*

It doesn't differ. The BBC are doing exactly what we're doing. Earlier on the BBC were entirely different from us. Now they're the same. Tuesday a feature film, Thursday a feature film, Sunday a feature film, variety on Saturday – exactly the same as we are – film on Sunday afternoon. Exactly the same as we are. The only different scheduling is BBC 2. That's a different type of scheduling entirely.

*If there was a fourth channel that went to ITV what do you think would happen to that?*

I think a second ITV channel is an essential part of freedom of choice for the country.

*Is the present structure of ITV viable? The fact is it costs ITV roughly £95 million to run one channel and the BBC £100 million to run two channels and radio.*

You've got to remember there are fifteen Managing Directors, fifteen Head Offices, fifteen Head of Sales, fifteen Chief Accountants. It just goes on *ad infinitum*. None of our studios are used to the maximum. Therefore, with all the present resources that are available with very little addition you can have two complete – *complete* – competing channels. So there'd be four choices.

*Do you think the set-up with the ITA is all right?*

I don't object to that. I mean, they do a good job. Everybody doesn't realize how tough they really are. People think that they just sit back and let you do what you like. They don't. They advise, let's put it that way. I mean, it's really more than advice – they virtually tell you.

## ITV Executives

*Have you felt the pressure very much?*

Well, it's not pressure. They have an argument, they have a point of view. They have a point of view of their responsibility and we take note of it and do it. They're not idiots as some people think, just sitting there and just wasting the time of day.

*Have you any criticism of the two-prong nature of television, BBC and ITV, in this country?*

Oh, no. I think it's a good thing. Very good. Competition. I mean, look at the BBC programmes in 1954. That's all you have to do. The better they are the better it is for us and the better for television world-wide, because the BBC are putting quite a bit of effort into selling overseas. I think they'll do better. The reason they don't sell as much as we do is because we gamble crazily in films, and with a film you get a perfect quality.

*Has the downward tide in advertising revenue turned now?*

It has a little. It's only the economic situation, that's all. I mean, there's a ceiling on borrowing. In the past when you had to develop things and do things and capitalize, you could always go to the bank and have another £10 million. Now you can't, and there comes a time when you're going to pay Corporation Tax and you must pay something to the shareholders. You can't borrow the money and continue with research, so you have to save the money somewhere, and once the economic situation changes it will flow like mad because there's no medium like television.

*Once a programme company is based on the profit motive, it's under commercial pressure. Do you think there's any conflict at all?*

I have never known such nonsense in my life. It's absolutely ridiculous. When you do a programme, you want to do a good programme. How can it be linked with a profit motive? I'm doing a series with Tony Curtis and Roger Moore which will cost me at least £2,500,000 for twenty-four one-hours. That means to say England is going to see a series which costs £100,000 or just over to produce one episode. Who can pay? Does the advertiser pay for that? It can't. I'm taking the risk of recouping the money in the rest of the world. I will.

*I was thinking of the award-winning quality programmes, outstanding programmes which you probably wouldn't feel did go for a mass audience.*

No. I'd say award-winning plays are written only for the critics. Our job is not to provide programmes for the critics. I've only said it's our responsibility to provide for the majority without ignoring the minority. It doesn't mean to say that you don't do a minority appeal play now and again. After all we're currently doing *Twelfth Night*; we are in production on *Hamlet*.

# Francis Essex

Production Controller, ATV.

*Would ATV buy packaged light entertainment shows?*

As a company we buy complete shows, obviously. But I doubt if we would allow another organization to come into our studios to make shows for our network. Frank Sinatra *might* say, 'I'll come and do a show for you and supply all the dancers, all the supporting artists and all else – all you have to do is pay me £60,000 and we will do the rest.' I hope we would say 'no' to that – we would love to pay Mr Sinatra his fee to sing for us, but in our show, not his.

*The edges of that situation get blurred where, in fact, a lot of the light entertainment artists are contracted to agents and agent companies in which the Grade Organization has got holdings. Doesn't that worry you?*

Not in the least, because artists are booked by producers. They can go to an agent that is in the Grade Organization or an agent that is not in the Grade Organization – and they go. If you look over the records you will find there isn't anything like an exclusive use made of the Grade Organization.

*I understand that at ATV the decision about what the programme looks like is made as a matter of company policy rather than being entrusted to the producer?*

We have a system here where once a producer has a show he is given a briefing. A briefing simply means that we tell the producer what we are hoping to see – a philosophy, if you like, of that particular programme or programme series. Next we have a budget meeting where the producer puts down what he wants to do and we all cost it and he then gets the budget. He always thinks that he doesn't get the budget that he's asked for. Now from that moment on he is really absolutely on his tod because the next time we see the programme, unless he wants to come to us, is when it's on the air. If it then appears on the screen and not only has he departed from his brief but it's not what you wanted and, moreover, is not what you've given the remainder of the network to understand you were going to supply on that night, then you can start getting disorientation.

*What would be the criteria for schedules; the tastes of the average viewer, or some higher standard?*

The criteria should surely be the taste of the producer. One way or another he will eventually get on the air what he wants and what he believes in.

There is no doubt that Sir Lew can drive this bus by the seat of his pants, and he does have this quite incredible instinct for knowing what the public wants. But ATV doesn't always put out what Sir Lew wants – he is a great deal more sensible than that. He himself has employed a Head of Documentary, a Head of Adult Education, a Head of Religious Broadcasts, a Head of Drama, and so on, and none of us would be in the business if we weren't achieving job satisfaction. So, in effect, we are all doing what we want to do. Because Sir Lew is extremely tolerant of us, it could be argued that his own personal taste does not always appear on the screen.

\*

*What then of the ITA? As the public body set up in the interests of viewers why have they not interfered more? Their powers as laid down in Section 3 (1) of the Independent Television Act give* them the responsibility for maintaining a proper balance in the subject matter and a high general standard of quality: for seeing that nothing is included in the programmes that offends against good taste or decency, is likely to encourage or incite to crime or lead to disorder: for ensuring that companies, appointed to serve particular areas, provide a range of programmes calculated to reflect the interests of the region. Sir Kenneth Clark, a former Chairman of the ITA, wrote to Pilkington, 'Personally I think that the ITA could have done more with the companies if it had tried.'

The Pilkington Report, 1960, agreed with him that the ITA had not dealt strongly enough with the companies. Today the conviction is widespread, that the ITA has upheld middle-brow values of conformity and discretion, that the programmes of daring and eccentricity are not encouraged on the network. Bill Ward of ATV believes that the ITA would not have sanctioned Till Death Us Do Part and Till Death played to sixteen million. ITV's claim to be the popular entertainment channel should be modified to 'popular, predictable and safe'. Selwyn Lloyd's idealistic pleading in 1949 for a range of choice and diversity of talent that only the introduction of ITV could bring, has rebounded. His allegations that the BBC monopoly would lead to more of the same, less daring, less freedom, are allegations that are being brought today against the commercially competitive structure of ITV.

# Sir Robert Fraser

1955–70, Director-General, ITA.

In the beginning, nobody could know whether it would prove possible to conduct a national television service in this country which was to be entirely dependent on its capacity to pay its bills from the sale of the advertising time. There were many who said we would be able to make ends meet only if we were basing the system on sponsored programmes, because the whole of the American experience of television's earning capacity was based on a system of sponsorship. There were experienced people who said that, selling spot advertising alone, we wouldn't be able to do it. So we had to just wait and see. Of course, it was the vital question. Before you worry about whether you have a good television service, you have to worry about whether you have a television service at all.

Before we went on the air, only the first of the Authority's three main responsibilities had to be faced – those three main responsibilities being the responsibility for planning the shape of the system, what you might call the institutions of Independent Television, what it is like as a structure irrespective of whether the service is good or bad; then its continuous responsibility for the quality of the service; and then its responsibility for the impartiality of the programmes and for what the Act calls taste and decency. I am in this context not dealing with the Authority's large and important responsibility for transmission.

On the institutional side, I suppose the first thing we saw was that, wherever you looked at television, you saw two types of organization – on the one hand, plural and decentralized forms, as with newspapers in the free world, with many producers; and on the other, centralized and unitary forms, with only one producer, as at the time in this country and generally in Europe. We designed plural forms. One also noticed that there were two entirely different kinds of television programme in the plural systems, though not necessarily or so much in the unitary ones. There were network programmes, which went in to national distribution and were used by the whole service, and there were strictly local programmes produced by local companies which almost by definition were not designed to travel outside their own areas.

Having these two basic distinctions in mind, between plural and unitary systems and between network and local programmes, we had a clear picture that we would first of all divide the networking responsibility between a number of companies which we would regard as the network companies. Once we moved outside the area in which they were operating, we would successively appoint local company after local company. They would be finding their reason for existence in their local programmes, not finding their reason for existence in the development of programmes which then they hope to put into national distribution.

*This is a perpetual complaint from regional companies, that they cannot get their programmes on the network, isn't it?*

Not perpetual, and by no means from all. It was never envisaged that they should be responsible for network production. They came into being to provide Independent Television with its enormously valuable local programmes. What happened, I think, was that most of them, in the golden years, were so extraordinarily prosperous that their surplus of expenditure over the costs of discharging their local functions was considerable, and they began to feel they had the resources to make national programmes. We never required them to produce network programmes. We did require them to produce local programmes. The most we thought would happen from time to time was that the regional companies would produce a programme that certainly deserved a national distribution. But in planning the network, you cannot rely on a systematic supply of such programmes from the regions, so that it takes some doing to find slots in the network schedules for local programmes. Clearly you must have a reliable, steady and complete supply of network programmes and charge specific companies with that responsibility. Once you do that, problems arise if the desire emerges amongst regional companies to put some of their own programmes into national distribution. How do you find the slots? We have found a workable solution. It was out of discussion between the Authority and the companies that the present arrangements for regular scrutiny of available programmes from the regions grew up. There are programmes from the regions in network distribution every week of the year, and the Authority is delighted that it is so.

The Authority always felt a strong aversion on broad social grounds to the concentration of power in any means of communication. I think also we felt that, quite apart from the division of power, it was likely that we would get a better standard of programmes from a competitive network than from a unitary one. And anybody who thinks there is a lack of competitive spirit in Independent Television should spend an hour or two at a listening post in the corridors of any one of the programme companies. The danger, as a matter of fact, with a system like this one is that it can become just a little too competitive, and not sufficiently cooperative.

283

ITV Executives

*How did you divide up the regions?*

We just went by local demand. If we felt we were dealing with a
region with its own life, and if there were a group of risk-takers
interested in television and prepared to take the risk and responsibility, we went ahead. And until the downward turn in the
economy of Independent Television a year ago, the judgement of
the initial risk-takers, even in smaller areas, was justified by the
results. Channel broke even for a while, and then began to earn a
small surplus. The Channel Island group never thought that they
would make a fortune. They wanted to have a television station
for the Channel Islands where they lived. And the same desire
emerged in Carlisle and the Borders. In the very beginning, it
looked for a while as if Independent Television might fail financially. It was touch and go in 1956. Then came prosperity, and
now times are hard. The Exchequer Levy is still absorbing £20
million of the income of Independent Television. The pressure on
some of the regional companies is severe.

*What effect did that early financial difficulty have on the present
structure of Independent Television: did it make any difference?*

What the disastrous start did was to slow down by about two or
three years the development of Independent Television as a
balanced and comprehensive television service. When the programmes first began, what was being offered was primarily an
entertainment service as distinct from an information service, as
indeed BBC television was at that time. None the less, there was
some component of news, information and current affairs programmes in the first television schedules. When the financial
troubles came, the serious content suffered in the struggle to find
an audience large enough to let us carry on. So if you look at the
programme schedules in the *TV Times* for 1957, what you see is a
popular entertainment service, what we would now regard as a
narrow service. And it was from that point that the programmes
as a whole widened into what they are now – under the leadership
of the Authority, let me make clear.

The Authority of course is the manager and the leader of Independent Television, responsible not only for its institutions, but
also for the quality of the programmes. The Act does not say that

the programme companies are responsible for the standards of Independent Television. It says that the Authority is responsible.

Now this is where the Authority's problems arise, and where there will always be found the central dilemma of whoever is Director-General, he being no more than the chief executive of the Authority. He finds himself in a position in which the organization directly responsible to him under the Act and in line of command to him makes no programmes at all. That is what Parliament intended, that is what Independent Television is all about, that is precisely why Independent Television is not a second BBC. Every single programme-maker in the BBC is directly in line of command underneath the Director-General. The Director-General of ITA knows and the Authority knows that the whole of programmes will be made by somebody else. Programmes cannot be better than the people who make them. Programmes in fact cannot be anything else than the people who make them. The Authority is responsible for the quality of the service. But what is the quality of the service except the sum total of the programmes that compose it?

This embodies a fundamental daily truth about Independent Television. The Authority must accept the responsibility of programme leadership. This responsibility for the quality of the service being accepted, you have to find some means of establishing programme leadership over the system. It seems to me very clear that this responsibility for programme standards and this programme leadership have to be discharged co-operatively with the companies. I once said they are partners to be trusted and not agents to be instructed. They are for the most part the first, and they occasionally may be the second. But I will defy anybody to produce a good television service on the basis that the programme companies are no more than agents to be instructed. They will develop no pride in their own work, they will develop no sense of responsibility. They will not be television companies responding to the standards of public service broadcasting. They would be programme factories.

*Isn't the one difference between the BBC and the ITV operation that the people running the programme companies have as their principle objective to make money?*

Since the programme companies are private enterprise companies, then how much importance they attach to performance and how much they attach to profit will depend on what kind of people they are. One of the mistakes in life, it seems to me, is to think that people act for only one motive; they act for a variety of motives. They want to do well; they develop their own pride if they are any good at all: they want to be respected; they want to be praised; they like to feel a sense of creative achievement, and at the same time, of course, they want to make some money – who doesn't? But all these motives exist together, and how they are blended in companies will vary a bit, just as that will vary in people.

From the start, the Authority made it its particular care to see that Independent Television was able to develop its own standards in its own way. It had to be done in co-operation with the companies, the vital creative producers in Independent Television, and that meant the establishment of some kind of co-operative planning team. That was brought into existence about the time the first companies were appointed, well before programme transmissions started. It took the form of the least publicly known and yet most significant committee in Independent Television – the Standing Consultative Committee. The Standing Consultative Committee is in a way the board of management of Independent Television. It meets every month with occasional sub-committees and occasional special meetings. The Director-General takes the chair, and it is attended by the principals of all the programme companies. It began as a tiny body of about five people. It is now rather large, with representatives of fifteen companies, the Director-General and various other senior officials all present. I have been myself chided from time to time for not going personally to meetings of the Network Programme Committee. The Network Programme Committee is an important committee, but it deals with special practical problems, and not the standards and balance of programmes. The Deputy Director-General on the programme side always attends it, and other ITA staff go to its sub-committees. Looking back on the evolution of Independent Television programmes, one can think of a large number of decisive acts which stemmed from the Standing Consultative Committee.

In the winter of 1957–8, we sat down and made up our minds what sort of balance and character we wanted the programmes of

Independent Television to attain. As a result of that, within two or three years, Independent Television had grown from being primarily an entertainment service into a much more rounded and comprehensive television service. News and current affairs assumed much greater significance; school programmes began, adult eduaction programmes began, religious programmes were developed, and drama became better. Though statistics tell you only part of any story, by the end of that period the proportion of programmes in Independent Television that you might label as serious had risen from less than 20 per cent towards 30 per cent and then by 1962 to over 30 per cent. At the same time, another important programme policy decision had been taken, this time exclusively by the Authority. This was the decision to introduce, as an important part of the total Independent Television output, local programmes everywhere, including the network areas. So substantial has been the development of local programmes that out of the 133 hours of programmes produced by all the companies in the aggregate each week, leaving out acquired material, over eighty hours consist of local programmes. Those are last year's figures. These range from a maximum of about twelve hours of local programming in Wales and West, ten or so from Scottish Television, down to Channel with its three or four.

Sometimes it will happen that the Authority becomes concerned not with questions of balance, but with some particular class of programmes that seem to be losing their appeal. Round about 1964, for example, audiences were beginning to desert the plays, to which we had always attached importance. Plays had become so allusive, and so elusive in meaning, that they were passing over the heads of the audience instead of making contact. This was the time when people began to ask again for plays that had a beginning, a middle and an end, you remember. So we thought we had better try to give some thought to ITV drama. We held one of our familiar consultations. We have one or two of these a year. All the programme companies send representatives and on the whole the plan is that they send their programme controllers, their producers and directors, and not just management. We did this to great effect with drama. As a result of it, ITV drama began to regain its appeal. Now, I think, it is one of the most creditable parts of the programmes.

287

A year or two later, it seemed to many that certain parts of the schedules had begun to have a rather old look. The Authority became particularly concerned about the programmes that were being shown in peak time. And it began by issuing a purely restrictive prescription. We will not have more than, I forget how many it was, Westerns in this period and we will not have more than, however many it was, adventure thrillers. But that was purely restrictive, and really was not going to do very much good by itself. We had begun to see that there was growing up, alongside the old form of television, a new one. Now in its old form, never mind at what cultural level it chose to operate, television, for most of those working in it or watching it, was an entertainment service. It was not until the early 1960s that one saw that a television information service was growing up alongside the television entertainment service, and that for some people this service was going to become more important than the entertainment service. Much middle-class interest in television seems to lie very largely in the information side. Looking for something positive to replace these earlier purely restrictive rules that we had introduced, we thought the time may have come for the introduction of a half-hour news programme into television. And that was the birth of *News at Ten*.

One reason why we put it at ten was that the schedules had become a bit too regular in pattern in the middle evening, and in part this seems due to the rigidity of a ten- or fifteen-minute news bulletin at about nine o'clock. We thought that ten was not too late, and might have the great advantage of clearing the hours leading up to ten o'clock for the best deployment that you could make of the best that you had. So at one and the same time, *News at Ten* was introduced, both *World in Action* and *This Week* were placed at changed times in peak, the frequency of the one-hour documentary was increased to become weekly, the position of the Monday play was stabilized, and later the weekend play was restored, to be joined by the weekend special.

*Would this sort of pressure have come from the companies anyway, without the ITA interfering, do you think?*

Possibly. The companies are as interested in improvements as the Authority is, and many changes for the better start with them.

But perhaps, in a plural system, it is an advantage to have a recognized central authority, a point of final leadership. At the end of 1968, for example, for the first time since it began, Independent Television fell under a 50 per cent viewing share. And if you examined the ratings and tried to find out why, you made the somewhat surprising discovery that we were failing in the very areas where before we had been most successful, and where most people would say it was easier for ITV to succeed. We were being surpassed in comedy; people were laughing a good deal more with the BBC than with us. We were slipping behind in Light Entertainment, where we had become a bit heavy and old-fashioned. We were failing in children's programmes where we had about a third of the audience, against the four fifths that we had in the 1950s. And though never markedly successful, we were doing a great deal worse in sport than we had ever done before; our Saturday afternoon audience share had fallen towards a third. But we had already had most of this out at the Standing Consultative Committee, or at the Programme Policy Committee, composed much as is the Standing Consultative Committee but with the programme controllers as well as the managing directors. It had gone over the whole of the areas of weakness with the companies, and had got it clear what needed to be done. New comedies and new children's programmes were already on the way, and by the spring of 1969 the programmes were better and the audience recovered. *Magpie* is a charming programme, continually gets better. The children's drama is excellent. *World of Sport*, to everybody's astonishment, began to break the Saturday afternoon audience in half with the BBC, and is now showing every sign of doing better still. And we now have some funny programmes. Comedy has recovered.

Don't let me for a moment give the impression that this is all the doing of the wonderful Authority: it isn't. This is all done co-operatively. Even if it was not one's temperament to do it co-operatively, it cannot be done any other way. The great difficulty that the chief executive of the Authority will always find is to steer a middle course. He can so easily be too authoritarian or too passive. No Director-General loses his amateur status by getting headlines, you know, 'Director-General lashes XYZ', 'Authority raps programme companies'. You can do it in your sleep. You will be in the morning newspapers, the easiest thing, like falling off a log. But what happens to the attitude and the spirit that the programme companies bring to their own work if you treat them like that; if they are put in that kind of a position? Even if you enjoyed that sort of style, and it's not my idea of pleasure, it wouldn't work. And on the other hand, the impression mustn't be given that the Authority is passive. If that happens, away we go into reams of 'toothless mastiff' and 'watchdog that never barks'. No, it is not the easiest thing in the world to steer a course which lets it be plain that the Authority is the Authority, but none the less that the programme companies play the key role they do in Independent Television.

*What sanctions have you got?*

Absolute. All programme schedules have to be composed in consultation with the Authority and approved by it before transmission. Of course, the Authority does not insist that it sees all programmes before transmission, though there is daily consultation about programmes, and very, very occasionally a programme is stopped.

*In the original Act, people envisaged advertising between programmes and not in the middle of programmes: how did the fact of having it in the middle grow up?*

The Act provides for advertising within programmes as well as between them. It is plainly easier to sell advertising effectively if you can place it in relatively small parcels rather than, to be absurd, have five continuous minutes of advertising. We have eliminated it from the inside of a number of programmes, not necessarily because you could not find a genuine natural break in them, but simply because they seem injurious to the programme.

# 11 · Conclusions

NICHOLAS GARNHAM

Any examination of the present state and future possibilities of broadcasting in Britain must begin with an examination of the role and status of the BBC. This is not to prejudge its value as a broadcasting instrument, but to recognize historical facts. This book can, I think, be accused of bias in favour of BBC experience. This is in part due to the fact that the broadcasting experience of its two authors has lain within the BBC, but it also reflects the realities of British television. It is said that one day the BBC continuity clock – the clock you see on your screens between the programmes – went wrong. There was nothing that BBC presentation could do but work the clock by hand and it was running about two minutes slow. ATV presentation saw this and immediately put their clock, which was running perfectly, back two minutes. This story may be apocryphal, but it is an accurate reflection of the way in which the BBC dominates the thoughts and actions of broadcasters and their critics.

The first thing to be said about the BBC is that it is very difficult to imagine a situation in which the BBC did not exist. The hardware of a broadcasting system can be set up very rapidly to a blueprint, the speed of its development depends upon economic decisions concerning the rate of capital investment. Programme content, on the other hand, the professional practice of broadcasters, evolves as programmes are made and transmitted. The BBC as an institution pre-existed the practice of broadcasting. As the sole instrument of broadcasting, both the virtues and faults of British broadcasters were looked upon as the virtues and faults of the BBC. It is the continuing strength of that identification that still enables the BBC, in spite of the break-up of its TV monopoly, to maintain with remarkable success that whatever it chooses to do at any one time is both right and inevitable. When the BBC was a monopoly, monopoly was the ideal system. Now that it has learnt to live with a competitor, competition is healthy. Now that it has two channels, the existence of the two-channel system is the very essence of its public service role.

It is essential to break free from this identification of the practice of broadcasting with the BBC as an institution, and to remember that the BBC was created in certain specific historical circumstances and shaped by very clear but arguable intellectual assumptions about the nature of broadcasting. The need now is to examine with a clear mind the present context, both intellectual and technical, and decide what broadcasting institutions we require.

The difficulties of making such an imaginative leap, however, are illustrated by the setting up of ITV. The successive Television Acts are increasingly frenzied legislative attempts to break the monopoly of the BBC without really doing so. It was clear to many people that monopoly was an indefensible concept in our society. As the Beveridge Report stated,

However admirable the past achievements of the BBC, what concerns us is the future. . . . How can a body with a monopoly of broadcasting be prevented from developing the faults of complacency, injustice, favouritism? How can we meet the undeniable dangers of monopoly, or concentration of power?

In spite of their misgivings, the Beveridge Committee, like all other inquiries into broadcasting in this country, came down in favour of the *status quo*, the *status quo* being the BBC. Those who examine broadcasting institutions show the same characteristics as the television audience. They prefer the safety of the known and predictable to the dangers of the new and unknown. In general people do not like their habits to be changed. So Parliament tried to set up a system which would preserve the ethos of public service broadcasting combined with the ethos of private enterprise capitalism. That the system has never worked should surprise no one. That it continues to surprise even the most knowledgeable is illustrated by the unhappy story of London Weekend, where a group of enthusiastic BBC programme-makers attempted to continue doing their thing and to make large sums of money at the same time. It is no coincidence that much of the impetus behind demands for the reform of ITV stems from the failure of that attempt, for it exposed ITV's inherent contradictions. You either put the money on the screen or you give it to shareholders. It is difficult to do both.

Commercial competitive broadcasting is based on a fundamentally different view of society to public service monopoly broadcasting. The original creation of the BBC monopoly and Reith's development of it in practice were based upon the assumption that broadcasting is influential, a powerful and potentially dangerous medium requiring the most careful control lest it get into the wrong hands. One of the strengths of the BBC has been the readiness of broadcasters to believe this. All professionals naturally tend to exaggerate their own importance. That tendency contributed in large part to the almost fanatical loyalty which, until recently, the BBC inspired in its staff. The current breakdown in that loyalty is, in part, the reaction to a growing awareness, sharpened by redundancy, that this sense of self-importance is threatened.

But is broadcasting, or in the context of this book, television, influential? Does it, in fact, matter, as much as those who set up the BBC thought it did? You cannot answer that question without examining in more detail the functions broadcasting is supposed to fulfil. In the BBC Charter these functions are defined as education, information and entertainment. The major problem facing broadcasting organizations throughout the world, not only the BBC, is that broadcasting, because of the limitation of frequencies, has come to be regarded as one entity. Television is supposed to provide not only the contents of the average station bookstall, but to fulfil also the functions of cinema, theatre, sports stadium, concert hall and classroom. All these activities satisfy different expectations and have different operational requirements. Being forced to amalgamate them places broadcasters in a difficult position. To avoid the dilemma, it is usually claimed that one informs and educates by entertaining. This is the 'there's no point in saying anything if no one is watching' argument. This argument begins to break down in the educational field and broadcasters are there-

*Conclusions*

fore suspicious of education. Stuart Hood in his book, *A Survey of Television*, pours some scorn on the Open University project. In examining the importance of broadcasting we must, therefore, examine these functions separately.

Entertainment is and always has been the prime function of television, from Cecil Madden's opening revue at the 1936 Radio Show to the days of *Steptoe, Callan* and *The Black and White Minstrel Show.* Assumptions about television's influence and power are based primarily upon its pervasiveness as an activity, upon the sheer amount watched, which averages in Britain about two hours per day per head. Most of this is undemanding escapist entertainment. Indeed, many who see TV as an influential medium, criticize it for being escapist and see its influence as debasing. But for what is this viewing a substitute? If it is a debasing influence it is presumably taking the place of something more worthy. It is partly a substitute for hard, soul-destroying work, for the spread of TV viewing has coincided with shorter working hours and is particularly heavy among those who do the most uninteresting jobs. It is also a substitute for street-corner gossip and the pub. It is not, I think, just coincidence that the BBC developed in a country with strict licensing laws; though to give brewers their due, they have never adopted that quasi-religious tone which broadcasters adopt when explaining their public service function.

TV viewing has also, of course, taken the place of the theatre, the cinema, the music-hall and much pulp literature. It has not, contrary to gloomy forecasts, killed any of these activities. The research set out in Belson's *The Impact of Television* shows that TV's effect on a wide range of activities from gardening to reading is, in the long term, i.e. within 4–6 years of buying a set, almost neutral.

The Reithian public service concept of the BBC was based upon an élitist notion that you could protect people from their own desires and in so doing improve them. But in the world of entertainment the audience has always been king. Showbiz has always been an industry. I can see no objection, within society's normal financial, political and legal constraints, to letting Lew Grade get on with it. Either he is good at it or he isn't. *Steptoe* is good, not because it is worthy, but because it is hugely popular. It makes millions laugh. Its success, and the success of *Till Death Us Do*

294

*Part* or *Hancock* or *Not in Front of the Children* or *Val Doonican* or *The Black and White Minstrel Show*, merely shows that the late Tom Sloan and his merry men were as good and probably better at their job than Lew Grade. But it has little to do with public service. If we now turn to TV's informational and educational functions we are clearly faced with a different set of social priorities. Many of the arguments about public service television, serious television, quality television, are really arguments about the proportion of education and information to entertainment.

There are not, I imagine, many who would contest the influence and increasing importance of education. It is a major social priority and in a world of growing complexity and rapid change, society's demands upon the educational system become ever more insistent. To meet these demands the teacher is being forced to call technology to his aid and in many areas of instruction teaching machines and television are taking over from traditional class-room teaching. If the Open University is seen to be a success, there may well be an explosive growth in this area, reinforced by the development of cassettes. Television networks, whether airwaves or cable, are and will remain social assets. It is for Parliament with the advice of the educational authorities to decide what proportion of that asset they require for educational purposes. The financing and staffing of educational television should then be placed in the hands of those same authorities, whether national or local. The setting up of the Open University, to which the BBC has partially handed over editorial control, is a step in this direction. The BBC moved into educational broadcasting on its own initiative. While broadcasting techniques were being developed, it was natural that the already constituted broadcasters of entertainment and information should be allowed to pioneer schools and adult educational broadcasting. To discontinue that arrangement now would be a positive advantage. At present educational television is very much the poor relation within both the BBC and ITV, low on the list of priorities when it comes to budgets and technical resources. Moreover, new centres of television production with different aims and ideals would help to break down the mystique still surrounding television and encourage new ideas and new ideals.

It is in the field of informational TV that the questions of function and public service responsibility become most acute. There is a traditional and largely unquestioned assumption that journalism is a necessary estate of the realm in a properly functioning democracy. The more complex our society becomes, the greater the need for clear channels of communication by which information can be transmitted; information without which society would simply cease to function at all. Television is clearly growing in importance as one of those channels. Many would claim that it had already become the dominant information medium. I would myself doubt this. Britain remains a nation of heavy newspaper readers and journalist after journalist stresses the superiority of print over picture as a carrier of information. In the field of broadcasting, radio can often be a more efficient and pervasive news medium, as, for instance, coverage of the Six-Day War demonstrated. What evidence there is shows that television exerts little influence, merely confirming people's already received ideas. We are certainly a better informed society than we used to be, but there are so many other factors, such as education and increased leisure, which are more likely to account for this. There are those who criticize television as a supporter of the *status quo*. As all social institutions, by definition, support the *status quo*, it would be surprising if television did not share this characteristic. Others, who dislike change, see television as a revolutionary force the cause of whatever manifestations of social stress they dislike, be it strikes, demonstrations, violent crime or sexual permissiveness. In so far as the dissemination of knowledge, the offer of other options, speeds the process of social change, it would be surprising if television did not play a small part in this process. In this area you have to take a gamble similar to Pascal's. He could not say whether God existed or not, so he worked on the assumption that He did, because the gain if God did exist far outweighed any possible gain from believing that He didn't. I do not know whether informational TV matters, one must assume that it does, because if it doesn't a large number of intelligent, energetic people are engaged at some expense in a meaningless activity and my mistaken assumption to the contrary will add little to that sum of futility.

Certainly informational TV is controlled by the politicians on the assumption that it is influential. The atmosphere in which television journalism operates is one of constant constraint rather than freedom. Its free development is inhibited by an attitude of mind and institutional controls that have grown directly out of an original situation of one-channel radio monopoly. In such a situation editorial control had to be carefully watched. But in the present situation with four-channel national radio, as well as local radio and with three, soon four and then countless television channels, the editorial control is still in too few hands. This gives the politicians a dangerous excuse for intervention and fear of this intervention is used as a weapon to cow the broadcasters. As a result television journalism, in general, is too timid.

Apart from political controls, informational television is seriously inhibited by its confusion with entertainment. It is here that it is most vulnerable to the charges of trivialization. Practitioners are aware all the time that a news bulletin, or a programme on George Eliot, is being asked to compete with a variety show. They are afraid of boring their audience, afraid that unless they jazz up their programmes the audience will switch over to another channel. But perhaps more importantly, there is an awareness that they are competing for scarce air-time and resources. Working for the same programme controller as light entertainment shows, there is a largely unconscious feeling all the time that they must justify their cost-per-thousand viewers. This leads to the creation of the pseudo event, to a stress on form rather than content, to a fear of seriousness. For there is a basic difference between entertainment and information. Entertainment is an escape from mundane reality. It satisfies the human desire to dream. It depends upon a suspension of disbelief. But information is concerned with mundane reality. It depends upon belief in an objective truth that precedes it and is more important than its presentation and transmission. To mix the two categories is highly dangerous as the debate about drama-documentaries shows.

But in a sense the value of the BBC as a public service monolith is based upon the idea of combining the two, so that by sugaring the pill of information with entertainment you will raise the nation's intellectual and moral standards. The classic statement of this position is by Sir William Haley, in a lecture on 'The Responsibilities of Broadcasting': 'It rests on the conception of the community as a broadly based cultural pyramid slowly aspiring upwards. This pyramid is served by three main programmes differentiated but broadly overlapping in levels and interest, each programme leading on to the other, the listener being induced through the years increasingly to discriminate in favour of the things that are more worthwhile.' Unfortunately even when the BBC could exert 'the brute force of monopoly' there is no evidence to show that listeners could be induced to discriminate. The influence of BBC radio on musical appreciation is usually held up as a shining example of public service broadcasting in action. But, as Dr Emmett, Head of BBC Audience Research has said, this influence is not measurable, and John Culshaw and John Drummond of BBC TV's Music Department both say that Stravinsky's *Rite of Spring* is still regarded as *avant-garde* outside London. The 'outside London' is significant. Broadcasting is nationwide. Musical activity in the conventional concert-hall sense is heavily concentrated in London. It would seem therefore that it was traditional concert-hall activity that was the decisive influence on musical appreciation, rather than broadcasting.

All this leads me to the conclusion that it is vital formally to separate the functions of entertainment and information. There is not only a clear social need for rigorous journalism and documentary programmes of all sorts, there is also a massive demand for them, so I am not suggesting forcing something down unwilling throats. I am suggesting that this demand could be better satisfied by reorganization. The history of ITN demonstrates the possibility of setting up programming companies responsible solely for informational broadcasting, giving them with complete social justification, guaranteed outlets and a guaranteed budget and letting them get on with their job. As it is impossible to legislate against the inevitable biases of the news media, the maximum editorial diversity should be the aim, so that the biases cancel themselves out. Therefore each available channel should have a separate, fully independent company responsible for its informational output. How these informational companies fit in with the rest of the network I will explain in a moment.

Another factor that everybody thinks they know about the BBC is that it is financed by a licence fee, and that this gives them freedom from government. This too is a myth. The BBC has always been financed by a government grant. Originally the government collected the licence as tax revenue, decided how much of this the BBC needed and doled it out. For a long time licence revenue kept well ahead of the sums required by the BBC. Only in 1963 did the BBC receive the full licence revenue. Since then it has been involved in a continual battle to push the licence fee up, which amounts to asking for ever-increasing government grants. Indeed, I believe it would be easier for a government to increase a straight grant than increase the licence which is both difficult and expensive to collect. The main argument in favour of the licence fee is that it provides an assured and known sum which will be unaffected in the short term by the BBC's performance. This is a real gain. But at present the future growth of BBC income is dependent on the growth of colour licences, which cannot be accurately computed. This means that the BBC is attempting five-year budgeting with no accurate forecast of income. Wouldn't it be preferable to negotiate a direct government grant, based on present known costs and output and pegged in some way to the cost of living index? If the BBC then wished to expand, into local radio for instance, they would have to give their reasons publicly and the government would have to give their reasons for either accepting or declining this request. This would avoid the situation in which the BBC started BBC 2 and went into colour without adequate funds to finance these developments. Under the present system the country refuses repeatedly, through its elected re-presentatives, to pay the true price for the services it demands.

Throughout the world the generally accepted alternative to licence or government financed broadcasting is advertising either by sponsor or, as we have in this country, by spot. Unfortunately the founding of ITV institutionalized two confusions. It confused the idea of competition with the idea of private enterprise finance, and it confused advertising finance with private profit. But neither are necessary conditions of the other. I believe it was correct to break up the monopoly, not because of the virtues of competition, but because of the need for the maximum diversity of broadcasting organizations. A monopoly is only justified in a society unified under a ruling *élite*. Living, as we do, in an increasingly pluralist society which accepts a wide range of both material and moral choice, we require a plurality in broadcasting also. But the need for this plurality must not be confused with a necessity to finance

299

*Conclusions*

alternative systems from advertising. It would have been possible in 1954 to finance the alternative channel out of an increased licence fee or straight government grants. That would still be possible, although now advertising has been developed as a source of revenue, it would be more difficult and would require great political courage.

The other alternative is to accept advertising, but to remove the possibilities of private profit. It would, for instance, be easy to turn the present programme companies in ITV into public non-profit-making corporations, thus removing the conflict that has always crippled ITV, between programme budgets and standards on the one hand and high dividends on the other. Although, as will be clear, I think reform should go much further, that is the most practicable short-term reform of the present unworkable ITV system. The great disadvantage of advertising revenue is that it fluctuates. As the recent history of the BBC shows, under the present system maximization of audiences is the aim, however the channel is financed. The BBC's advantage is that it can maximize over a longer time scale, whereas ITV's revenue is immediately affected by a drop in audience. It is not only advertising finance that makes it difficult for ITV companies to plan ahead, but the insecurity of their franchise. This insecurity is built into the system to counteract the dangers of monopoly capitalism. It seems to me better to build in security and remove monopoly capitalism. In the long term, fluctuations in advertising revenue would iron themselves out, and companies financed in this way could carry experimental programmes in the same way that an industrial corporation has a research and development budget. I personally favour keeping advertising off the screen, but so long as we live in our present mixed economy it is stupid to get morally stuffy about advertising, and it certainly doesn't make that much difference to the programmes.

Perhaps the most unfortunate result of the foundation of ITV was the reinforcement of the BBC's good opinion of itself. ITV has been so clearly unworkable as a system for producing good television, that it has seriously damaged the consideration of alternatives to the BBC. Ever since 1955 the BBC has found it all too easy to silence its critics by pointing at its rivals and saying, 'Look at the alternative.' The Pilkington Committee were forced

300

into this trap. Not allowed by their terms of reference to recommend radically different broadcasting organizations, in rightly criticizing ITV, they inevitably over-praised the BBC and over-consolidated its power and influence. Of course, ITV is worse than the BBC, but it is not the only alternative. Perhaps there are systems better than either.

The main requirement of any system is the maximum diversity with the minimum of competitive scheduling. Diversity is important, because what is transmitted will inevitably depend upon taste. Taste is very subjective. We do not all agree about what is good and bad, therefore the more people making these judgements the better. Diversity is also important to avoid large organizations interposing themselves between the programme-maker and the screen. On both these counts I believe that BBC television should be separated from radio and split up. Having also accepted the need to split entertainment and information as programming functions and having accepted a system of mixed financing, what national broadcasting structure do you erect to contain these elements?

In pursuit of diversity you open up the fourth available channel as soon as possible. Two of these channels would be London-based national networks and the other two would have a regional structure. In order to have the undoubted advantages of a co-ordinated two-channel system, one national channel would be linked with one regional channel under a body responsible for transmission and scheduling alone. These two bodies would own the transmitters and continuity studios and perhaps in certain cases the studios as well. Sitting on them would be representatives of the programme companies with an equal number of public appointees and a full-time chairman. Their scheduling powers would be purely in terms of either entertainment or information. This is in effect the only sort of co-ordinated planning possible between BBC 1 and BBC 2 at present. But by what God-like process would they decide on the right proportion? In the first instance by the same process as that used by existing programme controllers: tradition. The shape of television schedules has changed little since main evening viewing started at 6.00 P.M. instead of 7.00 P.M. with the abolition of the toddler's truce in 1957. So arguments would start from a solid basis of experience and the conflict between journalism and entertainment would be out in the open. Moreover, with the present pressures of competitive scheduling removed, there would be a chance for a radical change of schedules.

This body would see that news bulletins were spaced through the evening. They would also co-ordinate the informational companies on their two channels for the televising of major events, such as the World Cup, a moon shot or the General Election. This scheme has, I think, two advantages. By separating the bare bones of scheduling from programme-making, it would make it impossible to manipulate a whole evening's viewing, impossible to plan for inheritance or pre-echo and so free programme-makers from the more unreal and unhealthy ratings pressures. With four channels split in such a way it would make it impossible to compete. It would also make room for more public participation in television. Certainly on the regionally based networks time should be set aside for the use of interest groups; perhaps, as in Holland, groups with a given number of members could claim airtime. This could either be done under the auspices of the responsible information company, budgeted and staffed as part of their airtime, or the authority itself could allot airtime and technical facilities.

The basis for the two London-based national channels already exists in the present BBC and the present ITV London companies. The basis for the regional channels exists in the present ITV and BBC regional structure. Indeed there was a major opportunity lost when BBC 2 was not given a regional structure. The logic of the major investment in new studio complexes in Birmingham and Manchester was to move whole programming areas to these centres and give them real autonomy with London only acting as a co-ordinator. The BBC are now trying to do this with an existing department, moving Further Education to Manchester. But had they built up new departments in these centres from scratch, those applying for jobs would have known where they were going and why. The choice would have been willingly taken and not imposed.

Each independent regional network would consist of three major companies, one information company and two entertainment companies. The entertainment companies would each split into separate light entertainment and drama groups, each with different geographical bases. In the same way the information company would split into news and current affairs, documentary and OB groups. The news and current affairs group would almost certainly have to have a London base. However one may wish to support regionalism, one must face the facts of TV current affairs life. I do not believe you could run such an operation from anywhere but London; if the experts disagree, so much the better. But the aim on both the national and regionally based channels is to create as much diversity of editorial judgement in everything from light entertainment to news as is possible within the limits of four channels. There should be maximum competition for ideas and minimum competition for audiences.

Given the experience of ITV, in which four major seven-day-a-week companies are seen as the most viable structure, a three-company structure should be able to provide vigorous regional broadcasting and the two regional networks should be planned to avoid the present regional duplication of BBC Birmingham alongside ATV, BBC Manchester alongside Granada and so on.

Once time had been allotted in the schedules the creative groups would be allowed to get on with their job of making programmes. The transmission authority would exercise no control whatsoever over programme content. This would be controlled by the normal law of the land and by the normal social pressures of taste. Matters of dispute could be regulated by a body similar to the Press Council which would meet in public and on which would be represented, in equal numbers, programme-makers and members of the public with a lay chairman.

If the channels carried advertising, this should be controlled by a separate body appointed by Parliament to control all advertising. The aim at all times should be to avoid large monolithic controlling bodies with wide-ranging responsibilities.

The creative groups should be controlled and run by their own members. It is repeatedly said that public service means that the BBC's only interest is what is on the screen. This should be true of all broadcasting organizations. This is why such organizations should be controlled by those who put the programmes on the screen. When broadcasting started there was no body of broadcasters, no corpus of broadcasting opinion, no developed standards. Because the BBC and the ITV institutions pre-existed the broadcasters, these broadcasters became employees. In Raymond Williams's words, they were made agents rather than recognized as sources,

He is an agent, not a source, because the intention lies elsewhere. In social terms the agent will normally in fact be a subordinate of a government, a commercial firm, a newspaper proprietor. Agency, in the simple sense, is necessary in any complex administration. But it is always dangerous unless its function and intentions are not only openly declared, but commonly approved and controlled.

Charles Curran can claim with constitutional correctness that the BBC is the Board of Governors. It is into such realms of unreality that the historical development of broadcasting has led us.

Now that an established body of broadcasters exists, they can control themselves. As Huw Wheldon states, the object of public service broadcasting is excellence. The problem is, who decides what is excellent? As tastes differ the more people who are involved in the process the better. I see, therefore, the creative groups operating as co-operatives, electing a managing editor or group head to allot budgets and adjudicate between the claims of, for instance, series and single plays, in collaboration with an elected steering committee.

One of the advantages claimed by the BBC for its present size is that it enables it to stand up to political pressure. I would have thought that it would be harder for a government to nobble four news organizations than the present two, particularly when these four are democratically run, so that any censorship pressures would be brought instantly into the open. In a democratic society all broadcasters must accept the superior power of Parliament. As society's agents they are going to be controlled in some measure by society's representatives. What broadcasters must fight for is the openly exerted power of Parliament as opposed to the clandestine pressure of executive government. The present structure of both the BBC and the ITV encourages such clandestine pressure. Complaints are neither seen to be made nor seen to be rejected or accepted.

But the structure I have outlined will anyway be only transitional. The possible plurality of broadcasting is limited at the moment by the shortage of frequencies for transmitted TV. Therefore as soon as possible a push should be made at a national level to cover the whole country with a system of coaxial cables. The capital cost of such a scheme means that this decision will have to be taken at the highest level. But once that system is installed and linked to video-tape and film libraries, the range of choice becomes very wide indeed. With such a system we could make decisions about broadcasting priorities with more accuracy and sensitivity than at present. There would at last be a direct link between the audience and the programme-makers. Perhaps then we would find it desirable to pay directly for entertainment, perhaps subsidizing certain areas, and provide information and education free on different channels as national services.

The stresses experienced by our present broadcasting institutions are evidence that they are no longer suited to the society they are trying to serve. The Reithian BBC from which the present system has directly developed was an élitist concept, an attempt to construct a National Church for a united nation. We are rapidly moving into a pluralist society with little respect for élitism. A parallel movement took place in Western Christendom during the Reformation. The concept of the Catholic Church as the source of all authority was challenged. Rival interpretations of God's will flourished. The congregation no longer submitted to the will of the Church, but many Churches were founded as expressions of the will of varied congregations. In broadcasting our Reformation is in full flood.

## JOAN BAKEWELL

In 1924, two years before John L. Baird first demonstrated television, Lord Reith, then Managing Director of the BBC Ltd, was able to write about broadcasting: 'The preservation of a high moral standard is obviously paramount. Few would question the desirability of refraining from anything approaching vulgarity or directing attention to unsavoury subjects.'* Probably most people agreed with him. They certainly knew what he meant and undoubtedly would have drawn the limits in the same place. It is not

* Broadcast over Britain.

so simple today. Television has been partly contributory to the widespread expression and exchange of different points of view in our society. The absence today of any accepted set of moral or social values, or rather the existence of a variety of different moral systems, throws pressure on the television services and especially the people who produce the ideas.

Television today is itself a big industry – entirely apart from the manufacturing and selling of sets. The BBC employs 23,000 people, about 6,500 of them working directly in the making of TV programmes. In ITV there are 8,500 employees in the fifteen companies. The BBC's annual expenditure at the moment is near to £95 million; of this £64 million goes directly into the servicing and producing of television programmes for two networks. ITV's income is around £95 million from advertising, of which the Chancellor immediately takes away £23 million. With such an investment of labour and capital it's natural that questions are asked about the product that results.

The television product is strangely indefinable. It produces programmes, of course, and in various cupboards in various tins lie coils of film and tape to which one can point and say that is the product. But it isn't. Much of what television produces goes entirely unrecorded; what is initially recorded is usually wiped so that the tape may be used again; what is recorded and kept for the archives is so selective that it is in no way a record of what television is really like. Television is lost each night into the air: it exists and then it is over. It is so much more transient than the daily press which can at least point to a stack of back numbers, or where one can look up someone's series of articles. Television exists while it is being transmitted and is then dead.

Nevertheless one thing is definable and that is the amount of it. In the production of television programmes of native origin and native talent Britain is a leader. The BBC is the biggest producer of programmes in the world: far more than any European country, or any one of the American giant companies. Its output is around 7,000 hours of television a year. In just one year the BBC Drama Group alone produced 604 original productions providing 395 hours of television programming. The cost of this plus 136 hours of repeats came to about £7 million (April 1969– March 1970). The BBC voluntarily restricts its quota of foreign

programmes to 15 per cent of which about 12½ per cent come
from America. The ITV have an imposed quota of 14 per cent of
foreign originated material: so the entire ITV complex of fifteen
companies is itself originating about 135 hours of programmes
per week.

With the introduction of more hours and the fourth channel
which must come eventually, this can only increase. So we have a
booming industry supplying a product that defies being put on a
slab and defined – that is fluid, changing, elusive. It is not surprising that there are so many different attitudes towards it, nor that
television provokes so many arguments.

Television is, of course, particularly vulnerable to public response, because while being in one way nebulous, it is responsible
for one of the most fundamental currents of any society – the
exchange of ideas within it. When individual programmes, performances, events, have been forgotten, there remains the residue of
ideas and attitudes those programmes have produced. And it is the
new and disturbing ideas that stick in the mind and disturb the
public conscience. It would probably astound people to discover
what a high percentage of *Wednesday Plays* were not kitchen sink
or social realism. But it was because this style of play caught the
tempo of the times and crystallized the areas where society today
has a sense of conflict that they remain in the mind, in public
debate and at the centre of argument.

Television deals in ideas over a far wider area than any other
medium. It can communicate the entire output of Fleet Street,
Hollywood, the West End theatres, the world's libraries and the
world's speakers. It does each of those things less well and less
subtly than the best of the originals. The best TV news programmes
cannot convey the complex details and the subtleties of argument
of the best journalism; the TV Western is puny beside the Cinema-
scope epic; the TV debate is over-simplified compared with discussions or lectures among specialist groups. The TV opera cannot
match the personal experience of live opera; nor can TV drama
ever outclass the theatrical impact of a great actor giving a great
performance on stage. Only in the area of public events, pageant
and sport, could television possibly give, by the range of its
coverage, a satisfaction that might match that of being present.

Thus television is, at one time, transient, nebulous, comprehen-

Conclusions

sive, superficial and influential – all at once and in great quantity. What do the consumers, the viewers, make of it? Well, the equation runs: programmes plus audience reaction equals ratings. Ratings as an abstract statistic are the only clumsy and inadequate tool for measuring on a large scale public response to programmes. There is an evaluation called RI, Reaction Index, used in the BBC, which measures not just how many watched, but how many enjoyed a programme: but until there is a means of measuring what Brian Emmet of Audience Research calls programme 'grats' – gratifications – then the numerical response to a programme will still have the power to tyrannize the schedules. For this reason ratings tends to be an emotive word among television people – based on the unproved fear that you can always get higher and higher ratings with worse and worse programmes. What is certainly true for all networks is that actual ratings considered against rating expectations crystallize the arguments that come from both sides as to whether programmes are good or not.

Questions that agitate the television viewers, whether expressed individually or by politicians and pressure groups, centre around issues that exist outside television itself: violence, permissiveness, political loyalties (otherwise known as bias), the uniformity of society today and the hold of established values. The issues of television that concern the broadcasters are related to the structures of the two organizations: the BBC is too big, its schedules are as concerned with chasing ratings as those of ITV; it is sacrificing the old Reithian values of public service to business streamlining, and so losing its sense of purpose. The ITV structure is wasteful, uncoordinated and lacking in any philosophy at all other than that of pleasing its public. All these allegations have been made in this book: they may or may not be justified. But they make it worth carrying the argument a stage further.

The structure of television can be considered both historically and theoretically. Any suggestions about possible changes in the existing structure must be based on both approaches. Historically then, two structures exist: the BBC built on high moral tone and a dedication to the principles of informing, educating and entertaining, had the field to itself for three years before the war and from 1946 to 1955. In 1955 ITV broke the monopoly, brought in strong competition and quickly won over a majority of the audience. The

BBC fought back with ratings-winning programmes and in-augurated the present area of competitive scheduling in which the two split the audience about half and half between them.

The BBC is a public corporation set up by Royal Charter and operating under licence, which is periodically to be renewed. The members of the Corporation are the twelve Governors including the Chairman, who are all appointed by the Queen in Council, normally for a period of five years. They are not expected to make broadcasting their sole concern: they work through a permanent professional executive staff headed by the Director-General who presides over a Board of Management of ten, covering all the functions of the BBC, radio and television, domestic and foreign. The Director-General is the chief executive of the Corporation. The BBC is responsible in total for the entire broadcasting process – from engineering, planning, programme-making and trans-mission.

In ITV these functions are divided. The ITA is like the BBC, a public corporation set up by statute and, like the BBC, operating under licence from the Postmaster General (now the Minister of Posts and Telecommunications) for a limited period of time. This non-profit-making body owns and operates the transmitting stations and hires its facilities to the privately financed companies who provide the programmes and draw their revenue directly from advertisements. The Authority consists of a Chairman, Deputy Chairman, and nine members, all appointed by the Minister of Posts and Telecommunications. They head a staff of 880, and are aided, as is the BBC, by a number of Advisory Councils. The chief executive officer is the Director-General. It is the ITA who selects and appoints the programme companies, and distributes the licences to these or new companies when they come up for renewal.

The ITA is thus similar to the BBC in having a governing body appointed by the government and in operating under licence whose renewal will also be by government sanction. The major difference between them is that the ITA is separately constituted from the programme companies and not in clearly defined authority over them (see page 290) whereas the BBC governing body and executive body are both contained within the same organiza-tion.

## Conclusions

These two structures are financed from two sources: the BBC from a licence fee, ITV directly from advertising.

The BBC licence was finally approved as the source of BBC finance under the Licence and Agreement of 1927. This was an agreement between the BBC and the Postmaster General allowing his power to revoke the licence if at any time the BBC failed in its duty: he also had the power to veto any proposed programme or class of programme. Should he exercise this veto, the BBC has the right to state publicly that this has happened, and this is undoubtedly a major deterrent to direct government interference. In theory then, the BBC's finances are linked to government. It has so far been the agreed policy of successive governments to treat their powers as major reserve powers only and to allow the BBC total independence in the conduct of its day-to-day business. None the less the attempt to get an increase in the licence fee is regarded as a political manoeuvre in which the government of the day must be won over. Thus the critical state of BBC finance is linked from the very source of that income with government. The BBC's freedom of choice and programme policy are severely determined at the moment by financial pressures. It is natural that this should be so: there is no justification for broadcasting to exist in a vacuum and the producer who disregards his budget limitations is bad at his job. None the less, in the last resort, knowing the financial stringencies and the economies that have been observed, the BBC is still not free to put up the price it charges for its product. It must always wait for the government of the day to sanction any increase and this governments are loath and slow to do.

ITV's annual income stands at around £95 million and, because it is drawn from advertising revenue, gives viewers the feeling that ITV is 'free'. It is, of course, paid for in the sale of the goods advertised in its commercials. This is satisfactory as a source of income just as long as the advertisers favour TV with enough commercials to make programme production viable. The tendency recently has been for them to withdraw from TV advertising. Thus ITV's survival is rooted in its ability to attract advertising, and so in its ability to attract viewers. And pressure such as this is hardest on the smaller companies.

Any new structure for television considered by the successors to the now-cancelled Annan Inquiry must take these two existing

310

structures as starting points. Adaption and reform is likely: abolition is improbable. What must also be considered is what our society from the 1970s onward will need of its television service, where can the possibilities of the medium be improved and strengthened and how they can be safeguarded against abuse, uniformity and blandness.

The complexity of our social structure, political diversity and fundamental disagreement on moral and ethical matters make it imperative that as many channels of expression are open to as many opinions as possible. This was the ITV argument against the BBC monopoly: it is the argument for more channels and more hours today. However, the increase in opportunity that hours and channels would bring does not necessarily mean more choice. Commercial experience in America has shown how *more* usually results in more of the same things: competition for audience makes for conformity and a lowering of standards in the pursuit of ratings. This seems a strong reason why channels of broadcasting with the socially desirable opportunity to express the diversity of life and interest in a community should not be regarded as a source of business profit. It would immediately debase and devalue the role of television in our society. Malcolm Muggeridge would say this was a good thing. It has largely happened in America. Television there is a service in the sense that the water supply is a service: it has no character or contribution other than its abundant and continual outpouring. Its responsibility to ideas has been largely and fundamentally abdicated. It plays no consistent and continuing part on the debate of the nation's affairs: it merely reflects and reports brilliantly on its moments of crises. Otherwise its overriding influence is as a reflection of a materialist philosophy which excites a degree of consumer expectation that the realities of American society constantly fail to realize. To avoid a similar situation in this country it seems logical to suggest that we need many channels of communication not motivated by business profit.

To release both the BBC and the ITV companies from governmental and commercial pressures of finance their financial basis should be fundamentally revised. The BBC should be free to raise its licence fee independently of the Minister of Posts and Telecommunications. Just as in any other industry that costs its production processes and assesses its future capital needs, it could

311

be made responsible to the Prices and Incomes Board (always supposing it survives present economic changes). Within ITV the ITA should extend its powers and duties as a public body. The ITA should be the collector of advertising revenue from commercials, and it should plan the schedules of ITV including the fourth channel which should also be financed by advertising revenue. When the sale of colour sets starts to rise seriously the advertisers will return to investing heavily in colour commercials thus providing enough revenue for both. The structure of ITV as a whole should really bear the financial pressures and safeguard the smaller companies from the alternatives of ratings-grabbing or going out of business.

ITV would therefore retain its role as an advertising medium, but the income from such a source would go into programme production rather than to individual shareholders. The major criticism of these proposals is that, being financially more independent, the BBC would be answerable to no one, responsible to no body of public opinion and therefore under none of the checks and pressures that operate today. The fear might be that the BBC would go mad and give the viewers a runaway and increasingly expensive diet of what the programme-makers felt was good for us. The safeguards are two. The first, the dependence of both BBC and ITV on the renewal by statute of their Charter and licence. Secondly, the continuing competitiveness between the two systems for viewers: ITV's continuing dependence on advertising revenue would guarantee highly competitive scheduling between the two systems.

The ITV structure, the federal structure of five major networking companies and a number of regional companies provides a challenging alternative to the BBC. Under a more powerful ITA, these companies could become non-profit-making programme-producing companies under contract to supply programmes to the ITA. Regionalism, which is considered to be commercially so much in the balance today, would be guaranteed its place in the structure and encouraged by the ITA to serve and reflect the different regions. The programme companies would each be required to supply a mixed output of both informational and purely entertainment programmes. Any separation of the sources of documentary and comment from the sources of entertainment would be to split the system into the hands of different élitist groups growing further apart. The survival of the two together is essential to the survival of television as a mainstream of culture: the cross-fertilization of ideas between programme groups constantly revitalizes the ideas of both. Nevertheless it is probable that certain company strengths would lead to some specialization: at the moment, for example, Yorkshire, Granada and Anglia in Drama, ATV in light entertainment, Southern in children's programmes.

The proposed change to the BBC's financial structure would allow it to increase the licence more immediately in response to financial pressure. At the moment the combined BBC sound and television licence is £6, for colour television and sound £11. This is the lowest licence paid by any European country. The combined radio and black-and-white television licence in Belgium is the equivalent of £8, in Norway and Denmark, £11 13s., France £8 9s., Sweden £14 10s. In Australia it's £9 5s. and in Japan £4 8s. Yet the British licence supports a programme output far exceeding any other country.

McKinsey, the management consultants called in to report on the BBC, basically found the BBC to be well managed and carrying little fat. However, they were not required to comment on the very size of the BBC nor on the range, content and balance of programmes it produces. There is certainly, among both viewers and broadcasters, felt to be too narrow a range of points of view expressed on BBC television. There is an idea current of the BBC man and the BBC outlook. What bearing it has on reality will have already been demonstrated by this book. But the fact that the idea of the professional broadcaster as someone different from the rest, unbending to public criticism and arrogant in his assurance, is easily explained. The broadcasters who belong to the BBC hierarchy understand its management problems; they realize the extent to which these are not appreciated by the public and they identify with the difficulties and the problems rather than the public's over-simplified complaints. At some point, then, the creative man, the programme-maker, must disengage from the politics of management.

The playwrights, Hopkins, Mercer and Potter – all working freelance – expressed concern at audience reactions to their plays,

## Conclusions

the public's right to feel outraged if a programme made them un-comfortable. But the thought that such apprehension should govern their writing is unthinkable. They write as they do: their plays can then be either refused or accepted for transmission. That is the job of the management hierarchy. That same separation of responsibility is necessary for programme-makers. Within the BBC they stand too close to the financial dilemmas and the concern with ratings which are the justified preoccupations of management.

To state the problem is easy: the solutions, not surprisingly, are elusive. Abolish the BBC? To my mind this would be killing the patient to cure the symptom. All programme-producing units necessitate a hierarchy. To co-ordinate the programme output into schedules, these hierarchies must come together – and hierarchies proliferate. It is far better that they should belong inside the BBC where the managers are prepared and willing to be saddled with the problems their creative departments raise, than separated off, as the ITA is at the moment from the ITV companies, as an overseer body with no line of command, no identification with the process of making programmes and no powers of sanction it can effectively apply.

The fact of the BBC's survival then, need not restrict its total transformation. And a trend already evident might suggest where that transformation might be. Co-productions with television companies abroad are being increasingly undertaken by the BBC to help with budgets. In ITV, London Weekend had for a time as an affiliate a programme-producing company called Kestrel which has a two-year contract to produce sixteen plays. Allen King Associates is an independent group of programme-makers who sell to different companies. The independent producing unit may well be on the increase. There is no reason why *Man Alive*, *Chronicle*, *Wheelbase* should not be the output of independent working units under contract to the BBC but with access to its facilities, studios and libraries.

Such diversification, both within the BBC and throughout the ITV federal structures, will point the industry in the right direction for the future technical innovations. Within twenty years – some say earlier – programmes will not just come from the BBC and ITV channels on the screen. They will also come from cassettes

314

which will do for television what the LP did for music. They will come by cable into our homes so that dial-a-programme systems will link us with vast libraries of recorded material. And they will come finally from satellites, brought from all over the world to challenge home-produced material. Confronted with the threat of the TV output from, say, America, it will be necessary to strengthen the power and resolve of the public broadcasting bodies at the top while diversifying the creative contributors from below. It is finally, on the intelligence and integrity of them both that future standards of television depend. At the moment those standards are in jeopardy.